MENTAL HEALTH IN THE METROPOLIS

*the text of this book is printed
on 100% recycled paper*

THOMAS A. C. RENNIE
SERIES IN SOCIAL PSYCHIATRY

Mental Health in the Metropolis, 1962
Torchbook Revised and Enlarged Edition
   Book One, 1975
   Book Two, 1977

Life Stress and Mental Health
Thomas S. Langner
and Stanley T. Michael, 1963

Drawing by Saul Steinberg. From *Art of Living* (Harper & Row)
Copyright 1949 by Saul Steinberg

". . . the Midtown population . . . can be viewed as an emergent of a relatively
new, localized species of American. . . . adapted, albeit in an uneasy fashion,
to its chosen environment. . . ." (Book One, p. 81.)

Mental Health
In The Metropolis

The Midtown Manhattan Study

Book Two
Revised and Enlarged

LEO SROLE
THOMAS S. LANGNER • STANLEY T. MICHAEL
PRICE KIRKPATRICK • MARVIN K. OPLER
THOMAS A. C. RENNIE

EDITED BY

LEO SROLE / ANITA KASSEN FISCHER

HARPER TORCHBOOKS
HARPER & ROW, PUBLISHERS
NEW YORK • HAGERSTOWN • SAN FRANCISCO • LONDON

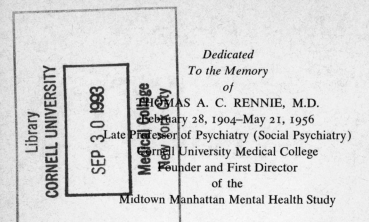

Dedicated
To the Memory
of
THOMAS A. C. RENNIE, M.D.
February 28, 1904–May 21, 1956
Late Professor of Psychiatry (Social Psychiatry)
Cornell University Medical College
Founder and First Director
of the
Midtown Manhattan Mental Health Study

This monograph was originally published in 1962 by McGraw-Hill Book Company in one volume. The senior author has added the following new material to the Torchbook edition:

Book One   Chapter 1, "Introduction to the Torchbook Edition"
Book Two   Chapter 15, "Parental Socioeconomic Status: Income Adequacy and Offspring Mental Health"
Chapter 20, "The City versus Town and Country: New Evidence on an Ancient Bias, 1975"
Chapter 21, "Summing Up, 1975"
Chapter 23, "Sociologist's Perspectives: Past and Future, 1975"
Appendix G, "Rural-Urban Diagnostic Issues"
Appendix H, "Midtown Critique of Previous Patient Enumeration Studies"

First HARPER TORCHBOOK edition published 1977

LIBRARY OF CONGRESS CATALOG CARD NUMBER: 76-54380

ISBN: 0-06-131915-5

77 78 79 80 81 10 9 8 7 6 5 4 3 2 1

TABLE OF CONTENTS

TABLES   *Book Two*

FIGURES *Book Two*

ILLUSTRATIONS *Book Two*

LEO SROLE, PH.D.
Professor of Social Sciences, Department of Psychiatry
  College of Physicians and Surgeons
  Columbia University
Chief of Psychiatric Research (Social Sciences)
  New York State Psychiatric Institute
Extraordinary Professor, Faculty of Psychology and Education
  University of Leuven (Louvain), Belgium

THOMAS S. LANGNER, PH.D.
Professor of Epidemiology
  School of Public Health and Administrative Medicine
  Columbia University

STANLEY T. MICHAEL, M.D.
Associate Professor of Psychiatry
  Cornell University Medical College

PRICE KIRKPATRICK, M.D.
Late Director, Kern County Mental Health Services
  Bakersfield, California

MARVIN K. OPLER, PH.D.
Professor of Social Psychiatry, School of Medicine
Professor and Chairman, Department of Anthropology
  State University of New York at Buffalo

THOMAS A. C. RENNIE, M.D.
Late Professor of Psychiatry (Social Psychiatry)
  Cornell University Medical College

ANITA KASSEN FISCHER, M.A.
Research Associate, Department of Psychiatry
  College of Physicians and Surgeons
  Columbia University

Book Two

Preparation of this revised and enlarged edition was facilitated by a research and teaching grant awarded to the senior author by the Foundations Fund for Research in Psychiatry.

FOREWORD: PRÉCIS OF BOOK ONE

In the opening chapter of Book One, we quote Saul Bellow, eminent American novelist and ex–New York resident, who, from first-hand experience, has written of that city: "Those who wish to feel its depths had better be careful."

The effort to sound those depths prompted a New York magazine writer to characterize the present investigation by a contrapuntal metaphor: "A massive study of the way New Yorkers react to stress, called the Midtown Manhattan Study, [is] only a little less complex and ambitious than a moonshot. . . ."

To employ a more mundane figure of speech, the care urged by Bellow was exercised in applying psychosocial instruments to uncover and delineate Midtown Manhattan's mental health and social vitals. The results of this exploratory surgery have been opened in the pages of this monograph, here published in twin softcover books.

Book One undertakes first to visualize New York City, the island of Manhattan, and Midtown in close-up as a man-made, high-rise habitat; as a population congeries drawn from the entire Western world; and as a going, round-the-clock, residential community. It next offers the reader opportunity to inspect the research methods and instruments, appropriated and newly devised, that were put to painstaking use in the course of the long exploration.

Finally, that Book reports the Study's first set of mental health data, presenting comparisons of Midtown and several other general populations. It closes with mental health probings of (1) Midtown's own prime-of-life age groups, (2) its men and women, and (3) its various stages of marital status.

Book Two carries that report farther into the community, turning to mental health comparisons of Midtown's enormous poor-to-rich range of socioeconomic differences, its immigrants and native Americans, and its unparalleled diversity of nationality and religious origin groups.

We also consider new evidence bearing on the millennial, ideologically charged controversy swirling around the city versus the town and country, and their differential health-linked qualities as human habitats. In the Epilogue we sum up and comment on the findings' implications.

The reader can then discern how far the Midtown Study complies with Mr. Bellow's admonition to explorers of New York's depths.

Part VI

Mental Health Composition and Psychiatric Care in Midtown's Sociocultural Groups

CHAPTER 13

SOCIOECONOMIC STATUS: MEASUREMENT IN A GOLD–COAST AND SLUM AREA

LEO SROLE

In many human societies, both simple and complex, the typical family is saturated with awareness of its relative "position," "standing," "station," or "status" in the communal scheme of social rank. There are few places where this is more evident as historical fact than on the American scene.

Writers in the literary vineyards, from Chaucer to Faulkner and Marquand, have been arrested by the individual's predicaments in the halter of social class status. On a higher level of abstraction, the concept of social class has engaged social philosophers and sociological theorists at least since Plato and Aristotle. Historians like Charles and Mary Beard, Daniel J. Boorstin, and analysts of American culture ranging from Alexis de Tocqueville to Max Lerner[1] have given it an important place in their observations.

Among the field research disciplines, anthropology from its beginnings has more or less systematically taken into account the patterning of social rank in societies other than our own. The research record of sociology on this front is rather less consistent. Starting in 1889 Charles Booth, the English sociologist, published his seventeen-volume research monograph *Life and Labour of the People in London*. A pioneer work of ground-breaking significance, its natural-history purpose was "to describe the general conditions under which each class lives." In contrast with its large influence on the social work field here, the Booth monograph found only slight resonance in the research interests of American (and British) academic sociology.[2]

Although exploring all manner of social problems associated with poverty and fruitfully mapping various facets of the heterogeneous city as a community type, American sociological research by and large did not fully awaken to the systemic and dynamic implications of social class processes until two empirical developments emerged under principal impetus from the field of anthropology. These took form (some forty years after Booth's first volume) in the Middletown studies of the Lynds and in the Yankee City investigation launched by Lloyd Warner in 1931, with the present writer as a coworker and coauthor.[3] These two studies had immediate and telling impact in directing American sociology's diverted attention to social stratification as a major specialty field of inquiry. By way of delayed recognition a massive and diffuse sociological literature in the English language has since burgeoned, of such proportions that a bibliography assembled in 1968 required a 440-page book to list its 7,000 items.[4]

Given the theoretical and technical diversities that pervade this literature, and the key importance of socioeconomic status (SES) to the present Study, the writer is prompted to indicate briefly the particular formulations, conceptual and operational, that guided his treatment of this complicated demographic variable while planning the design of the Midtown investigation. This effort will probably be better served if it starts with elementary processes discernible from the broad anthropological perspective.

FUNDAMENTALS OF SOCIOECONOMIC STATUS

All human societies utilize the biosocial factors of age, sex, and marital status to harness individuals to the conjugal family as it advances in the procession of generations. Within a given society, furthermore, family units are often categorized on various sociocultural criteria that operate to sort them along various axes of subgroup formations. Socioeconomic status is one of these axes. At the root of SES differences the world over are the commonplace facts that (1) to meet its creature needs the family must perform a productive work role within the local economy, and (2) the economy is organized around a division of labor, often manifested in technically specialized work roles or occupations that elicit and channel different kinds of individual skills.

It is axiomatic that the larger the diversification in occupations, the greater is the range of individual skills called into play. Although from society to society there are differences in the evaluation of corresponding occupations and the skills required, each society itself tends to place varying values on the several kinds of occupations represented in its own economic system. Such evaluations are usually expressed in the dissimilar "returns" associated with different occupations, returns both tangible and intangible. The intangible returns include differential respect and esteem, carrying the force of community consensus, and ranging from prestige commanding great behavioral deference to stigma seen in opprobrious behavior toward the pariah.

Of course, there are direct consequences of the differences in both types of returns. For example, varying tangible returns imply differential capacity to acquire consumer goods and services in the form of creature necessities, amenities, and luxuries. In American society especially, the highly visible level and style of family consumption or standard of living, although more or less dependent on the occupation that supports it, is itself one of several scales applied by the community in assaying the relative standing of different family units. In fact, the visible pattern of consumption, among other more basic motivations, is the family's most direct mode of symbolically validating the income value attached to its breadwinner's work role.

The varying returns of different occupations, both intangible and tangible, have further consequences (1) in the privileges and restrictions their holders are dealt and (2) in the relative control—through influence and power—that their members can or cannot exercise over community processes affecting the interests and well-being of their families. Thus family, economy, and polity interweave to form a closely knit trinity in the local social system.

Interfamily similarity of income and consumption is usually reflected in the spatial differentiation of housing areas, tending to make for residential contiguity and interaction of families in like economic circumstances. Such proximity, in combination with (1) similar life interests, problems, outlooks, and attitudes arising from like economic circumstances and (2) similar standing as status[5] equals, tends to make for close associations, beyond those of kinship, in friendship circles characterized by relatively intimate behavioral congruences. In the nation's capital, by way of illustration, we are told that "Federal employees move socially within their own salary brackets." As has been observed about a lady who has lived in the District of Columbia for a long time, "everyone she knows has an income within a thousand dollars of her husband['s]."[6]

Through overlapping memberships, these friendship circles are interlocked in an extended chain or network linking most families in the community who are in broadly similar economic circumstances. To the outside observer, this network can be seen as a loosely structured, informal kind of horizontal band, or status equivalents grouping. From the inside vantage point of the family unit, this grouping tends to be seen not as an inclusive whole, but rather as a series of three expanding, progressively less clearly delineated, concentric social rings. Bounding the innermost ring is the friendship circle or circles in which the family directly participates. In the next ring are the circles whose member units are partially known and defined as "friends of our friends." In the outer ring, the largest of the three, are the many other families of similar standing which, under the necessary face-to-face conditions, would normally be considered "socially our kind" and thus potentially eligible for friendship formation.[7] These three rings comprise a partially and loosely integrated social orbit and status domain, which is locally identified in various ways, descriptive or metaphorical. Illustrative of such modes of identification for one particular status category are such terms as "high and mighty," "top drawer," "upper crust," and "the cream."

Marking off families in different status categories are divergences in standards of consumption, in values and tastes, and in behavior patterns and group identifications. As a result, there is comparatively little interaction between such families; in fact, there may be actual avoidance.[8] When interaction happens to be unavoidable or required, this "distance" is manifested as a rule in relatively brief and formal behavior.[9]

The community's several horizontal categories of families that differ in status relate to each other in a higher-lower or vertical rank order continuum. These ranked categories have been variously referred to as strata, status levels, socioeconomic groups, social classes, etc.[10]

Thus, from the twin processes of occupational specialization and differential economic and social evaluation of occupations there emerges a third process, i.e., varying elaboration of status groups and categories based on the family as their fundamental unit and arranged in a stratified order designated as a social class system.

In an earlier period of European history, the class system was of the *closed* type, marked by lifetime fixity of family position within one or another of three sharply cleavaged categories or "estates," namely, peasantry, burghers, and nobility. Through processes of evolution and revolution, the American version of the system has emerged into one preeminently, but by no means completely, *open* to change of family position. However, the broad lines of the three estates remain discernible in the apparent behavioral distinctions (1) between the manual worker (or blue-collar) class and the white-collar classes, and (2) among the latter, between the "middle" class and the "top drawer" families of inherited or acquired wealth and power.

In certain well-studied, older American communities, each of these strata has discernibly proliferated an upper and lower segment that Warner and his associates have viewed as social class groupings in their own right. However, economic changes within families and fluidity in friendship circle formation tend to make it difficult, both for community residents and scientific observers, to identify firm lines of demarcation between certain of these more limited groupings. As Lerner has more generally remarked: "To draw the profile of the American social strata is more elusive than almost anything else in American life."[11]

Apparently, we have here something roughly analogous to the chromatic spectrum of light with its bands of well-defined primary colors, the latter blending into each other at their margins to produce the secondary colors. That a continuum of shadings, rather than a series of lines, characterizes such a spectrum does not place in question the identity or identifiability of each color, secondary or primary, despite its indistinct borders.[12]

THE METROPOLITAN SITUATION

In the case of the SES spectrum, this kind of difficulty, although real enough for the field investigator, has become grossly exaggerated in the generally cogent literature of theoretical criticism. A far more serious difficulty to this investigator was the fact that the documented picture we had available on the structure and dynamics of the status system had been derived almost entirely from studies of small and relatively stable communities in New England, the South, and the Middle West regions. We had impressionistic reasons to believe that this picture applied in the main, if with touches of caricature, to the metropolis of Washington, D.C., where rank (and its well-publicized salary tag) in the huge bureaucracy of Federal government, as in the military hierarchy and in the one-industry town, is ordinarily coded and directly translated into parallel social circle clusterings and rankings of families. In contrast with such rigid patterning of status groupings in the exact mold of the economic and political hierarchies, we had the definite impression that in industrially heterogeneous metropolitan cities, like New York and Chicago, the face-to-face processes of status evaluation, friendship circle crystallizations, and resulting group formations are far more diffuse and fluid.

One facet of this difference has been noted in the following observation:

In small towns of the United States, where every man may know almost every other, participation in the daily life of the community is widely evaluated. On the basis of such community-wide evaluations the participating person and his family may be assigned to a social class. . . . In contrast to the intimate and enduring appraisals of the small town may be placed the anonymous and often fleeting appraisals of the city [where] many social contacts are segmented and the participants often strangers. Consequently, the urbanite may frequently rely upon appearance rather than reputation: status may be temporarily appropriated by the "correct" display and manipulation of symbols.[13]

Our procedural detour around this problem can be more appropriately summarized in the instrumentation section below.

CONCOMITANTS AND CONSEQUENCES OF STATUS DIFFERENCES FOR THE CHILD

We have sketched the functional evolution of social rank systems out of fundamental economic and regulative (power) processes into varyingly circumscribed but interlocking clusters or groups of informal interpersonal associations.

Around the base of similar economic roles, resources, and capabilities each of the several social class groups elaborates its own standard of consumption, a more or less coherent framework of values and attitudes, a congruent set of behavior tendencies, and common patterns of intrafamily functioning. These form a constellation, or way of life, that, together with variant constellations in other groups, are often conceived as related subculture designs within the larger cultural tapestry of the community.[14]

For us the decisive point about each status group and its way of life is that it is also the form and content of the child's "little world" —the environment, intrafamilial and extrafamilial, that guides, channels, and marks his personality development with its own indelible stamp, as it were.

The second volume of the Rennie monograph series* focuses on certain highly specific experiences of our Midtown sample respondent and tests their connections on the one hand to social class differences and on the other to the mental health variable. Here we turn to several larger concomitants and consequences of status differences that impinge with particular force on the child and seem to provide preliminary conceptual sightlines to the connections between the socioeconomic patterning of the child's world and his subsequent mental health.

An inventory of differences among children belonging to the three broad bands (i.e., lower, middle, and upper) of the American status spectrum could list research-documented items in the hundreds. For present illustrative purposes, we shall confine ourselves to only a few of these, selected because they represent relatively recent research or conceptual developments that seem to be of large potential significance.

One set of important SES correlates is suggested by William Osler's observation that "tuberculosis is a social disease with medical symptoms." Medical epidemiology has long established that certain infectious and deficiency diseases are inversely correlated with socioeconomic status. A similar relationship has been suggested for the prevalence of major chronic disorders.[15]

Whatever the etiologies of the several genera of somatic diseases, for children in different status environments they pose varyingly dis-

* Thomas S. Langner and Stanley T. Michael, *Life Stress and Mental Health*, 1963.

criminatory risks of illness and disability, with potential untoward consequences for personality development. The cumulative effect of these differential risks on physical survival alone may be inferred from the fact that between newly born *white* males of highest and lowest SES parents the latter infants have an average life expectancy 7.4 *years fewer* than that of the former.[16] If the individual survives to the twentieth birthday, the chances of being dead by the twenty-fifth birthday are four times greater for the low-status person than for his status opposite.

Of particular relevance here is this reported finding:

. . . there are positive and probably etiologic relationships between low socioeconomic status and prenatal and paranatal abnormalities which may in turn serve as precursors to retarded behavioral development, and to certain neuropsychiatric disorders of childhood such as cerebral palsy, epilepsy, mental deficiency and behavior disorder. . . .[17]

A number of studies over the years have now uncovered a chain of malfunctions that arise from poverty-level status, lead through nutritional deficiencies into maternal organic complications surrounding birth and/or prematurity of birth, accompanied by infant's low birth weight, culminating in his early death, or survival with brain damage or central nervous system dysfunctions. The latter may also be induced or further aggravated by postnatal malnourishment.[18]

A large literature also testifies to SES-mediated differences in malfunctions within the child's interpersonal realm. With the interrelationship of father and mother one of the pillars in this domain, Goode cites evidence supporting the observation that "economic factors may be of importance in marital stability."[19] This supplements research confirming that maladjustments in husband-wife relationships increase in prevalence downward on the social class scale.[20]

The frequent deterioration of such maladjustments into broken homes has been repeatedly noted in the literature: "Lower class families exhibit the highest prevalence of instability of any class in the status structure. . . . In the Deep South and Elmtown studies, from 50 to 60 percent of lower class family groups are broken once, and more often, by desertion, divorce, death or separation . . . between marriage, legal or companionate, and its normal dissolution."[21] Evidence on the psychiatric effects of such broken homes has been comprehensively reviewed by Gregory.[22]

This carries us to the all-important parent-child dyad in the family structure. Since we must be highly selective, we shall not touch on the extensive series of studies bearing on specific infant training practices in the lower and middle classes but shall refer instead to several investigations that have focused on more global aspects of the parent-child relationship. Offering a suggestive portal to these aspects is a study reporting that middle-class children tend to feel themselves influenced in their behavior by parents perceived as a pair, whereas to lower-class children these influences are more often felt to be emanating from parents as separate individuals.[23]

For the latter child, apparently, the father-mother bond tends to be less an entity and more a case of "house divided." The potential implications of this interparental fracture for the personality of the growing child would seem to be considerable.

To a sample of 1,472 adolescents, Nye has applied a measure of child-parent adjustment. He finds that "adolescents from the higher socio-economic level families score higher [i.e., better] on feelings of being loved and secure, feelings that parents trust and have confidence in them, socialization including disciplinary relationships [i.e., more positive feelings about parents as disciplinarians], attitudes toward the parent's personality and . . . adjustment to groups outside the family."[24]

If these findings are worded in terms of children from lower-SES families, implied is a greater prevalence there of a fracture in the parent-child relationship. This inference is consistent with projective test data among lower-SES "normal" samples, where subjects "portray themselves as relatively isolated from parental figures whom they see as cold and rejecting."[25]

From his research in a lower-class metropolitan area, Miller observes:

The genesis of the intense concern over "toughness" in lower class culture is probably related to the fact that a significant proportion of lower class males are reared in a predominantly female household, and lack a consistently present male figure with whom to identify and from whom to learn essential components of a male role. Since women serve as a primary object of identification during preadolescent years, the almost obsessive lower class concern with "masculinity" probably resembles a type of compulsive reaction-formation.[26]

Employing "family rituals, as a relatively reliable index of family integration," Bossard and Boll assert: "Our overall conclusion is that family rituals increase in number, variety, richness and willing co-operation by individual family members as one moves upward in the economic scale."[27]

These sociologists see the lower-class family as having "little connection with the past. The present is composed of individuals crowded into a space too small for comfort. . . . Children see little if anything in their families to stimulate a desire to perpetuate what they see. Opportunities for emotional satisfactions in the home are few, even for adults. The rituals arising from these situations are, for the most part, rituals of expedience, to keep the home going, and to facilitate escape. . . ."

In the middle-class families, on the other hand, "the tone is one of hopefulness and optimism. . . . The rituals here show a cooperativeness, of a desire to reach these goals, as well as a genuine family 'togetherness' in a home where there is need and opportunity for it."

In a paper appropriately titled "Portrait of the Underdog," Knupfer "considers the disadvantages of low status, the restriction of 'life chances' which low status carries with it. From this point of view, the tendency of different aspects of status to 'cluster' together takes on the aspect of a vicious circle which recalls the Biblical dictum: 'to him that hath shall be given.' "[28] Knupfer then offers evidence "to show that closely linked with economic under-privilege is psychological under-privilege: habits of submission, little access to sources of information, lack of verbal facility. These things appear to produce a lack of self-confidence which increases the unwillingness of the low status person to participate in many phases of our predominantly middle-class culture, even beyond what would be a realistic withdrawal adapted to his reduced chances of being effective."

The problem, we consider, also goes deeper than a lack of self-confidence. The child of the slum, to concretize the urban version of low status, tends to find in his home few responses to his need to feel that he is valued or respected.[29] The self-image initially implanted in that important arena of his life, we can assume, is hardly a prepossessing one.

To an even lesser degree does he find this response outside the home—with the single exception of his street gang (wherein lies its potent hold on him). In a study of school children Neugarten reports that "social class differences in friendships and reputation are well established by age eleven years."[30] Lower-class children, this investigation revealed, were regarded with indifference or disfavor by schoolmates of higher status, and even more strikingly, they regarded themselves unfavorably. Moreover, they enjoyed no surcease even when they escaped to the movies, comic books, and television. In Hollywood films, "whether by omission or commission, there is an implicit but clear disparagement of anything that suggests 'dirty work' or anyone who labors. Such deprecation pervades all the popular culture media, assailing the worker (and his children) and tending to weaken his ego-image. . . ."[31]

The pieces of evidence just reviewed, among many others, all fit into a consistent picture. This picture reveals a life setting for the slum-level child heavily weighted with impoverishing burdens and deprivations of body, mind, and spirit, to an extent well beyond the more nurturing environment of the middle-class child and far beyond that of the "cushioned" upper-class child. However, what is perhaps the most serious core of the matter remains to be brought into sharper focus. In fact, this was only partially discerned when the Midtown Study was being designed.

The keystone of the democratic creed is the doctrine that, whatever their native endowments, all men are intrinsically of equal worth before God, the law, and their fellows. With considerable intensity, children tend to incorporate this canon as a bulwark in their still fragile image of themselves. As we have seen, however, in many areas of his experience the lower-class child encounters the contempt, implicit but palpable, in the nonverbal behavior of others who think of him in the symbolism of such words as rubbish, scum, dregs, riffraff, and trash. These devastating judgments inevitably force their way into his own self-evaluation processes. Thus, he is caught between grossly contradictory, mutually exclusive images of himself, torn by a conflict implanted through the agents of a society that professes equality and practices invidious discrimination.

Between the millstones of this jarring contradiction, the slum-dweller child grows into another, if related, conflict. Under the democratic guarantee of equal opportunity he may expect, given the requisite ability and effort, to rise to a social position of more comfort and respect.[32] But with economically and culturally disadvantaged parents and a school system unequipped to help him overcome his learning lags,[33] he is likely to get only the legal minimum of ten years' schooling. On the other hand, carrying no better native endowment but confronted with none of the objective barriers, his high-status schoolmate goes on to college. From that turning point forward the career opportunities are actuarially even more disparate than the differential longevity expectations of the two boys.[34]

The "poor" boy has a large chance of becoming an unskilled worker, the "rich" boy a corporation executive. By all economic criteria, with support from all the culture media, the latter is a success, the former decidedly less than that. But under the logic of equal opportunity, this difference in terminus is presumed to reflect differences in character and abilities; q.e.d., the laborer is inherently inferior to those in higher economic echelons. Thus, the contrast between the open-opportunities doctrine (seemingly validated by the successful) and his own meager career accomplishments is a second source of unresolved contention in the arena of his self-evaluation. Reinforcing each other, we hypothesize, the two conflicts have been induced at every step in the lower-class individual's life by a self-contradicting society, one that regularly feeds and uplifts him by the promise of its tenets as democratic writ, and that just as regularly cuts him down by the punishing inequalities and discriminations of its social class system. This, it is submitted, is a culturally designed approximation of the classical experiments in provoking animals to the point of paralyzing neurotic symptomatology.[35]

In a trail-blazing paper, Merton has delineated the disparity between culturally emphasized goals and socially inaccessible means to actualize them, a sociological condition of disjunction, or *anomie*, and one he postulates is conducive to behavioral deviation.[36]

The present writer has elsewhere conceptualized these phenomena of social conflict as one stream among others leading to the individual condition of self-to-group alienation, or *anomia*, and has shown that the frequency and intensity of this state vary inversely with socioeconomic status,[37] i.e., are most heavily concentrated at the lowest reaches of the social class scale. Parallel but more extensive data from the Midtown sample adults will appear in a separate publication by this author.[38]

Although not fully articulated to the social class framework, the work of psychiatrists Cleveland and Longaker has made a conceptual contribution in relating culturally derived value conflicts to the emergence of psychopathology. The intervening process of "disparagement" they locate

. . . on the level of individual development and personality integration [as a] pattern of extreme devaluation . . . which can arise . . . when the socializing agents, primarily the parents, hold out contradictory models of behavior (grounded on conflicting cultural values). . . . Disparagement can become a fixed tendency in the child to devalue certain facets of his own personality. . . . Moreover, the disparagement of self is often not confined to one's own individual capacities but radiates to disparagement of the defined behaviors and value systems of his culture. In short, it touches all that has been internalized by the individual, or with which he identifies. . . . Its corrosive implications stem from both the tendency to deny individual worth, with resultant crippling of selfhood, and to deny the worth of group values, and thus to cripple interaction.

The quoted authors delineate this situational nexus in the neurotic processes of three psychiatric patients from a single extended family.[39]

That the parents of the slum child may themselves be behaving under this self-defeating mechanism could account for the atmosphere of malaise often observed in such homes and for the affectional fractures discerned above in the father-mother and parent-child relationships. Given this kind of disarticulated family setting in infancy and early childhood, given the assaults on body, mind, and spirit in early and late childhood, and given the double-barreled, destructive conflict of self-image during adolescence, we can judge that chance and society have saddled the lower-class child with a cumulatively oppressive series of burdens. Compared with the more privileged child, we originally hypothesized that as an adult he would be more defenseless against the crises of life and therefore more susceptible to mental morbidity.

INDEPENDENT OR RECIPROCAL VARIABLE

Applying this hypothesis to our Home Survey adults brought a further problem of specification. Most previous investigations focusing on mental health as the dependent or response variable had in effect declared, as had one, that "the class status of individuals in the society is viewed as the independent or antecedent variable."[40]

The present writer from the start rejected this view as untenable. At the very least, an adult's socioeconomic status and his mental health are *concurrent* phenomena and no basis exists for assuming a priori which is antecedent and which is consequence. Moreover, realities strongly argued that sound preadult mental health is generally a favorable precondition to achieving higher adult status, just as chronic mental disturbance could make it difficult for a breadwinner even to match his parents' socioeconomic standing.

On the other hand, the adult's success or failure in meeting the standards of the SES group to which he is oriented may contribute its own discrete weight toward changing the subsequent course of his mental health development. As previously suggested, therefore, the adult's *own* status level must strictly be hypothesized as no more than a reciprocal variable relative to his current mental health.

For SES in a form that can be defended as antecedent to and independent of mental health we had to look to the status of the adult's *childhood* family, here designated as *parental SES* or *SES origin*, particularly as the weight of accumulated evidence suggests that (1) the childhood period may be crucial in shaping determinants of later mental health and (2) interfamily differences may be partially attributed to differential social class patterning of intrafamily processes and life conditions.

INSTRUMENTATION: HOME SURVEY OPERATION

Estimation of parental SES among our Home Survey sample of adults in turn raised several technical problems. Ruled out as data altogether inaccessible to us were the subjective indications of social standing, namely, (1) how member families of the community say they place each other on the social rank scale and (2) where member families behaviorally place themselves through participation in selected friendship circles, secular organizations, and religious institutions of known SES composition. These involve rating methods that have been particularly developed and systematized by Warner in his techniques of "evaluated participation."[41]

Accessible, however, were the objective indicators that themselves contribute to the community's determination of family status. For example, toward classifying respondent's own SES we used four such indicators, namely, his education, occupation, total family income, and rent—as a key to his style and standard of family living. Such yardsticks would have been preferred in any case because they are quantifiable, are simple to secure, and readily lend themselves to comparative uses in different communities.

For respondents' parents, who in largest numbers had lived in places big and small spread over the European and American continents, across a time span of a half century, neither income nor rent offered itself as a sufficiently standardized register of interfamily differences. The father's schooling, on the other hand, was somewhat less objectionable, and his occupational level was most acceptable of all for this purpose. However, for interview elicitation from the father's offspring, the latter datum in particular required a number of special precautions. First, for what stage of father's life did we want his occupation—at marriage, at retirement, at midlife? This could not be left to respondents to decide in their separate ways. And clearly it had to be specified at a stage that respondent could report from personal observation. Rephrasing the question in terms of respondent's age of observation suggested that we set this period at the *same* point in the life cycle for *all* respondents. The point we felt to be of maximum significance was the respondent at age 18 to 19, when he was near the launching of his own career and the father himself was probably near the middle of his work history.

Second, precautions had to be taken to minimize the widespread tendency to add a substantial dosage of wishful thinking in reporting occupations, for both the father and oneself. Accordingly, three separate questions were put to each respondent with reference to his and his father's occupation. In relation to the father these were: (1) "When you were about 18 to 19 years old, what kind of work was your father doing for a living?" (Here the interviewer recorded the work as described and the title of the job if named.) (2) "At that time did he work for himself or others?" (3) "About how many people did he have working for (under) him?"

Placement of father and respondent, each in his own occupational bracket, was made neither by the respondent nor by the interviewer. Instead, on the basis of the respondent's three replies and a framework of specifications developed for the purpose, office coders placed the father in one of 27 occupational rubrics. The latter were then collapsed on the line of the blue-collar–white-collar dichotomy, with each category in turn divided into a high, middle, and low grade. In the blue-collar range, these grades represented the usual skilled, semi-skilled, and unskilled kinds of manual work.

Within the white-collar range the allocations were somewhat more complicated. Into the high stratum were placed professionals and top-level executives, self-employed and otherwise. Semiprofessionals, intermediate managerial personnel, and highly specialized sales people (e.g., in real estate, stocks, insurance, wholesale trade) were assigned to the middle grade. To the lower bracket were allocated small shop (goods or services) proprietors, managers with relatively few subordinates, other sales people, and office and clerical help.[42]

The six grades were given score values from 1 to 6 proceeding upward in the scale. Fathers' schooling was similarly divided into six grades.[43] For each father the two scores, equally weighted, were summated. The distribution of 1,660 summated scores was then cut in a manner to produce six groups as equally populated as possible. This stratification will be our measure of respondent's *parental SES*.

It is readily apparent that this is an unusual yardstick in two respects. First, the lines of demarcation between the parental-SES levels emerge from the procedure of distributing families in nearly equal numbers among the six strata. On the one hand, this is an approximation of defining classes by the criterion of equally spaced intervals, an instrumentally desirable tactic whenever it is feasible. On the other hand, it lends itself readily to symmetrical mergers into fewer and larger categories when SES-origin differences must be applied as an analytical control.

Second, the six parental strata do *not* tell us how respondents' families stood in the prestige rank system of their respective home communities. This, of course, would have been beyond the practical powers of retrospective research to reconstruct. Instead, they suggest how these families would hypothetically have stood *relative to each other*, in socioeconomic respects, had they all been gathered together, at one time and place, to continue functioning as they had when their offspring-respondent was near the turn into adulthood. In effect, therefore, these families as stratified represent an analytically contrived social rank order.

However, each of the six aggregations of respondent families may not be quite as artificial as would appear at first glance. It was the writer's prediction that when economically equivalent SES classes in different Western countries were ultimately studied and compared in detail, this would be found: The specific status-linked similarities in outlook and behavior patterns would outnumber and significantly outweigh differences rooted in specific national traditions. The rationale for this prediction was the assumption that like economic and creature conditions of life, in countries within the broad Western compass, tend to evoke similar constellations of values, goals, and role patternings in both intrafamily and extrafamily settings of daily functioning.

Monographic studies of this general kind have since been made in England, Australia, Mexico, and the Soviet Union. In a summary of the Soviet study we are told: "It will perhaps come as a great surprise to many that there is a close correspondence between the pattern of experience and attitudes of Soviet citizens and their counterparts on the same level of education or occupation in a variety of other large scale industrial societies having markedly different culture and history and possessed of quite dissimilar political institutions."[44] Despite extreme differences in methods employed, the three other studies point in the same direction.[45]

Accordingly, the respondent families in each of our SES-origin strata, with their close similarities in education and occupation, would probably have shared a wide range of other common elements. Such a larger array of like characteristics would support our inference that each stratum of families has a core of homogeneity in intrafamily patterns, if not of interfamily linkages.

In moving on to the respondent's *own* status alignments we shall proceed on two separate tracks. First, to stratify respondent's own SES on the most refined and extended yardstick available to us, we have combined his total family income and dwelling rent with his education[46] and occupation.[47] Each of the former two indicators was also cut into six brackets and scored on a 1 to 6 scale. The sum of the scores for the four indicators, all given equal weight, was calculated for each respondent. The sample's distribution of these summated scores was then cut to yield twelve segments (collapsible into six or three levels as analytically required), as evenly populated as possible.

Second, to trace respondent status changes (mobility) from specific parental positions, we compare occupational level of father and of respondent.

INSTRUMENTATION: TREATMENT CENSUS OPERATION

In our Treatment Census operation we faced certain other difficulties. Working exclusively from institutional records, we found that data related to parental SES were available, in the nature of the situation, only for preadults. That did not matter, since our interest in the treatment variable in any case allotted primary relevance to the immediate own SES circumstances and settings of patients as they crossed into a therapeutic relationship. It was here in fact that we encountered problems. In the records of psychiatric hospitals and clinics, information on income or rent appeared infrequently; for the nonemployed, including housewives, occupation of family breadwinner was often missing; and for 10 percent of the adults no data on schooling were given. From office therapists it proved possible to ask only for patient's initials,[48] diagnosis, and home address. The latter item of information, in terms of verified residential buildings, was provided for 81 percent of the office patients reported to us. Together with home address of 99 percent of hospital and clinic patients, the largest possible common indicator of status we could apply to Midtown's patient population (as enumerated by our Treatment Census) was place of residence.

Other studies have given a rank order value to all homes in a small area unit with known economic characteristics, e.g., the census tract.[49] However, Midtown's extreme housing heterogeneity—even within the census tract subunit of the city block—made this expedient patently error-ridden. The only alternative, but a difficult one, was to use the individual residence as the unit of evaluation.[50] Fortunately, earlier in the Study a housing survey had been made by four volunteer businessmen who were experts in local residential properties.[51] Every tenanted building in Midtown was inspected by a team of two of these men and graded, by means of consensus judgment, on criteria of housing quality and condition of upkeep.

The validity of these judgments was later tested against the 1,660 Home Survey respondents. A Pearson coefficient of .73 was established between (1) the housing grades independently assigned to respondents' buildings by the above teams and (2) respondents' composite own SES scores as based on education, occupation, income, and rent. This is sufficiently high to warrant use of the former, divided into three categories, as a crude substitute own SES yardstick for our Treatment Census patients. As to the reported office patients of unknown address, we assumed that they were distributed among the housing categories in more or less the same manner as the office patients of known address. Actually, there may be a bias hidden in this allocation, to which we shall allude when the data are presented in chapter 16.

It should be added that to calculate patient rates in each housing category, the denominator figures needed were the total number of people living in each such grade of housing. That the United States census could not furnish. However, we did know the housing grades and total number of occupants in 2,060 randomly selected Midtown dwellings. From this sample it was possible to estimate the total population in each housing category, thereby permitting computation of patient rates per 100,000 people in each stratum.

SUMMARY

Substantively, the contents of the present chapter belong in Book One, chapters 7 and 8. However, unusual complexities and difficulties attending observation and measurement of the SES variable dictated that this discussion be held as stage setting for the data chapters that follow immediately.

To capture the essential, universal elements of socioeconomic status, its genesis was traced to this chain of fundamental processes: proliferating social division of labor, occupational specialization, differential evaluation of occupations and differential rewarding of the skills they require, economic shaping of family conditions and style of life, and the interactional sorting of economically similar families into friendship circles and status-peer groupings.

Note was taken of the evolution of the medieval European status system, closed and sharply cleavaged in structure, toward the open spectrum type of contemporary America.

The concept of the status group's way of life as a constellation or subculture was advanced and tied to the patterning of the child's world. Selected research evidence was introduced to indicate social class differences in patternings that were potentially significant for the direction of mental health development.

Focusing on the slum child, a formulation was offered of the development of conflicting self-images and evaluations, induced by self-contradictions in the doctrinal and behavioral realms of a democratic but prestige-discriminating society. These and other impoverishments of the lower-class family and environment provided the rationale for the test hypothesis that in the Midtown survey sample parental socioeconomic status and adult mental morbidity would be inversely related.

The grounds for the distinction between parental SES and own SES were defined. Discussed also were the various problems of and solutions to measuring socioeconomic status both in the Treatment Census and Home Survey operations.

NOTES

1. D. J. Boorstin, *The Americans: The Democratic Experience*, 1973; G. W. Pierson, *Tocqueville in America*, 1959; M. Lerner, *America as a Civilization*, 1957, pp. 465–540.

2. C. H. Page, *Class and American Sociology: From Ward to Ross*, 1940.

3. Robert Lynd and Helen Lynd, *Middletown* and *Middletown in Transition*, 1929 and 1937; and W. L. Warner, L. Srole, P. S. Lunt, and J. O. Low, Yankee City Series, 1941–1959, vols. 1–5. For a comprehensive account and balanced evaluation of the antecedents, contents, and repercussions of these community studies, see M. M. Gordon, *Social Class in American Sociology*, 1958.

4. See N. D. Glenn, et al., *Social Stratification: A Research Bibliography*, 1970.

5. For verbal convenience, the term *status*, when appearing without specification, will hereafter be used as shorthand reference to socioeconomic status.

6. I. Kapp, "Living in Washington, D.C.," *Commentary*, January 1957, p. 61.

7. Obviously, other criteria of eligibility also operate. Some base eligibility on inherited family lineage, a symbolic badge that may be more weighty to a rare few than economic and related circumstances. Some criteria refer to group alignments that cut across and tend to subdivide the economically grounded status-peer grouping, e.g., religious affiliation and national background. Other criteria relate to personal tastes and interests that combine into a test of aesthetic and intellectual congeniality, such as is conceptualized in Russell Lynes's typology of "highbrow," "middlebrow," and "lowbrow." (*The Tastemakers*, 1954.)

Of course, such religious, ethnic, and aesthetic criteria may draw together people of dissimilar economic characteristics, thereby interlacing and blurring the edges of adjoining economic-peer groupings. However, it is more often likely that such criteria will tend to recruit friendship circles from within, rather than from beyond, the same economic bracket.

8. "Individuals occupying certain statuses simply do not directly interact with persons in certain other statuses, or interact only minimally. . . . A 'map' of the interaction patterns of most American communities would unquestionably show definite clusters of frequent interaction, separated from other clusters by social

voids only lightly bridged by a few individuals." Robin Williams, *American Society*, 1970, p. 593.

9. "[One] type of [interstatus] insulation involves direct person-to-person interaction, but consists of formalized and limited patterns of relationships such as the constrained interaction of superiors and subordinates in rigidly hierarchical organizations." Ibid., p. 594.

However, those serving people of different social ranks learn to modulate the formality of their behavior, as enlisted men reveal in their interactions with the various ranks of officers. Similarly, a Washington columnist reports that the capital "is a place where the grocer knows precisely the standing, social and financial, of Mrs. Jones against Mrs. Smith . . . and intuitively treats each good lady with the exact degree of deference to which she is entitled."

10. In the interest of variety, we shall use these terms interchangeably.

11. Lerner, *America as a Civilization*, p. 473.

12. Implied in this question is the fallacy of discrete concreteness; that is, what does not have clear-cut boundaries does not qualify for identification as a conceptual entity.

13. W. H. Form and G. P. Stone, "Urbanism, Anonymity and Status Symbolism," *American Journal of Sociology* 57 (March 1957): 504.

14. The development of this concept in the work of the Lynds and Warner and his associates has been synthesized by C. Kluckhohn and F. R. Kluckhohn, "American Culture: Generalized Orientations and Class Patterns," in L. Bryson et al., eds., *Conflicts of Power in Modern Culture*, 1947, pp. 106–128. For related formulations see W. B. Miller, "Lower Class Culture as a Generating Milieu of Gang Delinquency," *Journal of Social Issues* 14 (1958): 5–19; and H. H. Hyman, "The Value Systems of Different Classes: A Social Psychological Contribution to the Analysis of Stratification," in R. Bendix and S. M. Lipset, eds., *Class, Status and Power: A Reader in Social Stratification*, 1966, pp. 488–499.

15. J. M. Ellis, "Socio-economic Differentials in Mortality from Chronic Diseases," in E. G. Jaco, ed., *Patients, Physicians and Illness*, 1958, pp. 30–36; "Chronic Conditions and Limitations of Activity and Mobility, 1965–1967," *Vital and Health Statistics*, Series 10, no. 61 (1971); M. Lerner, "Social Differences in Physical Health," in J. Kosa, A. Antonovsky, and I. K. Zola, eds., *Poverty and Health*, 1969, pp. 60–112; D. J. May and M. J. Wantman, "Selected Chronic Conditions: Estimates of Prevalence and of Physician Services, New York City, 1966," *Population Health Survey Research Bulletin*, RB–M8–69, 1969, p. 15. In the latter survey, the frequencies of heart conditions, hypertension, diabetes, arthritis, asthma, and bronchitis were inversely related to family income; peptic ulcer and hay fever were not. See also T. Rennie and L. Srole, "Social Class Prevalence and Distribution of Psychosomatic Conditions in an Urban Population [Midtown]," *Psychosomatic Medicine* 13 (1956): 449–456.

16. E. M. Kitagawa and P. Hauser, *Differential Mortality in the United States*, 1973, p. 71. In a comprehensive review of the evidence, A. Antonovsky writes, "The inescapable conclusion is that class [still] influences one's chances of staying alive." ("Social Class, Life Expectancy and Over-all Mortality," *Milbank Quarterly* 45 [April 1967]: 67.) For a challenge to the evidence prompting this conclusion, see C. Kadushin, "Social Class and Ill Health: The Need for Further Research," *Sociological Inquiry*, Spring 1967, pp. 323–332.

17. B. Pasamanick, H. Knobloch, and A. M. Lilienfeld, "Socioeconomic Status and Precursors of Neuropsychiatric Disorder," *American Journal of Orthopsychiatry* 26 (1956): 594–602.

18. H. Birch and J. Gussow, *Disadvantaged Children; Health, Nutrition and School Failure*, 1970; D. Amante, et al., "Epidemiological Distribution of CNS Dysfunction," *Journal of Social Issues* 26 (1970): 105–136; F. Shah and H. Abbey, "Effects of Some Factors on Neonatal and Postneonatal Mortality," *Milbank Quarterly* 49 (January 1971): 33–57; W. Shoemaker and R. Wurtman, "Perinatal Undernutrition: Accumulation of Catecholamines in Rat Brain," *Science* 171 (March 1971): 1017–1019.

19. W. J. Goode, "Economic Factors and Marital Stability," *American Sociological Review* 16 (December 1951): 802–812.

20. J. Roth and R. F. Peck, "Social Class and Social Mobility Factors Related to Marital Adjustment," *American Sociological Review* 16 (August 1951): 478–487.

21. A. B. Hollingshead, "Class Differences in Family Stability," *Annals of the American Academy of Political and Social Science* (November 1950): 39–46. See also *Journal of Marriage and the Family* 28 (November 1966), articles on marital stability and status variables, pp. 421–448.

22. I. Gregory, "Studies of Parental Deprivation in Psychiatric Patients," *American Journal of Psychiatry* 115 (November 1958): 432–442. See also E. Furman, *A Child's Parent Dies*, 1974.

23. F. Sabghir, "Relation between Consistency and Ego-Supportiveness of Influence Techniques Used by Parent and Behavior and Self-Acceptance of Children (Ph.D. dissertation, George Washington University, 1959).

24. I. Nye, "Adolescent-Parent Adjustment: Socio-economic Level as a Variable," *American Sociological Review* 16 (June 1951): 341–349.

25. J. L. Singer, "Projected Familial Attitudes as a Function of Socioeconomic Status and Psychopathology," *Journal of Consulting Psychology* 18, no. 2 (1954): 99–104. See also B. Rosen, "Social Class and the Child's Perception of the Parent," *Child Development* 35 (December 1964): 1147–1153.

26. Miller, "Lower Class Culture," pp. 5–19. A study of London slum families uncovered the identical linkages; cf. B. M. Spinley, *The Deprived and the Privileged: Personality Development in English Society*, 1953, p. 81.

27. J. H. S. Bossard and E. S. Boll, "Ritual in Family Living," *American Sociological Review* 14 (August 1949): 463–469.

28. G. Knupfer, in R. Bendix and S. M. Lipset, eds., *Class, Status and Power*, 1953, pp. 255–263.

29. In some part this may stem from the calculus of economic costs of a child relative to inadequate and unstable means and from the further fact that under lower-class fertility patterns children arrive far more frequently than they are wanted or can be accommodated into mother's economy of affect and energy.

30. B. L. Neugarten, "Social Class and Friendship among Children," *American Journal of Sociology* 51 (1946): 305–313.

31. S. Bellin and F. Riessman, Jr., "Education, Culture and the Anarchic Worker," *Journal of Social Issues* 5 (Winter 1949): 24–32.

32. This has been stated in extreme form by an inspirational nineteenth-century writer, as follows: "The road to fortune, like the public turnpike, is open alike to the children of the beggar and the descendants of kings." (A. C. McCurty, *Win Who Will*, 1872, p. 19; cited in H. M. Hodges, Jr., *Social Stratification*, 1964, p. 195.)

33. W. L. Warner, R. J. Havighurst, and M. Loeb, *Who Shall Be Educated?*, 1944.

34. B. K. Ecklynd, "Academic Ability, Higher Education and Occupational

Mobility," *American Sociological Review* 30 (October 1965): 735–746.

35. J. H. Masserman, "The Biodynamic Approaches," in S. Arieti, ed., *American Handbook of Psychiatry*, Vol. II, 1959, pp. 1686–1688.

36. R. K. Merton, *Social Theory and Social Structure*, 1949, pp. 125–129. The writer's indebtedness to this paper is apparent. The deviation Merton refers to is "in types of more or less enduring response, not types of personality organization." Emphasized in the present formulation are effects on the ego mechanisms of the child's developing character structure.

37. L. Srole, "Social Integration and Certain Corollaries: An Exploratory Study," *American Sociological Review* 21 (December 1956): 709–716.

38. L. Srole, "Anomia: Antecedents and Consequences," work in progress.

39. E. J. Cleveland and W. D. Longaker, "Neurotic Patterns in the Family," in A. H. Leighton, J. A. Clausen, and R. N. Wilson, eds., *Explorations in Social Psychiatry*, 1957, pp. 167–200. For a conceptually refined and empirical articulation of the process to SES differences in a general population sample of 500 adults, see H. B. Kaplan, "Social Class and Self- Derogation: A Conditional Relationship," *Sociometry* 34 (January 1971): 41–54.

40. A. B. Hollingshead and F. C. Redlich, *Social Class and Mental Illness*, 1958, p. 12.

41. W. L. Warner, M. Meeker, and K. Eells, *Social Class in America*, 1949.

42. In so stratifying the grades within the white-collar range, the writer was departing from the Edwards' United States Census scheme of occupational classification in the general direction taken by Warner's system (*Social Class in America*, pp. 140–141). However, in the absence of local evidence to indicate otherwise, we maintained the integrity of the blue-collar–white-collar dichotomy, as had Edwards.

43. That is, (1) some elementary school, (2) elementary school graduate, (3) some high school, (4) high school graduate, (5) some college, (6) college graduate. If father's schooling was uncertain or unknown, mother's schooling was used instead.

44. A. Inkeles and R. A. Bauer, *The Soviet Citizen: Daily Life in a Totalitarian Society*, 1959.

45. Spinley, *The Deprived and the Privileged*; O. S. Oeser and S. B. Hammond, *Social Structure and Personality in a City* [Melbourne], 1954; and O. Lewis, *Five Families*, 1959.

46. However, wives are classified by composite score of *own* schooling, occupation of husband, total family income, and dwelling rent.

47. In the present edition of this monograph attention can be called to the Kansas City investigation reported in R. Coleman and B. Neugarten, *Social Status in the City*, 1971. This investigation was directed to analysis of the status structure in the subject city by methods adapted from studies of small communities (principally by W. L. Warner and his colleagues). It empirically arrived at a measure called "the Index of Kansas City Status" (IKCS). Three of the component indicators incorporated in the IKCS (p. 81)—namely, education, occupation of head of household, and total family income—had been included in our composite measure of respondent's own SES. Also included in the IKCS were classification of "neighborhood of residence and quality of housing." These were both represented in the Midtown measure by the single indicator of household rent. However, novel in the IKCS was the inclusion of three other indicators—based on "evaluations made by Kansas Citians"—namely, "education of wife, church affiliation, and community associations [including the factor of ethnic identity]." We have found that schooling of husband and that of spouse

are sufficiently correlated (Gamma = .75) that the latter is largely redundant. For purposes of the Midtown Study, moreover, religious and ethnic affiliations stand on very different conceptual planes relative to metropolitan SES as we had observed it. Above all other considerations, our hypotheses about these affiliations as potential predictors of mental health required that they be analyzed with controls for SES as usually defined, precluding their merger with the latter.

48. These were needed to check against multiple reporting of the same patient.

49. The New Haven Study of psychiatric patients used a residential area scale of this kind, but the specific nature of the area unit employed has not been clearly identified. Hollingshead and Redlich, *Social Class and Mental Illness*, p. 390.

50. See R. W. Mack, "Housing as an Index of Social Class," *Social Forces* 29, no. 4 (May 1951): 391–399. Also, Warner et al., *Social Class in America*, pp. 143–150.

51. These were Messrs. Kurt Porges, Percival Perkins, René Hoguet, and Maurice Bloch, to whom the Midtown Study is indebted for this and other highly skilled services.

CHAPTER 14

SOCIOECONOMIC STRATA: THEIR MENTAL HEALTH MAKE-UP

LEO SROLE AND THOMAS LANGNER

Change as it may, socioeconomic status is a lifelong motif in the individual's web of daily experience. One of the dominating designs in the vast tapestry of the nation's culture, it also weaves itself into the dreams, calculations, strivings, triumphs, and defeats of many Americans from childhood on.

Accordingly, the hypothesis linking frequency of mental disorder to SES differences was inevitable, and indeed has drawn the attention of numerous investigations. Their reports provide convenient points of departure for the present chapter.

In largest numbers these researchers chose to test the hypothesis by the relatively simple expedient of enumerating psychiatric patients recorded on treatment rosters as their measure of the extent of mental morbidity. With several notable exceptions, these efforts did not explicitly distinguish between *treated* frequency and *overall* (untreated and treated) frequency of mental impairment as very different yardsticks of morbidity. They therefore applied the former but fell into the error of drawing generalizations as if they had measured the latter.

We hold that socioeconomic status as linked on one hand to *overall* frequency of mental impairment and on the other to frequency of *psychiatric treatment* among the Impaired present rather different questions that require discrete hypotheses and separate testing. In the next chapter we take up the SES-and-treatment hypothesis, where the previous studies of patient populations can claim direct relevance. To our top-priority hypothesis connecting status and *overall* mental morbidity, these limited studies do not offer tests that satisfy the criterion of relevance.

Potentially offering a more adequate test of the latter hypothesis are the investigations that have looked beyond patients inscribed on institutional records and, in search of both untreated and treated cases of morbidity, reached with a far wider, albeit crude, net into the lifestream of a general population at large. Relatively few in number, these published studies deserve brief examination for any light they can throw on the state of knowledge bearing on this particular hypothesis.

Probably the first and the largest of these was the National Health Survey conducted in 1936 under Federal auspices. Using the interview method and covering, in one of its aspects, a sample of 703,092 households (2,502,391 individuals) in 83 cities,[1] this study included a wide range of medical disabilities reported active on the day of interview. Included was the category "nervous and mental diseases," specifically "neurasthenia, nervous breakdown, epilepsy, chorea, locomotor ataxia, paresis, other diseases of the nervous system." Occupation was the SES indicator (among the employed in the age range 15 to 64), and was dichotomized on the line of the white-collar and blue-collar distinction. In frequencies of "nervous and mental disease," so defined, the data for employed females revealed no difference by occupation category. Among males, on the other hand, the white-collar rate exceeded that of the blue-collar category by about 3:2.

A check of the latter finding is at hand in several World War II studies of Selective Service male registrants, with rejections for "mental and personality disorders" as the criterion of morbidity. One of these investigations involved a national sample clinically examined during November–December 1943, with occupation again the status indicator.[2] With the exclusion of farmers, students, and the unemployed, no significant differences in psychiatric rejection rates were found among the several occupational categories there defined.

A second Selective Service study was conducted with 60,000 male registrants examined at the Boston Area Induction Station in 1942.[3] The Boston psychiatric rejection rates by socioeconomic level of registrants, as indexed by area of residence, were as follows:

Socioeconomic level	Rejected in each level
A (highest)	7.3%
B	9.2
C	9.4
D	10.0
E	12.7
F (lowest)	16.6

Clearly the lower the SES stratum, the larger was the rejection rate.

A more recent study relevant here was conducted in Baltimore.[4] From our discussion in chapter 10 it will be remembered that this investigation involved a clinical examination and evaluation of a sample of 809 men and women (approximately 30 percent of these were nonwhites) and covered a broad spectrum of some 30 somatic disorders. The mental disorder rates by income level are reported only for whites and nonwhites combined. If we assume that the non-whites of Baltimore, as elsewhere, were highly concentrated in the lowest of the four income brackets defined, then the other income groups, inferred to be predominantly white, have mental disorder rates reported as follows:

Income level	Disorders in each level
$6,000 and over	13.6%
$4,000–$5,999	8.9
$2,000–$3,999	8.9

The four inquiries just considered had in common the distinguishing feature of covering a general population, rather than an aggregate of patients. However, on the issue of a connection between SES and overall prevalence of psychiatric disability, the findings of these studies point in almost all possible directions. In the national Selective Service investigation the correlation was practically zero; in the Boston Selective Service survey it was inverse, i.e., the lower the SES level, the higher the morbidity rate; among the Baltimore sample whites it was apparently positive, i.e., highest morbidity rate in the top-income category; and in the National Health Survey the correlation was zero among females and positive among males.

Although the four inquiries used different SES indicators—occupation, area of residence, or income—these are standard measures that are known to be highly correlated with and predictive of each other. Accordingly, it is unlikely that the contradictory findings arise from the different socioeconomic yardsticks applied. Note in particular that the same indicator, occupation, was used in the two national investigations, yet divergent morbidity trends were obtained for the males in the two samples.

In the absence of sufficient evidence to explain or reconcile the inconsistent yields in the four studies reviewed,[5] we viewed the suggested hypothesis linking socioeconomic status and overall mental morbidity in the general population as an open question.

PARENTAL SES: MENTAL HEALTH DISTRIBUTIONS

During childhood, the individual shares the socioeconomic status of his parents and its many fateful consequences. This factor of SES origin we postulated as an independent precondition related inversely to variations in adult mental health.* We look to the Midtown Home Survey and its sample, representing some 100,000 adult "in residence" Midtowners, for a test of this hypothesis.[6] From the previous chapter it will be remembered that respondents' SES origins are distributed among six strata according to composite scores derived from their father's schooling and occupational level. With the SES-origin strata designated A through F in a sequence from highest to lowest position, table 14–1 arranges the Midtown sample adults in each stratum as they are distributed on the gradient classification of mental health assigned by the Study psychiatrists.

Reading table 14–1 horizontally from left to right in order to discern the nature of the trends, we might direct first attention to the Mild and Moderate categories. It is readily apparent that the frequencies of these two mental health conditions are remarkably uniform across the entire SES-origin range. These categories, it will be remembered, encompass more or less adequate functioning in the adult life spheres, although some signs and symptoms of mental disturbance in presumably subclinical forms are present. Equally prevalent along the entire continuum of parental SES, these two mental health types emerge here as generalized phenomena, much as they did with the age variable in chapter 11.

We also note in table 14–1 that around these numerically

---

* To our knowledge, the present investigation has so far been the only one in the adult mental health field to propose and test this hypothesis.

TABLE 14–1. HOME SURVEY SAMPLE (AGE 20–59), DISTRIBUTIONS OF
RESPONDENTS ON MENTAL HEALTH CLASSIFICATION BY PARENTAL-SES STRATA

Mental health categories	Parental-SES strata					
	A (highest)	B	C	D	E	F (lowest)
Well	24.4%	23.3%	19.9%	18.8%	13.6%	9.7%
Mild symptom formation	36.0	38.3	36.6	36.6	36.6	32.7
Moderate symptom formation	22.1	22.0	22.6	20.1	20.4	24.9
Impaired*	17.5	16.4	20.9	24.5	29.4	32.7
Marked symptom formation ..	11.8	8.6	11.8	13.3	16.2	18.0
Severe symptom formation ..	3.8	4.5	8.1	8.3	10.2	10.1
Incapacitated .	1.9	3.3	1.0	2.9	3.0	4.6
N = 100%	(262)	(245)	(287)	(384)	(265)	(217)

* $x^2 = 28.81$, $5df$, $p < .001$.

stable mental health categories the Well and Impaired frequencies
vary on the SES-origin scale in diametrically opposite directions.
From the highest (A) to the lowest (F) of the status groups the Well
proportions recede gradually from 24.4 to 9.7 percent, whereas the
Impaired rate mounts from about one in every six (17.5 percent) to
almost one in every three (32.7 percent).[7]

These countertrends can be more efficiently communicated by converting them into a single standard value that expresses the number of
Impaired cases accompanying every 100 Well people in a given
group. In the Midtown sample as a whole, this Impaired-Well ratio[8]
emerges with a value of 127, a norm available for comparative uses
in the pages to come. In bar chart form figure 1 presents the Impaired-
Well values translated from table 14–1.

With the top SES-origin levels (A and B) as our points of comparison, we observe in figure 1 that the Impaired-Well ratio is half
again larger in the adjoining group C, almost twice higher in the D
stratum, three times greater in the E level, and at a point of five-
power magnification in the bottom (F) group. Phrased somewhat
differently, the two highest strata (A and B) taken together constitute

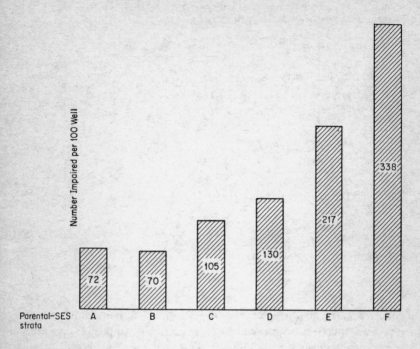

FIGURE I.   HOME SURVEY SAMPLE (AGE 20–59), IMPAIRED-WELL RATIOS OF PARENTAL-SES STRATA.

about 30 percent of the sample but account for 40 percent of the Well and for only 22 percent of the Impaired. On the other hand, the two lowest strata (E and F) taken together constitute 29 percent of the sample but account for only 19 percent of the Well and for fully 39 percent of the Impaired.[9] Through these variously expressed data a connection seems to be apparent between parental SES and mental health in Midtown's adults.

But before we accept such a conclusion, we must give precautionary consideration to this question: Could not the above differences be the result of biasing factors that intruded in the research process? Four major points of potential intrusion can be identified, namely, (1) selection of a sample unrepresentative in SES composition, (2) bias on the part of the interviewing staff, (3) status-linked differences in reporting symptoms on the part of respondents, and (4) preconceptions about social class held by the Study psychiatrists. These error potentials are too serious to be briefly dismissed and too technical for lengthy digression here. Accordingly, they are being held for evaluation in appendix F below. In fine, that evaluation presents firm evidence indicating that two of the four potential sources of bias (1, 4) had left no discernible traces of intrusion. Another possible source (2) is unlikely to have contributed significantly to such error, and the last (3) probably operated in a direction to *understate* the SES differences seen in table 14–1. On balance, therefore, the chances seem large that the connection observed between SES origin and adult mental health is authentic rather than a spurious consequence of biases brought out by the research process. If so, the data reported appear to offer an adequate test of the following hypothesis as originally stated: Parental socioeconomic status during childhood is an independent variable that is *inversely* related to the prevalence of mental morbidity among Midtown adults. However, the data produced force us to elaborate that hypothesis as follows: The stated independent variable of parental SES is related (1) inversely to the frequency of the Impaired condition of mental health, (2) directly to the frequency of the Well state, and (3) not at all to the frequencies of the Mild and Moderate types of symptom formation.

The first part of this proposition asserts that successively lower parental status carries for the child progressively *larger* risk of impaired mental health during adulthood. For those who may hold reservations about the clinical identity of the Impaired category of mental health, the second part of the proposition refers to the asymptomatic state as beyond cavil the minimal form of good mental health; and it asserts that successively lower parental SES tends to carry for the child progressively *smaller* chances of achieving the Well state during adulthood.[10]

The above proposition attributes some share of responsibility for adult mental health to differences in family socioeconomic status during childhood. Notwithstanding respondents' real differences in parental SES, however, it is altogether possible that the decisive factors influencing their current mental health had occurred not during childhood but since they have become adults.

The only approximate test of this possibility open to us here is to isolate the sample segment that has most recently turned adult, i.e., the age 20 to 29 respondents, who, on the average, are only five years removed from the end point of the teen-age phase. If childhood factors associated with parental socioeconomic status carry little weight for adult mental health, then we would expect that among these youngest sample respondents the parental-SES subgroups will emerge with relatively minor differences in Impaired and Well rates. For each of the three parental-SES "classes"[11] among the age 20 to 29 respondents the actual frequencies and the Impaired-Well ratios are seen in table 14–2.

TABLE 14–2. HOME SURVEY SAMPLE (AGE 20–59), DISTRIBUTIONS ON MENTAL HEALTH CLASSIFICATION OF AGE 20–29 RESPONDENTS BY PARENTAL-SES CLASSES

Mental health categories	Parental-SES classes		
	Upper (A–B)	Middle (C–D)	Lower (E–F)
Well	34.1%	21.4%	12.9%
Mild symptom formation	35.5	38.1	39.6
Moderate symptom formation	20.5	23.7	27.7
Impaired	9.9*	16.8	19.8*
N = 100%	(132)	(132)	(101)
Impaired-Well ratio	29	82	154

* $t = 2.1$ (.05 level of confidence).

Table 14–2 shows that the theoretical possibility defined is not fulfilled. On the contrary, among these young people recently out of adolescence,[12] significant differences in Impaired-Well balances are plainly tied to variations in SES origin. We can therefore plausibly infer that these differences were predominantly implanted during the preadult stage of dependency upon parents and were brought into early adulthood rather than initially generated there.

PARENTAL SES AND NATURE OF SYMPTOMS

We can here take certain limited steps toward eliciting clues about the qualitative nature of these differential implantations. From the technical discussion in chapter 8 it may be remembered that the questionnaire used to structure the Home Survey interviews covered a number of symptom clusters or dimensions. Each dimension was represented by a series of specific questions ranging from three to eight in number. The number of symptomatic replies that a respondent gives under each dimension can be expressed as a score, which permits examination of the SES-origin strata in their distributions on that score range. Without detouring systematically into all the quantitative details of such psychometric data, we can here indicate the general nature of their trends.

For example, one of these dimensions had reference to signs of tension and anxiety.[13] It can be reported that there were no significant differences in tension-anxiety scores among the six parental-SES strata. In all of these groups about 30 percent reported one or another of these symptoms, i.e., score of 1, and another one-third acknowledged two or more symptoms in this series. It can therefore be inferred that tension and anxiety scores are a generalized rather than a status-linked phenomenon in the Midtown population. The same inference is indicated for the "excessive intake" dimension, which refers to partaking "more than is good for you" of food, coffee, liquor, or smoking—each asked as a separate question. Again, about one-third of the respondents in all parental-SES groups reported overindulging in two or more of the four forms indicated. (Some 23 percent of the sample replied affirmatively to the liquor question.)

However, on all other symptom dimensions there was a highly significant *inverse* correlation with SES origin; that is, downward on the parental-SES scale the symptomatic tendencies increased. This trend obtained on such types of somatization as appetite-stomach or vasolability disturbances, dyspnea, heart palpitations, frequent headaches, and back pains. The trend registered similarly on the energy-deficit dimension of neurasthenic symptoms and on the affect dimensions of depression and hostile suspiciousness. It was manifest in the series of behavioral signs suggesting self-isolating tendencies. The high inverse correlation also appeared on two character dimensions that for the Study psychiatrists carried little weight in themselves as criteria of functional impairment, namely, rigidity and immaturity. Both of these suggest difficulties in impulse control.

Moreover, on the basis of interviewers' observations there were 41 intellectually retarded individuals apparent in the sample, ranging from 5.5 percent in the lowest parental stratum to 0.4 percent in the highest.

Finally, where the protocol evidence suggested a passive-dependent character structure or a schizophrenic thought process, these were also recorded by the Study psychiatrists. The former dimension was observed with a prevalence of 40 percent in the bottom parental stratum and only 15 percent in the top. The corresponding rates of the schizophrenic thought process were 7.8 and 4.6 percent, respectively, but this difference is not statistically significant.[14]

From an unreported number of clinic patients, we might recall that Ruesch projected the following symptomatic tendencies to two of the major social classes in American society: "We can state that the lower class culture favors conduct disorders and rebellion, the middle class culture physical symptom formations and psychosomatic reactions. . . ."[15] Even if the Ruesch sample of patients offered a basis for generalization about the universes of the American lower and middle classes, as it does not, the data we have reported above suggest that the corresponding parental-SES strata in the community sample of Midtown adults do not support that generalization. A more plausible interpretation of Ruesch's observations is that (1) rebellious lower-class individuals with "acting out" character disorders tend to be shunted to psychiatric facilities by action of community authorities or agencies; (2) their status peers with psychosomatic reactions get strictly medical or no attention; (3) middle-class individuals with psychosomatic disorders tend to be referred to psychiatric outpatient services, generally on the advice of their own physician.

In all, among Midtown's parental-SES groups there appear to be no frequency disparities in signs of a schizophrenic process, in symptoms of anxiety and tension, or in tendency toward excessive intake. However, on all other pathognomonic dimensions covered there is evidence among these groups of consistent variation in frequencies of disturbances in functioning—intellectual, affective, somatic, characterological, and interpersonal.

PARENTAL SES, AGE, SEX, AND MENTAL HEALTH

A definite relationship between parental socioeconomic status and adult mental health, sound and impaired, has been tentatively established in Midtown. We emphasize the word *tentative* because the possibilities that this finding is spurious are far from exhausted. Beyond technical artifacts, the correlation observed would be spurious if it evaporates when a third factor is analytically introduced and controlled. In the chapters to follow we shall test the relationship to mental health of other independent demographic variables of the sociocultural type. In those chapters it will be systematic procedure to assess the multiple ties linking parental SES and other such factors to the Study's dependent variable.

As a first step in this direction we ask: What is the outcome when we analyze adult mental health simultaneously against parental SES, sex, and age? Chapter 12 noted that in the Midtown sample as a whole there are no significant differences between males and females in their mental health composition. This situation persists, we can report, when both age and parental SES are controlled; conversely, control of the sex factor does not affect the relationship of parental SES and mental health. In future chapters, therefore, we shall drop sex as a control variable in dissecting factors potentially entangled with mental health.

In chapter 11, it will be remembered, we saw the Impaired-Well ratio rise from 65 in the age 20 to 29 segment to 205 in the age 50 to 59 group. In the light of this clear trend, it may be that age is the dominant variable and that the observed correlation between parental SES and respondent mental health is a spurious result of the contingencies that (1) groups with low SES origins may be "loaded" with older people and (2) those of high SES origins are heavily weighted with younger people.

To test this possibility, figure 2 has been prepared. And to avoid imposing undue burdens on the graph, only the Impaired-Well magnitudes are there presented for each of 12 subgroups of respondents representing a particular conjunction of respondent age and parental SES. Of course, with so many subgroups the number of Impairment cases in each is unduly attenuated. However, we emphasize again our interest in the *direction* rather than the *size* of the Impaired-Well differences, especially when pressing our finite sample to its utmost analytic limits.

Inspection of figure 2 reveals that on all age levels the Impaired-Well values—with only one exception—are progressively larger downward on the SES-origin scale.[16] In short, the connection between parental SES and mental health persists when the age factor is held constant.

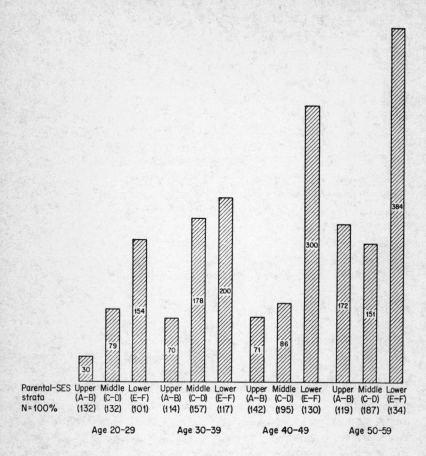

Parental-SES strata	Upper (A–B)	Middle (C–D)	Lower (E–F)	Upper (A–B)	Middle (C–D)	Lower (E–F)	Upper (A–B)	Middle (C–D)	Lower (E–F)	Upper (A–B)	Middle (C–D)	Lower (E–F)
N=100%	(132)	(132)	(101)	(114)	(157)	(117)	(142)	(195)	(130)	(119)	(187)	(134)
	30	79	154	70	178	200	71	86	300	172	151	384
	Age 20–29			Age 30–39			Age 40–49			Age 50–59		

FIGURE 2. HOME SURVEY SAMPLE (AGE 20–59), IMPAIRED-WELL RATIOS OF LIKE-AGE RESPONDENTS BY PARENTAL-SES CLASSES

The reader may also wish to trace the age trend within like SES-origin classes. For example, proceeding from the youngest through the oldest subgroup within the upper-origin class (A–B), the Impaired-Well ratios are 30, 70, 71, and 172 respectively. Within the lower-origin class (E–F), similarly, the corresponding values are 154, 200, 300, and 384, respectively. Finally, within the middle-origin class (C–D), the age progression shows values of 79, 178, 86, and 151, respectively. The trend-deviant subgroup here appears to be the age 30 to 39 respondents who, in fact, are quite close in mental health composition to their age peers of lower-class origin.[17]

We can summarize the two trends just disentangled with the single general statement that in the Midtown sample parental SES and respondent age are *both* related, quite *separately of each other*, to the frequencies of sound (Well) and Impaired mental health.[18] Stated in more dynamic terms, we can infer first that parental-SES differences were somehow involved in differential childhood implantings of potentialities for mental wellness and impairment. By the end of the teen years these susceptibilities were already differentially crystallized in the overt mental health conditions of the several SES-origin strata. Second, we can surmise that subsequent progression through adulthood carries in its wake further precipitating or aggravating pathogenic effects for the vulnerable people *from all SES-origin groups*.

The power of the two demographic factors when joined together can be seen in the extreme contrast of Impaired-Well values between the pair of most favorable variants, i.e., upper-SES origin and age 20 to 29, and the combination of most unfavorable variants, i.e., lower-SES origin and age 50 to 59. Among the former subgroup there are 30 Impaired cases for every 100 Well respondents; among the latter there are 384—a joint magnification power, by this measure, in the order of almost 13 times.

Given the "collaboration" of SES origin and age in their impacts on adult mental health, question arises about the generality of their interrelationship. And given that approximately three-fourths of Midtown's adults are migrants from beyond the City's five boroughs, might it not be that Midtown attracts migrants of a particular atypical kind—in whom the interlocking triad of SES origin, age, and mental health happens to be an idiosyncratic conjunction? On its face, this suggestion appears to be implausible but not impossible, and therefore cannot be ignored.

To consider the question, we need of course the evidence of independent observation. Fortunately, three quite different shreds of evidence of this kind are available to be fitted together in somewhat the fashion of a jigsaw puzzle.

First, is the study at an Eastern college, that reported a "six-year mean prevalence rate of 11.5 percent for clinically significant emotional impairment," a finding supported by a 12 percent rate of "clinically disturbed cases" at a second college.[19] In the Midtown sample, the closest single counterpart of the broad college population just referred to are the 132 age 20 to 29 upper-SES-origin (A–B) respondents. Included in this subgroup, as a matter of fact, are 29 current college or postgraduate students and five wives of such current students; among the remainder, most have attended or completed college training. It is therefore pertinent to recall that the impairment rate in this delimited age-and-SES subgroup is 9.9 percent.

The second source of evidence is a wartime study focused on white enlisted men who had not yet served overseas.[20] Used were one cross-section sample of 6,869 on-duty personnel and a separate sample of 563 psychoneurotic patients in Army hospitals. On the one hand, the latter represented mental impairment as judged by the criterion of behavioral incapacity for military duty. On the other hand, because of the constant surveillance and command powers of "noncoms," officers, and Army doctors these patients probably constitute a far closer approximation of overall prevalence of impairment than do mental patients in civil life.[21]

The particular relevance of this investigation is to be seen in two of its aspects. First, it calculated the number of hospitalized psychoneurotics per 100 nonhospitalized men, producing a "PN ratio," which, in fact, suggested our own Impaired-Well measure. Second, it tested the variability of this ratio with age and education *simultaneously*. To be sure, a person's education is generally treated as an own-SES indicator, a precedent we ourselves followed. However, by reason of its direct dependence on, and high correlation with, parents' socioeconomic position, schooling level of offspring can also be considered as an alternative, crudely approximate, indicator of the latter.

In the Army study, the educational range was trichotomized into three levels, namely, high school graduation or more, some high school (short of graduation), and grade school only. In the 20 to 24 age group the PN ratios for these successive schooling levels were 29, 99, and 129, respectively. In the 25 to 29 age group the corresponding ratios were 51, 104, and 156, respectively. And in the 30-and-over age group they were 119, 214, and 284, respectively.

Thus, when age is held constant, the PN ratio progressively *increases* downward on the education scale; and when these ratios are rearranged to hold schooling level constant, they are found to *increase* progressively with each age increment.

The third source of evidence is the study conducted by Bellin and

Hardt, involving a noninstitutional community sample of 1,537 elderly people dichotomized into two age groups, 65 to 74 and over 74.[22] The focus was *overall* prevalence of mental morbidity, the latter as judged by "evidence suggestive of certifiability" to a mental hospital. With own SES, in this instance dichotomized into a high and a low stratum, the morbidity rate was larger for low-status people than for those of high SES in both age groups and larger for older people than for those younger in both SES strata.

There are gross differences in the observed population segments just cited and in the nature of the evidence drawn from them. Nevertheless, these varied pieces fit into a congruent pattern consistent with the Midtown finding that SES origin and age stand in separate but convergent relationships to adult mental health. Accordingly, this complex triad uncovered in the Midtown sample of adults gives the definite appearance of a general rather than a local or idiosyncratic phenomenon.

This has since been supported in a national survey. Employing a large sample, dichotomized by schooling and sorted into five age categories, the frequency of reported "nervous breakdown" was greater with low education among *all* age groups, and larger with progressive age in *both* schooling groups.[23]

STATUS MOBILITY AND MENTAL HEALTH

We have thus far concentrated attention on *parental* socioeconomic status, postulated as embracing overarching constellations of different life conditions during childhood. However, there is a generalized cultural mandate binding all social classes in American society. Rising from impoverished immigrant parents to the summit of an industrial empire, Andrew Carnegie gave utterance to this mandate in ringing words: "Be a King in your dreams. Say to yourself 'My place is at the top.' " [24]

A more realistic injunction and one more widely accepted is this: Whatever your status inheritance from parents as a point of departure, strive to "do better," i.e., advance beyond it. In due course, the adult settles into his own position, at a level that may be higher, lower, or more or less the same as his father's. These three parent-offspring sequences are technically designated as the variable of *intergeneration status mobility.* The status mobility variable circumscribes an extremely complicated and dynamic set of processes that operate in the individual's life history between childhood under the roof of parental-SES conditions and his own status shelter built in adulthood for his spouse and children.

What light does published research shed on the mental health aspects of such mobility differences? In their literature-synthesizing book *Social Mobility in Industrial Society*, Lipset and Bendix devote separate sections to (1) "the consequences of social mobility" for the individual and (2) varying individual orientations that spur different directions of status change.[25] In the former discussion they conclude that "studies of mental illness have suggested that people moving up in America are more likely to have mental breakdowns than the nonmobile." An examination of the New Haven study used as the principal source of this inference shows that Lipset and Bendix appear to have misread the evidence. The New Haven reports on status mobility covered 847 schizophrenics in treatment, who were found to be 88 percent nonmobile, about 4 percent upward-mobile, and 1.2 percent downward-mobile.[26] (The remainder were in the category of "insufficient family history.") Contrary to the Lipset-Bendix reading, these data do not suggest a picture of upward mobility as a major trend among the New Haven cases. More important, even if their reading were correct, trends among treated schizophrenics, whatever their direction, can hardly be generalized to apply to treated nonschizophrenics (unreported in the New Haven publications), or to untreated schizophrenics, or to the untreated with other disorders. Above all, these trends cannot be extrapolated, as Lipset and Bendix have done, to "mental breakdown" trends in the universe of "people moving up in America" as compared with trends in the universe of nonmobile Americans. In point of fact, there is some question whether it is possible to extrapolate from the New Haven treated schizophrenics to schizophrenic patients generally. In a New Orleans study, such patients were reported to be predominantly (45.7 percent) downward-mobile—in striking contrast with the New Haven cases.[27]

In further fact, single-point-of-time studies, whether of treated or overall mental morbidity, offer no basis for the inference that status mobility "may cause difficulties in personal adjustment."[28] Such investigations cannot parcel out the discrete mental health *conse-*

quences of individual changes in socioeconomic status from the specific personality *preconditions* of different self-determined mobility paths.

However, citing the *same* New Haven treated schizophrenic rates, Lipset and Bendix assert in their later section on differential motivations for mobility that "mental illness rates would seem to provide additional data for the notion that the upwardly mobile [population] tend to be deprived psychodynamically."[29] In its context, this statement seems to suggest that psychic deprivation tends to induce status climbing. But clearly no study of patients can tell us about the psychically deprived and nondeprived segments of the nonpatient population and their respective mobility tendencies.

In a relevant research paper, Douvan and Adelson preface their data report with the observation that in the large literature on social mobility

. . . only limited attention has been given to studying the motivational sources of mobility. What we do find is a general disposition to treat *upward* mobility in a vaguely invidious fashion. It would seem that, in this country, the Horatio Alger tradition and the "dream of success" motif have been pervasive and distasteful enough to have alienated, among others, a good many social scientists. The upwardly aspiring individual has apparently become associated with the pathetic seeker after success* or with the ruthless tycoon. This image of success is, much of it, implicit—assumption and attitude, and not quite conviction—but it seems to have dominated the thinking of our intellectual community.[30]

In their insightful study of a national cross-section sample of 1,000 age 14 to 16 boys, Douvan and Adelson tested their ego-theory conceptualizations on personality determinants of precareer mobility aspirations. To draw on the summary of their findings:

The upward aspiring boy is characterized by a high energy level, the presence of autonomy, and a relatively advanced social maturity. These attributes may be viewed as derivatives of a generally effective ego organization.

[In the] downward mobile boys . . . we see an apparent blocking or impoverishment of energy which should ideally be available to the ego. There is a relatively poor articulation among the psychic systems; impulses

---

* Playwright Arthur Miller has embodied the type in his *Death of A Salesman* character Willy Loman.—Eds.

threaten the ego's integrity; the superego seems overly severe and yet incompletely incorporated. These boys seem humorless, gauche, disorganized—relatively so, at least. Perhaps the most telling and poignant datum which the study locates is their response to the possibility of personal change, their tendency to want to change intractable aspects of the self, and the degree of alienation revealed by their desire to modify major and fundamental personal qualities.

The study just cited was focused on mobility aspirations among a general sample of adolescents, and their personality correlates. As contrast to this prospective approach to adult developments, in the Midtown sample of adults we are focusing retrospectively on status mobility, completed or in process, and current mental health. In the planning phase of the Study we were clear that from the latter we could not dissect (1) what the level of mental health had been at the threshold of the respondent's career and (2) what increments of mental health change were subsequently added as a specific result of the struggle for one's own place in the socioeconomic sun.

In the face of this empirical limitation we hypothesized as follows:[31]

1. Upward mobility requires not only appropriate aspirations but also efficient personal mobilization, such that to actually "make the grade," sound mental health is a decided preparatory asset and impaired health is not. Downward mobility, on the other hand, is culturally so deviant from group and typical self-expectations that it can only happen under some initial, predisposing handicap in physical or mental health.

2. In turn, given adequate preparation in the preadult stage, accomplished upward mobility and its rewards tend to have constructive consequences for subsequent adult mental health;[32] whereas the consequences of downward mobility and its deprivations would tend to be in the opposite direction.

3. However, countervailing tendencies also operate. For some people, status climbing may have costly pathogenic effects that would have been avoided had they remained stationary, i.e., nonmobile, relative to father. Similarly, downward mobility may conserve or stabilize mental health in certain special, limited circumstances, when other courses would have been taxing or damaging to the individual.

As to the relative importance of these postulated elements in the resultant current mental health of sample respondents, we believe that those subsumed under hypothesis 3 are relatively rare and partially offset those suggested in hypothesis 2. The latter, in our view, are secondary to the dominant contribution of the forces emphasized in hypothesis 1, namely, the psychosocial selection of different kinds of preadult mental health for adult replication, advance, or retreat from parental status.

In testing the relationship of status mobility, as a reciprocal-type variable, to current adult mental health, we faced a number of alternatives in choosing a common yardstick to measure SES of both the respondent and his father. The decision finally taken was that for this specific purpose occupation level by itself, though not accounting for all socioeconomic variability, is more useful in identifying specific father-offspring sequences than any two status indicators arithmetically averaged. From the previous chapter it will be remembered that a series of three questions was used with each respondent to elicit (1) the nature of his own work and (2) that of his father when the respondent was age 18. On the basis of these data, father and respondent were separately placed within the identical occupational framework of six levels, numerically scored 1 to 6. Where respondent and father have a like score, the former is classified nonmobile. If the respondent has a higher score, he is classified upward-mobile, and if a lower score, downward-mobile.

It can now be reported that the 911 sample males and never-married females[33] who could be placed in terms of both father's and own occupation were distributed among the three forms of mobility approximately in a 1:1:1 ratio. However, the mental health compositions of these three groups present significant differences in the hypothesized directions, as table 14–3 below reveals.

We note first in table 14–3 that the stable nonmobile group presents an even balance in its number of Impaired and Well members. With this as a point of comparison, we further observe that among the "climbers" there is an imbalance, with the Well outnumbering the Impaired by about 3:2. Finally, among the "descenders" the imbalance is tipped sharply to the other side, the Impaired exceeding the Well by almost 5:2.[34]

Two qualifications must be weighed in considering these trends. First, the relationship between occupational mobility and mental health would be at least partially spurious if the up-moving people were largely younger adults of higher status origins and those moving in the opposite direction were principally older adults of lower paren-

TABLE 14-3. HOME SURVEY SAMPLE (AGE 20–59), RESPONDENTS'
DISTRIBUTIONS ON MENTAL HEALTH CLASSIFICATION OF MEN AND SINGLE
WOMEN BY OCCUPATIONAL MOBILITY TYPES

Mental health categories	Mobility types		
	Up	Stable	Down
Well	21.0%	22.6%	12.7%
Mild symptom formation	41.6	37.0	33.8
Moderate symptom formation	23.8	16.8	23.4
Impaired*	13.6	23.6	30.1
N = 100%	(315)	(297)	(299)
Impaired-Well ratio	65	104	235

* $x^2 = 24.57$, $2df$, $p < .001$.

tal SES. The fact is that the climbers are split below and above the 40-
year line exactly 50–50, whereas the descenders are split 40–60.
The latter *are* a somewhat older group. On the other hand, the climbers are predominantly (67 percent) from blue-collar fathers, whereas
the descenders are mainly (55 percent) from white-collar fathers.
Thus, the two potentially masking factors approximately serve to
cancel each other out.

Second, our data may actually understate the strength of the relationship. An optimal test would focus on self-supporting adults at an
age when occupational change is largely over, i.e., beyond the age of
40. Among younger adults, particularly in bureaucratic organizations,
further reaches of work upgrading may still lie ahead. If so, mobility
tendencies among younger adults would expectedly have a lesser
linkage with mental health than among older people. This inference is
actually supported by a comparison of the younger (age 20 to 39)
and older (age 40 to 59) male and single women respondents. That
is, the contrast in Impaired-Well balance between the upward- and
downward-mobile types is considerably sharper in the senior than in
the junior group.

We can look more closely at the character of the changes by focusing down to the 442 U.S.-born male respondents known in terms both
of own and of father's occupation. This particular segment of the
population is of purified relevance because it excludes single women,
who are limited in their occupational movements by an intracultural

bias. Also excluded are the foreign-born males, whose mobility can be measured only by their occupational place in the American economy as compared with their father's occupational level in the economy of the homeland. Here various intercultural biases probably operate.

We might start with the high white-collar level of business executives and professionals. Sixty-three fathers have been in this stratum. Of their 63 sampled sons, 33 established themselves in the same occupational bracket; the other 30 dropped to lower levels—several in fact to the bottom of the blue-collar range. However, more than offsetting the latter were 65 men who climbed into this stratum from fathers in lower occupations. (Fifteen of these men had blue-collar fathers.) Now let us consider the respondent mental health differences selectively carried in these shifts. To be emphasized is that the number of cases involved is small and accordingly the Impaired-Well values are to be regarded as suggestive only. In figure 3 the arrow suggests the direction of mobility (horizontal arrow signifies nonmobility), and the number in the circle attached represents the Impaired-Well ratio of the men who moved in that direction.

As figure 3 indicates, the healthier sons replicated their father's top

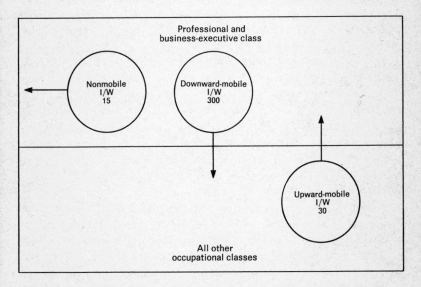

FIGURE 3.   HOME SURVEY SAMPLE (AGE 20–59), IMPAIRED-WELL RATIOS OF SONS ORIGINATING IN OR ASCENDING INTO THE TOP OCCUPATIONAL CLASS.

occupational position. On the other hand, the less healthy sons more often moved down, to be replaced by far healthier men ascending from fathers at lower levels. Thus, all 63 sons of top-level fathers present an Impaired-Well value of 70, whereas for all 98 men *now* in that occupational bracket the corresponding value is 24.

At the opposite pole is the unskilled class of blue-collar occupations. Fifty of our U.S.-born male respondents were from fathers at this level. Of these sons, 14 remain in the same kind of occupation; 6 of these have impaired mental health, 3 are "well." Thirty-six other sons have climbed to higher points—14 to the low and middle white-collar strata, 6 to the executive-professional ranks—and have an approximate balance in number of Impaired and Well respondents (Impaired-Well ratio of 120). Replacing these climbers are 37 descenders from fathers in higher positions.[35] With the out-climbers healthier in composition than the nonmobile men and the in-descenders least favorable of all in mental health (Impaired-Well ratio of 240), the 51 men now in the unskilled class have an Impaired-Well ratio of 225. This compares with a value of 150 for the group of 50 offspring of unskilled fathers.

In the intervening occupational levels the mobility traffic is at once more balanced and more complicated. For example, there are 135 male respondents with fathers in the middle (managerial and semi-professional) white-collar stratum. Of the sons, 65 (48 percent) were nonmobile, 46 (34 percent) were climbers, and 24 (18 percent) descenders. However, the latter two types of out-movers from the class were replaced by two types of in-movers, namely, 43 climbers from fathers of lower occupational standing and 26 descenders from executive-professional fathers. As net effect of these four-way counterbalancing movements, the mental health composition of American-born male respondents who are *themselves* in the middle white-collar category is little different from that of the group of men *deriving* from fathers who had been in this category.

We would emphasize again that the mental health differences reported for the three mobility types of respondents probably represent the convergence of two sets of factors: (1) original (preadult) mental health differences among those carried in different own-SES directions and (2) subsequent mental health shifts along the several mobility courses.

A longitudinal study design is required to bridge the Douvan-Adelson data from adolescents and our own from Midtown adults. To such a prospective study, both sets of data offer the hypothesis that on the whole healthier adolescents tend to be more heavily drawn into the traffic of upward-moving adults, whereas more disturbed adolescents tend to be shunted into the downward traffic. We suggest the further hypothesis that on the whole those in the ascending traffic stream are subsequently less likely to show exogenous deterioration in mental health than those in the descending stream.

It may be asked how these hypotheses are to be articulated to the postulates in the previous chapter bearing on the child of low-status families. Among sample respondents derived from blue-collar fathers we know that about two in every five have been upward-mobile on our six-level occupation scale. Whether or not these Midtowners are in this respect typical of blue-collar offspring elsewhere is not yet known; but from evidence presented in chapter 5 there are intimations that they may be more upward-oriented than their occupation peers elsewhere seem to be. Even here, however, the nonclimbers outnumber the ascenders. That there are climbers at all would seem to reflect two factors: (1) The dynamic New York economy had open places at the requisite occupational levels, and (2) the objective goads to escape to a more comfortable and respected style of life probably sort out the climbers from the nonclimbers along such personality dimensions as were delineated in the Douvan-Adelson study and were briefly sketched earlier in this chapter. The latter inference raises the unanswered question whether differences within lower-class families yield personality variations among their *own* offspring which issue in subsequent status-mobility divergences among siblings.

OWN SES AND MENTAL HEALTH

From the unraveling of father-son occupational changes we can better grasp the results when the entire Midtown sample of adults is examined for mental health composition as classified on the scale of own socioeconomic status. In figure 1 we charted the Impaired-Well ratios of the sample arranged by SES origin as indexed by father's schooling and occupation. These are reproduced in figure 4, but they

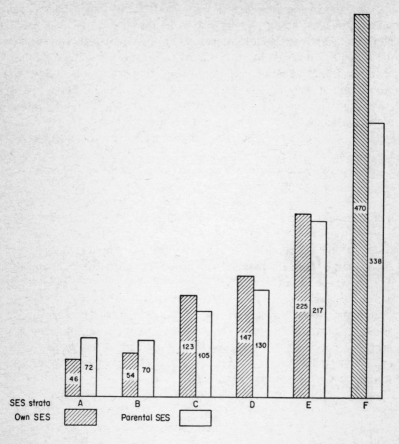

FIGURE 4.   HOME SURVEY SAMPLE (AGE 20–59), IMPAIRED-WELL RATIOS OF OWN-SES AND PARENTAL-SES STRATA.

now accompany bars representing the Impaired-Well values of the entire sample when sorted by own SES as indexed in this instance only, strictly for comparison, by respondent's own education and own occupation.[36]

Reflecting the greater tendency of the Well to move upward and the Impaired downward, figure 4 for the first time reveals that own SES stands to adult mental health in a relationship even more sharply accentuated than does parental SES. In other words, if parental socioeconomic status plays any contributory part in mental health determination, own SES tends to overstate the magnitude of that contribution.

For all other purposes of classifying respondent's own SES, we inquired about his/her family income and household rent as well as his/her education and occupation. From the sum of the scores on these four indicators, the sample was divided into twelve own-SES strata, as nearly equal in numbers of respondents as possible.

In the strata at the top and bottom extremes of this twelve-way range are 7.0 and 6.5 percent of the sample, respectively. Table 14–4 gives the complete distributions of these two sets of respondents on the Study psychiatrists' classification of mental health.

TABLE 14–4. HOME SURVEY SAMPLE (AGE 20–59), RESPONDENTS' DISTRIBUTIONS ON MENTAL HEALTH CLASSIFICATION OF TOP AND BOTTOM STRATA IN TWELVE-WAY OWN-SES RANGE

Mental health categories	Highest stratum		Lowest stratum	
Well	30.0%		4.6%	
Mild symptom formation	37.5		25.0	
Moderate symptom formation ...	20.0		23.1	
Impaired	12.5*		47.3*	
Marked symptom formation ...		6.7		16.7
Severe symptom formation		5.8		21.3
Incapacitated		0.0		9.3
N = 100%	(120)		(108)	
Impaired-Well ratio	42		1,020	

* $t = 6.0$ (.001 level of confidence).

The Moderate and Mild categories of symptom formation aside, the mental health contrast between the top and bottom strata could hardly be more sharply drawn. The story is partially told in their Severe and Incapacitated totals (5.8 and 30.6 percent, respectively) and above all in their respective Impaired-Well ratios of 42 and 1,020.

Of even larger interest perhaps is the shape of the Impaired-Well trend line across the entire range of the twelve-way own-SES continuum. This is profiled in figure 5.

Confronting data like those underlying figure 5, some investigators would defer to a statistical device (like chi square) for a yes-or-no dictum about the existence of a relationship between two vari-

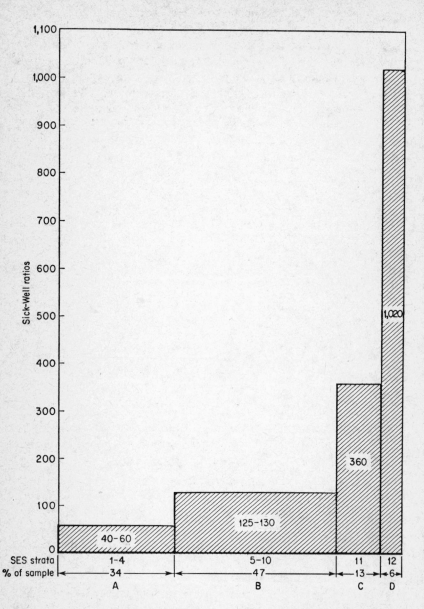

FIGURE 5. HOME SURVEY SAMPLE (AGE 20–59), IMPAIRED-WELL RATIOS OF TWELVE-WAY OWN-SES STRATA.

ables, beyond that producible by chance, and consider their work done if the answer is "yes" at a given level of confidence. Since such an answer conveys nothing whatever about the relative strength or weakness of the relationship so affirmed, other investigators apply more specialized statistical devices to measure closeness of the correlation.

However, both kinds of statistical yardsticks are completely insensitive to something potentially important in the data which are given in figure 5. That is, on the overall spread of the trend there is a wide socioeconomic span (strata 1 to 4) devoid of any notable differences in mental health composition until a line of change is crossed. Rising to the 125 to 130 level at this crossing point, the Impaired-Well ratio next remains in a flat trend across another broad span of own-SES differences (strata 5 to 10). These two large plateaus are followed toward the bottom of the own-SES range by two Impaired-Well peaks (strata 11 and 12).

The precise extent to which Midtown's mental health distributions statistically vary with differences in own socioeconomic status is of negligible moment compared to this demand of sheer curiosity: Given that each of the graph's four SES zones has its own inner similitude of mental health composition, how can these segments be concretely identified? We have already seen that the adult own-SES groupings are the residues of rise and fall of status around the parental-SES points of departure. However, our present interest in identifying the four own-SES zones is directed not to their past but rather to their present life circumstances. These are large contemporary "worlds," we can assume, that are the scene or the source of morbidity-precipitating events for the more vulnerable people in their midst. On the basis of data culled for this monograph we can indicate the approximate boundaries of these four worlds only in the most elementary economic terms.

In order of size, the largest is zone B, embracing strata 5 to 10 and roughly half of the entire sample. These six strata are quite uniform in mental health composition, with Impaired-Well ratios that stand near the whole sample's value of 127. They are broadly spread across the lesser ranks of the middle managerial and semiprofessional occupations, through the lower white-collar, the skilled blue-collar, and the higher-wage ranks of the semiskilled factory workers. The family income span, in 1954 dollars, was in the main from $3,000 to

$6,000, permitting a tolerable but hardly ample standard of consumption and certainly not permitting the accumulation of any significant reserve funds. With this "tightrope" living standard as the foundation of their claim to respectability, these respondents are close to the line of insecurity. When family crises jeopardize the economic supports of this way of life, the strain placed upon personality resources may be great.

Since these people are numerically the dominant and psychosocially the pivotal segment in the Midtown population, they have a potentially large influence on the mental health climate of the community, above all at times of collective crisis.[37]

Noteworthy also is the large representation of blue-collar respondents in this zone. In recent decades they have caught up with the lower white-collar class[38] in both income and level of consumption and now also match their mental health composition. A tantalizing question they pose is this: Has their documented economic and social progress through these decades been accompanied by an unobserved improvement in mental health, i.e., improvement sufficient to close what had previously been an unfavorable difference? This is a question to which we will return in chapter 23.

Second in sample representation (34 percent) are zone A's own-SES strata 1 to 4, covering the more affluent managerial and professional classes. Here we cross into a world characterized by a more secure, expansive, and ego-nurturing style of life, with larger buffers or cushions against the inevitable abrasions and hard knocks of human existence. It is striking that above roughly $6,000 annual income (in 1954 dollars) further increments toward $15,000 and far beyond, with all the accompanying socioeconomic correlates, do not appear to register any further gains in group mental health composition. (One 1954 dollar is about equivalent to two in 1974.) However, it can be hypothesized that without the common denominator "prophylactics" of these strata their latent store of mental pathology would probably emerge in more overt and impairing forms.

At the other side of the own-SES range we find that zone C absorbs a relatively narrow 13 percent segment of the Midtown sample. Occupationally they are semiskilled workers in the City's newer, marginal low-wage industries and workers in the more stable forms of unskilled labor, e.g., domestics, sweepers, window washers, and janitors. Weekly family income may at times reach the $60 point but more often hovers around $50. Here, we move into a zone of "struggle to keep head above water." The entire style and tone of life bear the marks of strain from constant struggle at the edge of poverty. The mental health situation here is suggested by the spike in the Impaired-Well ratio to the 360 point.

In zone D there is breakthrough to still another psychosocial realm, namely, poverty itself. Stemming in the main from parents in unskilled and semiskilled manual occupations, people in zone D are in or near the bottom bracket on every one of our four status indicators. Probably of first significance is that most of them did not complete elementary school. For some respondents this default doubtless was determined by such exogenous barriers as extreme poverty, a disabled or departed parent, or an otherwise acutely deprived family; for other respondents the default may reflect childhood endogenous disabilities, physical or mental.

Whatever the specific source of the barrier, subliminal schooling on its own account sets off a chain of other restrictions: (1) restriction largely to marginal, temporary forms of unskilled labor; (2) restriction to a low, unstable income[39] that at best is beneath the minimal necessary to shelter, clothe, and feed a family (total 1954 income in zone D households almost without exception was in a range between $15 to $40 weekly); (3) restriction to cramped quarters in the most deteriorated slum tenements.

Such noxious life burdens, together with handicapped or vulnerable personalities developed in childhood, often combine to produce a break in the intolerable struggle. Chronic poverty has at some time brought almost all zone D respondents to the City Welfare Department for financial assistance; and many belong to "multiproblem" families that are known to the police, courts, private social agencies, and mental hospitals.

From this group's mental health distribution reported in table 14–4 above, it is seen that exceedingly few (4.6 percent) are Well and nearly half (47.3 percent) are Impaired.[40] Segregated with others in like circumstances and mental health conditions, the numerically dominant Impaired of zone D doubtless help to create an unstable slum community that often carries its own pathogenic "contagion," in particular for the children in its midst. It is hardly surprising, therefore, to hear of a contemporary (1956) New York City Youth Board Survey that covered 825 children of needy families and reported that 40 percent of these children manifest "serious behavior problems." It was predicted that another 10 percent, principally in the youngest segment of the sample, would likely develop such problems.

Here the frequency of adult mental pathology is probably of unprecedented proportions. And here the environmental contamination of children very likely ensures that the epidemic shall continue to reproduce itself in the generation ahead, as it apparently has from the generation preceding.

Reviewing the four zones observed in figure 5, we can infer that certain turning points in the quality and weight of adult life conditions emerge along the status continuum represented in our twelve-way own-SES scale.

SUMMARY

In this sweep across the front defined by socioeconomic status with its multiform salients, we probed a number of discrete hypotheses with the following returns:

1. On the parental-SES range the frequency of impairment varies inversely and the Well rate varies directly.

2. This trend in Impaired-Well balance also characterizes those in the sample's youngest age group, who only recently have crossed the threshold from adolescence. It was thus possible to reject the hypothesis that SES-origin differentials in mental health had almost entirely been generated during adult life.

3. Among the several SES-origin groups no significant differences appear in the frequency of schizophrenic signs, anxiety-tension symptoms, or excessive intake behaviors. In all other pathognomonic dimensions covered, however, there is an *inverse* correlation with parental SES. These dimensions included disturbances in intellectual, affective, somatic, characterological, and interpersonal functioning.

4. Simultaneous analysis of age and status-origin against respondent mental health revealed that *both* independent variables are related to mental health, each in its own right. This suggested first that parental-SES differences had implanted varying mental health potentialities among sample respondents during childhood; and second,

that during the temporal course of adolescence and adulthood, precipitating factors had provoked overt morbidity among the more vulnerable people from all SES-origin strata. The combined power of these two demographic variables, as reflected in the index of Impaired-Well magnitudes, is substantial.

5. The hypothesis was suggested that this triad of age, parental SES, and adult mental health was specific to the kinds of people who choose to live in an area like Midtown. That is, the identified nexus lacked wider currency in the American population. Evidence from four radically different populations indicated rejection of this hypothesis. Positively stated, the complex triad isolated in the Midtown sample may well characterize larger reaches of the American people.

6. Intergeneration status mobility, as read in a single point-of-time study, is a reciprocal factor relative to adult mental health. In the Midtown sample's coverage of three mobility types, the climbers had the smallest Impaired-Well values and the descenders had the largest by far. For prospective longitudinal studies these data suggested the two-part hypothesis: (a) Preadult personality differences partially determine directions of status change in adulthood; (b) *on the whole*, upward status mobility is rewarding psychically as well as materially, whereas downward status mobility is depriving in both respects.

7. Reflecting the selective escalator effects of status mobility, own-SES shows an even stronger relationship to adult mental health than does respondent status origin.

8. Using four status indicators it is possible to divide the own-SES range into 12 finer strata. Revealed in these strata are four mental health zones, or contemporary worlds, seemingly marked at their boundaries by breakthrough points of differences in the size and security of economic underpinnings, in styles of life, in ego nurturance, and in their psychosocial atmospheres. In zones C and D, near or at the poverty level, we discern particularly heavy pathogenic weights currently bearing on the especially vulnerable people.

For targeting of social policy, Midtown zones C and D, and likely their psychosocioeconomic counterparts elsewhere on the national scene, convey highest priority claims for milieu therapy in its broadest sense. Ultimately indicated here may be interventions into the downward spiral of compounded tragedy, wherein those handicapped in personality or social assets from childhood on are trapped as adults at or near the poverty level, there to find themselves enmeshed in a web of burdens that tend to precipitate (or intensify) mental and somatic morbidity; in turn, such precipitations propel the descent deeper into chronic, personality-crushing indigency. Here, we would suggest, is America's own displaced-persons problem.

For basic research, the joint evidence of this chapter and of several collateral studies of general populations here reviewed highlights the status system as an apparatus that differentially sows, reaps, sifts, and redistributes the community's crops of mental morbidity and of sound personalities.

In no way have we claimed that the mental health effects produced by this apparatus are determined by sociocultural processes alone. Nevertheless, in line with our field of professional competence and responsibility to future investigators, we have advanced a number of hypotheses that implicate certain specific forms of sociocultural processes operating within the framework of the social class system. These hypotheses focus on the four mental health zones we have found dividing Midtown's own SES range. Distinguishing these zones, the hypotheses suggest, are economic factors linked to mechanisms of invidious discrimination that pervade the zones' respective way-of-life constellations. These postulates hold that toward one pole of the status range, in both preadult and adult life, such processes tend to penetrate the family unit with eugenic or prophylactic effects for personality development, whereas toward the opposite pole they more often work with pathogenic or precipitating effects.

These hypotheses chart paths of further necessary exploration. They can thereby lay reasonable claim to the attention of research programs of community psychiatry and psychiatric sociology.[41]

NOTES

1. David E. Hailman, *The Prevalence of Illness among Male and Female Workers and Housewives*, Public Health Bulletin 260, United States Public Health Service, 1941.

2. L. G. Rowntree, K. H. McGill, and L. P. Hellman, "Mental and Personality Disorders in Selective Service Registrants," *Journal of the American Medical Association* 128 (August 11, 1945): 1084–1087.

3 R. W. Hyde and L. V. Kingsley, "Studies in Medical Sociology: The Relation of Mental Disorder to the Community Socioeconomic Level," *New England Journal of Medicine* 231 (October 19, 1944): 543–548. Subjects were classified by place of residence, the residential unit being "the area under the jurisdiction of each local selection board." Each area was rated by criteria of "attractiveness

as a residential section." The highest (A) of the six rating categories covered "wealthy suburban communities" and the lowest (F) covered "the worst Boston slums."

4. Reported in *Chronic Illness in a Large City: The Baltimore Study*, 1957. The SES indicator employed was annual family income, as classified in four categories: Under $2,000, $2,000–$3,999, $4,000–$5,999, $6,000 and over. Overlooked in this investigation was the following consideration: to the extent that the sick are, or should be, family breadwinners, and are impaired in their earnings capabilities, their income is a variable contaminated by, rather than independent of, their mental health status.

5. It should be observed that three of the investigations had a second common characteristic—namely, psychiatric evaluation of the sample individuals was quite peripheral in emphasis to a physical examination. In the Boston Selective Service investigation, Hyde and Kingsley report that each psychiatrist examined about fifty men in a five-hour day, averaging in fact a few minutes per man. In the Baltimore study, a large number of chronic and acute somatic conditions were in the purview of the examining internists, who also made the psychiatric evaluation—if they were so inclined and scarce time permitted. Thus, the possibilities of judgmental error in the mental morbidity rates of all three studies loom large. Furthermore, when enmeshed in a variable like socioeconomic status, such an element of error can unwittingly work to bias the findings in various directions among different studies.

We can assume that validity of mental health determination in a general population study partially depends on primacy of the psychiatric focus in the research design and also upon measures for controlling potential bias in the classification process.

6. This hypothesis, it must be emphasized, cannot be tested in the patient aggregate counted by the Midtown Treatment Census nor in the patient aggregate enumerated by the earlier, parallel New Haven Psychiatric Census conducted by Hollingshead and Redlich. Both sets of patients are being held for later discussion of the treatment variable in the chapter that follows.

7. To be sure, the trend in incapacitation rates—except between the extreme strata—is not altogether consistent. It should be remembered, however, that Midtown's mental hospital patients have been drawn principally from the incapacitated group. These patients were excluded from the Home Interview Survey but were included in the Midtown Treatment Census. In the latter operation, we could determine only own SES of patients, in a form allowing delineation of three status levels. As we shall see presently, the hospitalization rates in the upper, middle, and lower of these levels are 0.2, 0.4, and 0.7 percent, respectively. Accordingly, we can infer that if the hospitalized patients could be added to the several columns in table 14–1, the trend in incapacitation rates on the SES-origin scale would probably be somewhat smoother and sharper than now appears to be the case.

In any event, the smaller the frequency values in a distribution, the more prone they are to magnify chance fluctuations due to sampling. Thus, with small frequencies some irregularity of trend is a negligible matter if the overall direction of the trend is clear. Such a trend is discernible in the above incapacitation rates, especially when corrected for the hospitalized patients.

8. Needless to say, this measure carries no claim to a place in the armamentarium of statistics. It is a supplementary reporting device for arithmetical summary of two rates and is employed for the convenience of the reader when intergroup comparisons of such paired rates become too complicated and cumbersome to juggle.

9. The intermediate (C and D) levels number 41 percent of the sample and account for 41 and 39 percent of the Well and Impaired categories, respectively.

10. Thus, parenthetically, our findings do not rest entirely on the impairment band of the Study's mental health spectrum. The frequency of impairment usually varies in a counterpoint congruence with the Well category, in such a way that a generalization about one category often applies in reverse to the other. This seesaw bond seems to reinforce the apparent significance of both mental health types.

11. The three classes are mergers of the six SES-origin strata and carry their original A to F notations. Only by such merger can the progressive shrinkage of cases in subgroups be partially compensated. The price paid, of course, is reduction in the range of SES differences.

12. Of the four age groups in the sample it will be remembered that this is also by far the most favored in mental health composition (cf. chapter 11).

13. The five specific signs were: (1) I often have trouble in getting to sleep or staying asleep. (2) I am often bothered by nervousness. (3) I have periods of such great restlessness that I cannot sit long in a chair. (4) I am the worrying type. (5) I have personal worries that get me down physically.

14. However, when respondents are classified according to own SES, the prevalence rates in the bottom and top strata are 7.4 and 1.8 percent, respectively, a difference that is statistically significant. Reflected thereby is the fact that in their own status these particular "schizophrenic thought-process" respondents tend to be lower than their parents were.

15. J. Ruesch, "Social Techniques, Social Status and Social Change," in C. Kluckhohn and H. A. Murray, eds., *Personality in Nature, Society and Culture*, 1949, pp. 117–130.

16. Among the 12 subgroups the only exception to this consistent trend is to be found on the 50 to 59 age level, where the respondents of middle-class origin stand at an Impaired-Well point somewhat below that of their upper-class neighbors. Beyond the possibilities of chance fluctuations, the explanation for this exception is not yet apparent.

17. One possible accounting for this particular exception, beyond that of sampling variability, goes back to a problem sketched in chapter 5. We there discussed the pressures of inadequate living-and-play space on Midtown families with young children and the consequent exodus of middle-class families (in particular) to city and suburban areas of less horizontal and vertical congestion. Accordingly, it seems possible that the age 30 to 39 parents of middle-class origin are a self-selected residue who have resisted these pressures bearing on the well-being of their children. If so, the question of why their age 40 to 49 SES-origin peers, with older children, do not reflect the same processes is one for which no immediate answer is at hand.

18. This means, of course, that both of these factors must be controlled simultaneously, so far as possible, in analyzing the other sociocultural variables covered in the data chapters that follow.

19. R. J. Weiss et al., "Epidemiology of Emotional Disturbance in a Men's College," *Journal of Nervous and Mental Disease* 141 (1965): 240–250; and W. G. Smith et al., "Psychiatric Disorder in a College Population," *Archives of General Psychiatry* 9 (1963): 351–361.

20. S. Stouffer et al., *The American Soldier*, 1949, vol. II, table 2, pp. 423–425.

21. If the universe of white Army men in the enlisted ranks was more general than the Midtown universe in its national, rural-urban, and ethnic-origin

dimensions, it was less general in age, sex, socioeconomic status, and in screening out of grosser pathologies at the point of Selective Service examination.

22. S. S. Bellin and R. H. Hardt, "Marital Status and Mental Disorders among the Aged," *American Sociological Review* 23 (April, 1958): table 4, p. 160.

23. H. J. Dupuy et al., "Selected Symptoms of Psychological Distress," *National Center for Health Statistics,* Series 11, no. 37, 1970.

24. Quoted in R. K. Merton, *Social Theory and Social Structure,* 1968, p. 192. So ingrained is the emphasis upon status change in the *upward* direction that it can operate as a reflex in seemingly unrelated kinds of spatial situations. Referring to changes in tenancy, for example, a prominent New York realtor reports that in Manhattan "many tenants, commercial as well as residential, have a great reluctance to move down. When they move to new quarters, the space *must be* [italics added] on a higher floor than that which they leave." (*New York Times,* April 27, 1958.) Because of street noises and lack of vistas, avoidance of quarters at low floors is of course utilitarian. However, this rationale is hardly involved in upward changes from quarters on the higher floors of Manhattan's skyscraper apartment houses and office buildings. The penthouse and the executive suite at the crown of the tower are of course physical embodiments symbolizing Carnegie's phrase, "My place is at the top."

25. S. M. Lipset and R. Bendix, *Social Mobility in Industrial Society,* 1959, pp. 65, 251.

26. A. B. Hollingshead and F. C. Redlich, "Schizophrenia and Social Structure," *American Journal of Psychiatry* 110 (March 1954): 695–701.

27. M. H. Lystad, "Social Mobility among Selected Groups of Schizophrenic Patients," *American Sociological Review* 22 (June 1957): 280–292.

28. Lipset and Bendix, *Social Mobility in Industrial Society,* p. 65.

29. Ibid., pp. 251–252.

30. E. Douvan and J. Adelson, "The Psychodynamics of Social Mobility in Adolescent Boys," *Journal of Abnormal and Social Psychology* 56 (January 1958): 31–44.

31. These hypotheses had been influenced by the promising conceptualizations of Ruesch bearing on (1) mobility motivations as emergents from "attitudes toward one's parents" and (2) the distinction between "climbers," and "strainers" as the upward aspiring who did not quite succeed. (Ruesch, "Social Techniques, Social Status and Social Change," p. 125.)

32. Some writers, Ruesch included, tend to view the consequences of upward mobility in terms of stresses that we can subsume under the concept of role discontinuity. As employed in chapter 11, this concept refers to the disjunctive predicament enveloping an individual when he acquires a rather new kind of role without adequate preparation of the requisite psychic defenses and social skills. This concept would probably apply in the main to the relatively rare instances of individuals who rise far economically in a relatively short period of time. However, our observations suggest that in most cases status mobility tendencies go back to the child's socialization in family, age-peer, and school settings. In such instances, furthermore, adolescence tends to be a period of informal apprenticeship in developing skills for the higher-status goal envisaged. Indeed, one of the major functions of high school and college life is to offer just such an apprenticeship. Thus, the usual gradual transition from parental SES to higher own status seems to us to be rather more continuous than discontinuous. See relevant data in L. Srole and A. K. Fischer, "The Social Epidemiology of Smoking Behavior, 1953 and 1970: The Midtown Manhattan Study," *Social Science and Medicine* 7 (May 1973): 341–358.

33. Married women were excluded from this analysis because intergeneration status mobility was usually accomplished in their case through their choice of husband. The wife's effect on his status movement was expected to be secondary to his own personality determinants. Indeed, when we classify wives according to occupational differences between their father and their husband, we find relatively small variations in mental health composition among the three mobility types.

34. The schizophrenic-process respondents form only a small fraction of the down-mobile group.

35. Nine of the latter fathers were in the white-collar category and two in the executive-professional class. If the latter sons represent the extreme type of downward mobility, the six sons who rose from unskilled fathers to top-drawer careers exemplify maximal upward mobility. In this particular sample of American-born males such "rags-to-riches" movement occurred once in every 75 men. It is a plausible guess that the latter is an exceptionally high rate, probably to be found in few populations outside of New York City.

36. In the case of married women, the indicators used were own education and husband's occupation.

37. As evidence of one possible facet in this crisis potentiality, the history of collective pathology is not likely to minimize the significance of industrial Germany's Nazi period.

38. It is not to be assumed that this group has been economically static. Reflecting not unionization but shortages in the local white-collar market, city-wide data on clerical office workers indicated that between 1949 and 1960 their salaries increased 59 percent in dollars and 21 percent in buying power.

39. Applying as a criterion the frequency of *steady* employment during the minor economic recession of 1958, a national survey revealed a frequency of only 50 percent among workers with less than nine years school, 75 percent among high school graduates, and 90 percent among holders of a college degree. (Unpublished study by the University of Michigan Survey Research Center and United States Census Bureau.)

40. A New York study has revealed that "67% of public welfare recipients [had] known or suspected psychological disorders." (Violet G. Bemmels, "Survey of Mental Health Problems in Social Agency Caseloads," *American Journal of Psychiatry* 121 [August 1964]: 136–147.)

41. For differential definitions of these two fields see L. Srole, "Sociology and Psychiatry: Fusions and Fissions of Identity," in P. Roman and H. Trice, eds., *Explorations in Psychiatric Sociology*, 1974, pp. 5–17.

CHAPTER 15

PARENTAL SOCIOECONOMIC STATUS: INCOME ADEQUACY AND OFFSPRING MENTAL HEALTH
LEO SROLE

In constructing the measure of respondents' parental socioeconomic status during childhood, we used as components father's years of schooling and occupational level but not family income. The latter was excluded because of the Midtown sample's enormous diversity in parental income standards for any given occupation across time and space. How, for example, could we possibly transform into a single monetary yardstick the incomes of three respondents' fathers of the very same occupation—e.g., plumber, one in Rome, Italy, during the 1890's; the second in Rome, New York, during the 1920's; and the third in Manhattan's "Little Italy" during the 1940's—even if our adult respondents could remember the actual figures approximately, if at all?

We assumed that they would more likely recall from childhood, with some vividness, as we shall see, the felt deprivational vacuums of the family's empty cupboards and pockets. Accordingly we asked a two-part question: "During the years you were growing up (age 6 to 18) did your parents (or those who brought you up) ever have a hard time making ends meet, i.e., making a living, buying what the family needed?" If the reply was "Yes," this followed: "Did they have such a hard time—often, sometimes, or rarely?" Analysis indicates the feasibility of a dichotomy counterposing the "often hard times" category against the "sometimes," "rarely" and "no/never" replies, combined into a "not often" category.

In figure 1 (page 322) above, a bar graph represents the ratios of

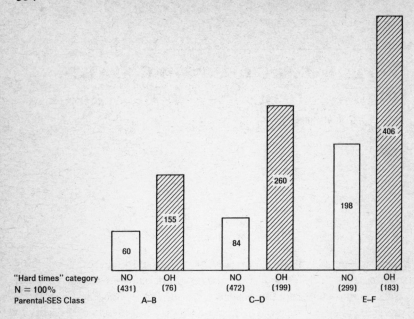

FIGURE 6. HOME SURVEY SAMPLE (AGE 20–59), IMPAIRED-WELL RATIOS OF PARENTAL-SES CLASSES DIVIDED INTO "OFTEN HARD TIMES" AND "NOT OFTEN" CATEGORIES.

number of Impaired per 100 Wells in each of the respondents' six parental-SES strata. In figure 6 these six strata are telescoped into three classes; represented are the Impaired-Well ratios when each class is split into an "often hard times" ("OH") and a "not often" ("NO") category.

We see above that whatever the father's weight of schooling and occupation (with corresponding expected standard of living), chronically insufficient income for that standard, and accompanying thwarting of legitimate expectations, are followed in his grown offspring by a tipping of the balance in their mental health composition toward a higher risk of Impairment and a lower chance of Wellness.[1]

Attention is drawn in particular to the middle (C–D) class, where the OH–NO difference of 3:1 is greater than the 2:1 difference in the lower (E–F) class. It would appear therefore that chronic financial insufficiency for a middle-class standard of living places a family in the hierarchically interstitial niche of "middle-class poor." That is a painfully anomalous, marginal position in a social class group that at best appears to be never altogether free of a lingering sense of economic insecurity, and one that seems to be somewhat more pathogenic for its children than even the NO, unpressured lower class family (I–W ratios of 260 and 198, respectively).

Similarly, grown offspring of upper-class parents who in earlier years had been chronically pressed for money to meet their normative social class prerogatives are somewhat less favorable in mental health composition than even their counterparts from middle-class families with incomes more or less approximating their class norms (I–W ratios of 155 and 84, respectively).

An excellently documented case study of this relatively rare upper-class predicament is offered us in novelist John Marquand's early life history and its life-long reverberations in his character and behavior. Marquand's parents were of "old money" Massachusetts "Brahmin" origin, originally presenting a domestic picture broadly resembling TV's turn-of-the-century "Upstairs" Bellamy family ambiance, with a full complement of "Downstairs" household staff—except that John's father, a personable but financially irresponsible man, dissipated all of his inherited, modest wealth. As a result, while John's still amply moneyed cousins were off to "fashionable" prep schools, John, in a reversal of his long-held plans, had to suffer through Newburyport's lackluster public high school, deprived, writes his biographer, of "all things [he] might once have expected but now could never enjoy. . . . there was no need for him even to look forward to anything like that. There was no money for it [he was told] and that was that. It was what happened when one's father was a failure."[2] The father's profligacy took on the proportions to the son of a hero fallen and a Paradise lost, grievous and forever irrevocable, a Horatio Alger story literally turned upside down.

"Throughout his life," adds biographer Birmingham, "John Marquand liked [as a tireless audience seeker] to make the point that much of his childhood and young manhood had been hard and poor." The resulting character disfigurations in Marquand's extreme "obsession" with money were later reflected in the fact that, even at the peak of his munificently rewarding career as a popular writer, he was an "exceptionally frugal, even tightfisted man—[manifesting] a preoccupation with thrift and spending [that] was almost neurotic. . . . He once had a violent scene with a woman he loved over an air mail stamp. To keep himself from spending money he adopted the practice of carrying no money on his person. As a result, he was a slight [the biographer's understatement] annoyance to his friends, who were forever having to make him small loans."[3]

The deeper trauma of his early family's financial stringencies are reflected in the clinically significant fact that "John had always been something of a hypochondriac."[4] In 1953, "convinced that he had an ulcer . . . he spent close to two weeks . . . undergoing a series of tests and x-rays which revealed an 'ulcerous condition' but no frank or apparent ulcer. . . . his doctor pronounced his problems largely psychosomatic."[5]

Of the early family impacts projected into Marquand's fictional works, Birmingham writes, "Failure and lost chances . . . would become linked themes in John Marquand's best [indeed almost all] novels . . . in which the villain was most often his father."[6]

Although Marquand went on to Harvard on a scholarship the College offered him, "he felt acutely embarrassed [there] at being the poor relation of a well-off [extended] family."[7] "Sometimes," during those college years, in what is pure Horatio Alger imagery, "Marquand would . . . stand quietly in the shadows," writes his biographer, "watching the bold young blades in their tail coats and silk hats . . . as they emerged from [Harvard's] Gold Coast parties [and] see himself not only as the poor relation but also the social outcast, the lonely boy with his nose pressed against the window pane, watching the shimmering life that was led by the handsome, the witty and the rich."[8]

In the light of figure 6 it is now necessary to refine the finding revealed in figure 1 to read as follows: Relative poverty and felt deprivation by the standards of one's social class reference group are heavy burdens that can descend on and distress children at all SES levels, including the topmost one, with possible adverse consequences for their subsequent mental health chances. This is not to suggest, of course, that the implicated factor is purely economic in character. Chronic parental underachievement of financial and related expectations is always mortifying to a family caught in its immobilizing web, but if it operates as a pathogenic input into children's subsequent personality development, it may itself also be a symptomatic manifestation of malfunctions, emotional and/or somatic, in either or both parents.

If so, what we have been reading in figure 6 may be the "sleeper effects" of chronic economic pressures and frustrations, compounded by mental and/or physical disabilities of parents, on children during the formative years of life. Certainly, the elder Marquand's gambling compulsions, restless itinerancy and relatively early signs of senility suggest that he played such a compounded role during his son's adolescent period.[9] A remarkably parallel case in point is Eugene O'Neill's "storm-swept" family history that is repeatedly reenacted in many of his plays. O'Neill came from middle-class parents of Irish origin who fell economically during his boyhood under the devastating weights of both parents' problems.[10]

Figure 6 seems to show cross-SES traces of the financial adequacy strand[11] in the tangle of parental characteristics that are implicated in offsprings' mental health, perhaps the first evidence of this kind on a general population-wide scale to be reported in the relevant scientific literature, evidence that in fact had been isolated too late for inclusion in the earlier (1962) edition of the present monograph.[12]

In conclusion, while it may be something of a discovery to learn that about 13 percent of A-stratum SES-origin respondents report an "often hard times" childhood, we must not overlook that the corresponding proportions in the five parental-SES strata successively lower are 16.5, 26, 33, 36.6 and 41.4 percent, respectively. Certainly the facts that this deprivational trauma is experienced among three times as many F-origin as A-origin families, and in the former at far lower, and substantively thinner, levels of accessible material resources, account in no small way for their contrasting Impaired-Well ratios (figure 1) of 338 and 72, respectively, with an OH Impaired-Well ratio (figure 6) of 406 at one extreme and an NO ratio of 60 at the opposite extreme.

After all, John Marquand, with extra-family help, did make it to and through Harvard. On the other hand, his F-origin boyhood acquaintance from a Newburyport riverfront family of clammers never got through the doors of the town's high school. And thereafter, Marquand could go "onward and upward" to a Pulitzer Prize, the cover of *Time* magazine, and a photographic appearance as "Man of Distinction" in a widely displayed liquor ad, whereas his boyhood acquaintance from the Newburyport riverfront was progressively hammered down into knee-crawling dependency on degrading welfare client hand-outs.

In these contrasting life outcomes of two boys, both traumatized and damaged by economically unsupportive and psychologically disturbed fathers, we can glimpse the vastly different compensatory forces operating at different SES-origin levels to carry them as adults to absolutely opposite kinds of career rewards and climaxes.

The converging evidence of this chapter suggests that parents' social class position and income-earning adequacy, as well as personalities, determine to an appalling extent the mental health fates of their adult children. If specific gene linkages lie hidden beneath this empirically established knot of manifestly specific parental characteristics, as some hypothesize, the sociologist must leave it entirely to the geneticist to carry on the slow and extraordinarily refractory scientific work of uncovering and clearly delineating them for us.

NOTES

1. This tipping is apparent in all six parental-SES strata, which are merged above into three classes, both to avoid crowding of graphic space and to counteract undue numerical attenuation of Impaired and Well cases when the OH–NO dichotomy is superimposed on each stratum.

2. S. Birmingham, *The Late John Marquand*, 1972, pp. 15, 28. See also W. L. Warner et al., *Yankee City*, Volumes 1–5, 1941–1959, which reports the pioneer community study of Newburyport with which the present writer was associated as field researcher and coauthor of Volume 3.

3. Birmingham, *The Late John Marquand*, pp. 12–13.

4. Ibid., p. 215.

5. Ibid., p. 243.

6. Ibid., pp. 15, 28.

7. Ibid., p. 32.

8. Ibid., p. 34.

9. Ibid., pp. 17–21, 103–105.

10. For the definitive biography see A. Gelb and B. Gelb, *O'Neill*, 1960.

11. See M. H. Brenner, *Mental Illness and the Economy*, 1973, where long-term rates of psychiatric hospital admissions and changes in the economy are found correlated. This finding seems to partially explain why some hospitalizations occur when they do, but not why the psychopathologies warranting such institutionalization have taken root in some people but not in others.

12. For a different statistical treatment of the same Midtown information see T. S. Langner and S. T. Michael, *Life Stress and Mental Health*, 1963, pp. 227–228.

CHAPTER 16

SOCIOECONOMIC STRATA: THEIR PSYCHIATRIC TREATMENT

LEO SROLE AND THOMAS LANGNER

In the Midtown sample of age 20 to 59 adults the overall prevalence of mental morbidity is inversely related to the independent variable of parental socioeconomic status and related even more closely in this direction to the reciprocal variable of adults' present (own) SES.

We must turn now to another facet of the total complex, namely, how the frequency of psychiatric care varies with socioeconomic status. In this instance we shall apply own SES rather than SES origin as our test variable. We shall do so in part because the latter information is not available in certain segments of the treatment data gathered, but principally because current status, if only in its economic aspects, is certainly the more relevant precondition of movement into prolonged professional care.

For present purposes we can first call upon the one-day prevalence data secured by our Treatment Census operation. The latter, it may be remembered, entailed the systematic effort to circumscribe the universe of Midtown residents, across the entire age range, who on May 1, 1953, were psychiatric patients in the care of public or private hospitals (institutionalized under five continuous years) or of outpatient clinics or office therapists. For reasons outlined in chapter 13, the own-SES indicator we shall use in this particular analysis is a threefold classification of the housing quality observed at the last residence recorded for each patient.

Table 16–1 presents the one-day prevalence of Midtown patients in each status group (per 100,000 of its estimated population) as

TABLE 16–1. TREATMENT CENSUS (AGE INCLUSIVE), PREVALENCE RATES (PER 100,000 CORRESPONDING POPULATION) OF MIDTOWN PATIENTS IN OWN-SES STRATA BY TREATMENT SITE

Treatment site	Own SES (housing indicator)		
	Upper	Middle	Lower
Hospitals:			
Public	98	383	646
Private	104	39	18
Combined inpatients ...	202	422	664
Clinics	61	160	218
Office therapists*	1,440	596	178
Combined outpatients	1,501	756	396
Total Patients rate	1,703	1,178	1,060
N = No. of patients	(575)	(604)	(934)

* These rates are uncorrected for the unreported patients of noncooperating office therapists. They are corrected for patients reported with addresses lacking or verifiably false.

distributed through four kinds of psychiatric facilities, together constituting the Total Patients rate.

Given the costs of private hospitals and office therapists, there can be no surprise that the Midtown prevalence rates for these sites *decrease* downward on the socioeconomic scale, or that the patients in lower-cost public hospitals and clinics should *increase* downward on this SES scale.[1] As a result of these cross tendencies, at least in Midtown, Total Patients rate is largest at the top of the status range and smallest at the bottom.

The latter finding is in a direction quite the reverse of that observed in chapter 14 (table 14–1), where mental impairment was seen to be least prevalent in the highest SES-origin stratum (A) and most concentrated in the lowest stratum (F). This is a paradox, seemingly, to which we shall return presently.

The SES trend in table 16–1 is also in direct contradiction to that reported for the Psychiatric Census undertaken by the New Haven investigation. In their monograph, Hollingshead and Redlich concluded that "the lower the [socioeconomic] class, the greater the proportion of psychiatric patients."[2]

So striking a contrast warrants careful exploration. The New

Haven authors record[3] Total Patients rate per 100,000 population in each of their several social class groups,[4] as follows:

New Haven SES Class	Total Patients Rate per 100,000
I–II (highest)	556
III	538
IV	642
V (lowest)	1,659
All New Haven	798

This series of rates,[5] as published in the New Haven monograph, hardly represents the linear progression claimed in the conclusion just cited. Instead, it appears to conform more to a dichotomy in which class V for all practical purposes stands counterposed to the rest of the SES range.[6]

As for the seeming direction of the rate differences in the above series, two observations may be in order. First, the New Haven monograph estimates that approximately 40 to 50 office patients were not reported by therapists, principally New York practitioners, who refused to cooperate[7] with the study. These commuting Connecticut patients of New York City psychiatrists were not included in the above New Haven rates. However, it seems most likely that such shielded patients were predominantly from New Haven's highest social class levels. If so, they represent a pinpointed error of understatement, one that by our estimate could conceivably raise New Haven's combined class I–II patient rate from 556, as reported, toward 700.[8]

Several pertinent reservations also attach themselves to New Haven's class V patient count. Included in this enumeration were transients committed to a state hospital by New Haven police with key information about their home community undeterminable.[9] Not revealed is the number of such rootless transients charged to New Haven's count as class V. Moreover, the sample of New Haven's general population, drawn to estimate the city's inclusive social class distribution (for service as denominators in calculating rates per 100,000 population), explicitly included no transients.[10]

Second, the New Haven investigators make this observation: "Once a class V person is committed to a mental institution, the likelihood of his return to the family is small."[11] In terms of our present concern, this would seem to imply that the exceptionally high prevalence rate of New Haven's class V is in part a result of the cumulative pile-up of its unmoving sick as the more or less permanent "slag heap" deposit of custodial patients in public hospitals. To probe this inference we would need a New Haven counterpart of our table 16–1 above. This has not been published, but for such a purpose it is possible to regroup several New Haven tabulations[12] and convert their percentages into patients per 100,000 estimated population in each of the social class groups. These are presented in table 16–2.

TABLE 16–2. NEW HAVEN PSYCHIATRIC CENSUS (AGE INCLUSIVE), PREVALENCE RATES* (PER 100,000 CORRESPONDING POPULATION) OF NEW HAVEN PATIENTS IN OWN SOCIAL CLASS GROUPS BY TREATMENT SITE

Treatment site	Social class group			
	I–II	III	IV	V
Hospitals:				
Public	89	242	464	1,500
Private	85	17	6	—
Combined inpatients .	174	259	470	1,500
Clinics	30	66	53	115
Office therapists	352	213	119	44
Combined outpatients ..	382	279	172	159
Total Patients rate ..	556	538	642	1,659
N = No. of patients	(150)	(260)	(758)	(723)

* Adapted from A. B. Hollingshead and F. C. Redlich, *Social Class and Mental Illness*, pp. 265, 419. Source data are used by permission of John Wiley & Sons, Inc., New York.

Inspection of table 16–2 frequencies reveals the same SES trends in New Haven as were observed for like treatment sites in Midtown (table 16–1). That is, patient rates for the low-cost facilities (public hospitals and clinics) *increase* downward on the socioeconomic scale, whereas for the high-cost services (private hospitals and office therapists) the trend is for the patient frequencies to *diminish* with descending SES. The parallel Midtown and New Haven evidence on these countertrends suggests anew that if the inescapable calculus of cost relative to financial means is not the only factor determining whether and where psychiatric care is sought and secured, it probably is one of the most important.

A closer comparison is warranted of New Haven's classes IV and

V in table 16–2. These two groups do not differ in either private hospital rate or combined outpatient frequency. However, they *do* diverge in their public hospital rates by a decisive margin of 3.2:1.

Noteworthy in the comparison next of the public hospital frequencies in tables 16–1 and 16–2 is the general *numeric* similarity of these rates between the Midtown pair of upper and middle strata on the one hand and the New Haven series of classes I–II, III, and IV on the other. Residually highlighted thereby is the sharp contrast differentiating the public hospital rate in the bottom stratum of the two communities, i.e., 646 for Midtown's lower SES group and 1,500 for New Haven's class V.

If the "permanently" hospitalized (by our definition those confined continuously for five years or more) are predominantly drawn from the lowest socioeconomic level, then the pinpointed intercommunity contrast just mentioned is in part a consequence of the facts that (1) in its patient prevalence count one investigation (New Haven) included these piled-up people in limbo and (2) the other (Midtown) excluded them on grounds that they could no longer be meaningfully considered bona fide residents of the study area.

On two lines of analysis, accordingly, the extraordinarily high public hospital rate of New Haven's class V appears to be a function, at least in part, of the accumulation and stagnation in state hospitals of the terminally confined, who mainly originate in this group.

If class V has the standout Total Patients rate (1,659) of all SES groups in New Haven, in Midtown this distinction belongs to the top stratum (rate: 1,703) at the opposite end of the socioeconomic hierarchy. Table 16–1 tells us that accounting for seven-eighths of this peak frequency are the patients reported by Manhattan office therapists,[13] who by a 4.4:1 margin outnumbered (per 100,000 local population) their fellow professionals in New Haven at the time. Office patients all told represent nearly half of Midtown's inclusive patient universe reported to us, and by their numbers they have imposed their skewed SES composition on the trend in Total Patients rates among Midtown's several SES groups.

On the other hand, with New Haven's office therapy cases numbering only about 20 percent of all local patients, Total Patients rates in that community are dominated to a greater degree by the public hospital occupants and *their* particular kind of skewed SES make-up.

In chapter 10 (Book One) we offered the seemingly obvious but often overlooked point that intercommunity variations in the treatment capacities of their psychiatric facilities place different ceiling limits on their patient rates, thereby tending to conceal any real differences in their overall prevalence of mental disorder.

This can now be given the obvious amplification that intercommunity variations in the development of high-cost and low-cost psychiatric facilities will inevitably place differential ceilings on the number of people in like-SES groups who can get psychiatric care. All in all, it is difficult to avoid the conclusion that divergences in Total Patients rates among a community's several socioeconomic groups have a significance decidedly less etiological than that seemingly attributed to them at some points in the New Haven monograph's earlier chapters.

The issue of ambulatory versus hospital sites of treatment, earlier discussed, becomes programmatically sharpened when narrowed down to the psychotic patients uncovered by our Treatment Census. In table 16–3 we present Midtown's psychotic patients in each status group as they divide on the ambulatory-hospital line of psychiatric facilities.

TABLE 16–3. TREATMENT CENSUS (AGE INCLUSIVE), DISTRIBUTIONS OF MIDTOWN'S PSYCHOTIC PATIENTS IN OWN-SES STRATA BY TREATMENT SITES

Treatment sites	Own SES		
	Upper	Middle	Lower
Outpatient	49.6%	25.2%	10.0%
Inpatient	50.4	74.8	90.0
N = 100%	(113)	(274)	(598)

As expected, of course, Midtown's large outpatient facilities, or more particularly its corps of office therapists, operate to the far greater service advantage of the high-status psychotic needing treatment than to fellow psychotics on SES levels below him. Suggested thereby is the *urgent importance of low-cost outpatient clinics and day-care, night-care, foster family, and home treatment facilities to correct this service imbalance among the more seriously impaired in the community.*

PSYCHIATRIC ATTENTION AMONG THE HOME SURVEY'S IMPAIRED RESPONDENTS

In the preceding section, patient rates yielded by our Treatment Census were calculated relative to the total number of Midtown people making up each status group. If all the afflicted came under treatment, as generally happens with a dread infection like polio, such rates could stand for the frequency of a disorder in a given group per 100,000 of its total population. With mental pathology, however, we have every reason to believe that the treated represent merely a fraction of all the impaired, whose numbers are generally unknown. Under this circumstance, the count of patient numbers is the product of at least two unknowns: (1) the *overall* frequency of the disorder and (2) the extent to which the impaired manage to get psychiatric care.

However, the count of patient numbers can break out of its besetting clouds of ambiguity if it is converted into a rate per 100 in presumptive need of professional help. Such a rate acquires significance by giving at least some rough inkling of the number and character of the help-needy who get professional attention as compared with those who go unattended. The unmet needs so uncovered, if sizable in extent, would be an action challenge to both the healing professions and the communities they serve.

In view of the specific mission assigned to the Midtown Treatment Census operation, it was felt that the treatment factor could be given only a brief glance during Home Survey interviews with a representative sample of Midtown adults. Given the hard-won wisdom of hindsight, we concede this short cut to have been an error.

In any event, every respondent in the Home Survey sample was asked whether he had ever gone to a psychiatrist or a "nerve specialist."[14] Affirming respondents were then asked only one other question, namely, when the therapist was last seen.

Such affirming respondents were subsequently pressed into service as the Home Survey's particular criterion of a patient, under a definition considerably wider than that applied in our Treatment Census operation. Those counted by the latter's methods had been admitted into a program of psychiatric care, however diverse or brief may have been the treatment content. However, by the Home Survey's broad-spectrum definition, patients included not only respondents who had received intensive treatment, but also those who in seeing a psychotherapist had not progressed beyond (1) a consultation, (2) one or more diagnostic sessions, or (3) unsuccessful application for treatment. Instances such as these three indicate the Home Survey's criterion of a patient to be a respondent who, however briefly, secured and directed the attention of a psychotherapist to his felt need for help. This liberal definition should be taken into account as we extract the patient-history variable from the Home Survey sample. We divide respondents into three categories: (1) current patients, ambulatory of course, who had last seen the therapist during the thirty-day period preceding the interview; (2) ex-patients, covering all others who had been in either a hospital or an ambulatory service; and (3) never-patients.

We now seek the connection between this patient-history variable and socioeconomic status, not on the broad base of the inclusive community population (as in table 16–1), but only among Midtown adults who are in a mental condition of probable help-need, at the very least for professional consultation, diagnosis, or prophylaxis. These we find represented by the Home Survey's 389 (age 20 to 59) sample respondents who were judged by the Study psychiatrists to be in the Impaired category of the mental health classification scheme. In table 16–4 the own-SES yardstick is a composite derived from scored rankings of respondent's education, occupation, income, and rent. However, given the relatively small number of Impaired people, the six A to F strata used in chapter 14 must be merged into three.[15]

TABLE 16–4. HOME SURVEY SAMPLE (AGE 20–59), DISTRIBUTIONS OF IMPAIRED CATEGORY RESPONDENTS IN MIDTOWN OWN-SES GROUPS BY PATIENT-HISTORY CLASSIFICATION

	Own SES (four indicators)		
	Upper (A–B)	Middle (C–D)	Lower (E–F)
Current patients (ambulatory)..	19.1%	4.5%	1.1%
Ex-patients (ambulatory or hospital)	32.4	18.0	19.9
Ever-patients	51.5	22.5	21.0
Never-patients	48.5	77.5	79.0
N = 100%	(68)	(134)	(187)

Relative to the lower stratum's Impaired people, the current patient rate in the middle and upper group is greater by 4 and 18 times, respectively. This trend in the probable "at need" segment of the general population reveals more clearly than before the highly selective nature of the current patient traffic to the doors of the ambulatory facilities.

The ex-patients, on the other hand, are more heterogeneous in terms of service site, including as they do the clients of both ambulatory facilities and hospitals. From clues provided by our Treatment Census data, we estimate in table 16–5 that these ex-patients were divided between hospital and ambulatory sites roughly as follows on the own-SES range:

TABLE 16–5. HOME SURVEY SAMPLE (AGE 20–59), DISTRIBUTIONS OF IMPAIRED EX-PATIENTS BY TREATMENT SITE AND SES

	Upper	Middle	Lower
Ex-patients:			
Hospital	4.4%	6.0%	12.3%
Ambulatory	28.0	12.0	7.6
Total ex-patients of Impaired group	32.4%	18.0%	19.9%

Thus, within the circumscribed confines of the Impaired category of respondents, almost half (the above 28.0 percent + 19.1 percent in table 16–4) of those belonging in the upper-SES stratum are estimated to be ambulatory ever-patients, as compared with one-sixth (the above 12.0 percent + 4.5 percent in table 16–4) and one-twelfth (the above 7.6 percent + 1.1 percent in table 16–4) of the middle and lower SES groups respectively.

We can now confront the seeming paradox, posed by tables 14–1 and 16–1, where on the one hand overall prevalence of mental morbidity was seen to *expand* downward on the SES pyramid and, on the other, treatment rates (per 100,000 total population) tended to *shrink* with descending socioeconomic status. From the previous paragraph it becomes apparent that if the top SES stratum has the fewest cases of mental morbidity, these cases present an even chance of sooner or later seeking ambulatory psychiatric service. The lower status group, on the contrary, has by far the largest prevalence of Impaired respondents, but the latter have only a slight chance (1 in

12) of ever coming to the professional attention of an outpatient facility. As net effect, into the traffic going through the community's psychiatric services the inclusive upper stratum, although healthier on the whole, *pours more patients*, relative to its numbers, than does the most impairment-laden bottom SES group.

HELP–NEED AND PROFESSIONAL ORIENTATION

In what remains a significant opening discussion of the matter, the New Haven investigators[16] have extracted this important point from observations on 50 intensively studied psychiatric patients: beyond the play of economic factors, there are SES-linked divergences in orientation to psychiatry that may partially explain the varying patient rates of the several social class groups. We did not attempt to retrace their pioneering steps in this direction. However, in our Home Survey sample we did explore respondents' readiness to advise, and presumably to accept, several relevant forms of professional help in instances of behavioral disturbance. By their replies, all sample respondents have been placed in one of these four professional orientation categories: (1) those advising a psychiatrist, a psychologist, or an institutional equivalent; (2) those others recommending a physician or an institutional equivalent; (3) those remaining who would call upon a member of some other remedial profession, e.g., social worker or clergyman; (4) the residue, who made no reference to professional intervention of any kind.

TABLE 16–6. HOME SURVEY SAMPLE (AGE 20–59), DISTRIBUTIONS OF MIDTOWN SAMPLE RESPONDENTS IN OWN-SES STRATA BY PROFESSIONAL ORIENTATION

Respondent recommendation	Own SES		
	Upper (A–B)	Middle (C–D)	Lower (E–F)
Psychotherapist	51.2%	26.4%	12.3%
Physician	11.8	11.2	12.3
Other professional	6.3	10.4	12.3
No professional	30.7	52.0	63.1
N = 100%	(560)	(556)	(544)

Of course, readiness of the help-needy person to accept professional service is only one element in the highly complicated total situation that determines what, if any, steps he takes to get help. Another element is the prevailing view or attitude climate that his group tends to press upon him and his family toward taking a certain course of action. From table 16–6 we can surmise that the Impaired never-patient of the upper-SES bracket would find a majority of his status peers urging him to see a psychiatrist.* If he is of middle or lower status the predominant tendency of his peers would apparently be in a direction other than advising professional assistance. However, compared to the lower-SES stratum a substantially bigger minority of the middle-class group would suggest a psychotherapist, namely, 12.3 and 26.4 percent, respectively. These data from a large sample of community residents may supplement the New Haven observations on a small sample of psychiatric patients. Seemingly implied is that SES-linked attitude climates operate differentially to facilitate or complicate the path a help-needy person must take if he is to find his way into a patient-therapist relationship.

OUTCOME OF EXPOSING IMPAIRMENT CASES TO PSYCHIATRIC ATTENTION

Our final question poses this issue: For those who do get psychiatric attention, what SES-mediated effects differentially accrue to patients from exposure to a therapist in a service setting? This is an exceedingly difficult empirical question—one not remotely contemplated when we designed the Home Survey operation. Nevertheless, a suggestive clue may emerge from the circumstance that this survey encountered 182 sample respondents who, by the criteria of our

---

* The *Psychiatric Dictionary*, by Hinsie and Campbell (1970), defines psychotherapy as "any form of treatment for mental illness, behavioral maladaptions, and/or other problems that are assumed to be of an emotional nature. . . . There are numerous forms of psychotherapy—ranging from guidance, counselling, persuasion, and hypnosis to reeducation and psychoanalytic reconstructive therapy." Although there are narrower definitions than this one, the authors of the present monograph emphasize that we use the terms "psychotherapy" and "psychiatric care" in the comprehensive sense just quoted, which we extend to cover the practices of clinical and pastoral psychologists, counselors, and psychiatric social workers, whether they work with individuals singly or in family or nonconsanguineous groups.

patient-history classification, are ex-patients. In the interest of expanding on this clue, let us assume that the reported relationship with a therapist probably would not have been arranged by, or for, these respondents unless a condition of Impaired mental health was believed to be present or imminent.

If this assumption is correct, and we have nothing to support it except plausibility, then we can take note that of these 182 ex-patients 83 are currently still in an Impaired state of mental health, whereas 99 are now functioning more or less adequately despite symptoms of underlying pathology. Of considerable interest at this point are the following differences among the ex-patients when sorted by their own-SES level:

1. Of 78 upper-SES ex-patients, the non-Impaired number 71.8 percent (the Impaired, 28.2 percent).

2. Of 50 middle-SES ex-patients, the non-Impaired number 52 percent (the Impaired, 48 percent).

3. Of 54 lower-SES ex-patients, the non-Impaired number 31.5 percent (the Impaired, 68.5 percent).

The potential clue buried in these data may be stated as follows: Within the universe of patient-therapist relationships, the chances of a successful outcome (as judged by the operational criterion of reversal from a state of Impaired to a state of non-Impaired mental health) seem to vary considerably among the several socioeconomic segments of the patient population, in a range from about 7 in 10 of the top segment to 3 in 10 of the bottom one.

If this clue should prove to be substantive, a number of factors could be adduced to explain the outcome differences. In fact, some of these variables have already been insightfully discussed in parts 4 and 5 of the New Haven monograph. Here we would only add our view that if the American patterning of socioeconomic status performs central social system functions, it also has serious dysfunctional aspects that remain a challenge to its powers of self-correction. The unequal consequences of these aspects for the development of mental health were discernible in the preceding chapter. Here we have presented clues and evidence attesting to another specific dysfunction in the social order: the conflict between the status system as it actually operates and a bedrock value on which the healing professions are founded, namely, that the sick shall have ready access to the ministrations of these professionals irrespective of their social differences.

SUMMARY

In the previous chapter our efforts were directed toward uncovering the lines of association between group mental health composition and socioeconomic status in several of its major aspects. Our point of focus in this chapter has been narrower, namely, the connection between psychiatric attention or care and adults' present (own) SES. On this level, the earlier New Haven Psychiatric Census study has made possible some illuminating intercommunity comparisons. However, our own sightings on this nexus have come from the twin vantage points provided by our Treatment Census and Home Survey operations.

Comparison of the Midtown and New Haven patient rates indicated like SES trends for like treatment sites. Notwithstanding this parallelism, the anomaly emerged that the SES trend in Total Patients rates of the two communities seemed to move in opposite directions.

Analysis suggested first that New Haven's inverse trend was beset on the one hand with some technical artifacts and, on the other, with a special tendency of the lowest (V) stratum's public hospital patients to become permanently institutionalized. In Midtown the opposite SES trend was shown to be a consequence of the numerical dominance of office therapy patients in this universe of patients and the overshadowing impact of their high socioeconomic status on the SES differences in Total Patients rates.

Thus, the relative development of high-cost and low-cost facilities in a community's treatment apparatus will variously affect people at different SES levels in their chances of securing psychiatric care.

Opposite SES trends were also encountered in comparing the Midtown Study's two field operations. The Home Survey revealed that overall prevalence of mental morbidity varied inversely with socioeconomic status. On the other hand, the Treatment Census reported Total Patients rates rising between the lower and upper socioeconomic strata. Using a broader definition of patient history as its criterion of psychiatric attention, the Home Survey Impaired respondents who satisfied this definition also showed the latter kind of SES trend. Integrating these separate findings, we observed that as we descend the continuum of socioeconomic status, Midtown's Treatment Census rates represent progressively smaller fractions of progressively larger reservoirs of mental morbidity.

In comprehensive terms, compared to the "affluent" group the "poor" have many more mentally impaired people; their help-needy people far less often get psychiatric attention; and when their impaired members do get such attention, the outcome, to judge from an elicited clue, rather less often appears to be a significant and sustained gain.

Indicated were the implications of sociological dysfunctions to be drawn from the large picture sketched in this and the preceding chapter.

NOTES

1. This SES trend of patient rates in publicly supported mental hospitals has been reported in other studies of patients, usually of the first-admission category. Cf. A. J. Jaffe and E. Shanas, "Economic Differentials in the Probability of Insanity," *American Journal of Sociology* 44 (January 1935): 534–539; R. E. L. Faris and H. W. Dunham, *Mental Disorders in Urban Areas*, 1939; C. W. Schroeder, "Mental Disorders in Cities," *American Journal of Sociology* 48 (July 1942): 40–48; R. E. Clark, "Psychoses, Income and Occupational Prestige," *American Journal of Sociology* 54 (March 1949): 433–440; R. M. Frumkin, "Occupation and Major Mental Disorders," in A. M. Rose, ed., *Mental Health and Mental Disorders*, 1955, pp. 136–160; B. Malzberg, "Mental Disease in Relation to Economic Status," *Journal of Nervous and Mental Disease* 123 (March 1956): 257–261; and B. Kaplan, R. B. Reed, and W. Richardson, "A Comparison of the Incidence of Hospitalized and Non-hospitalized Cases of Psychoses in Two Communities," *American Sociological Review* 21 (August 1956): 472–479. However, the trend was not found, at least for first-hospital-admission schizophrenics, in the study reported by J. A. Clausen and M. L. Kohn, "Relation of Schizophrenia to the Social Structure of a Small City," in B. Pasamanick, ed., *Epidemiology of Mental Disorder*, 1959, pp. 69–86.

2. A. B. Hollingshead and F. C. Redlich, *Social Class and Mental Illness*, 1958, p. 207.

3. Ibid., p. 210.

4. These groups were based on scored, differentially weighted rankings of education, occupation, and area of residence. Partly because institutional files were found to be markedly irregular in recording occupation and schooling, the Midtown Treatment Census has used only quality of residence as its indicator of patients' SES. Despite this difference and differences in dividing the socioeconomic range of the two patient populations, the Midtown and New Haven sets of data lend themselves to critical comparison of their SES trends.

5. When we undertake computations for classes I and II separately, the rates

we secure are 267 and 668, respectively, based on data (p. 199) in the New Haven monograph.

6. From notes taken of Redlich's report ("Social Class and Psychiatry," p. 181) given at the New York Academy of Medicine, March 9, 1955, it seems clear that he himself viewed the New Haven social class rates, group V excepted, as essentially describing a plateau.

7. Hollingshead and Redlich, *Social Class and Mental Illness*, pp. 22–24.

8. See also S. W. Ginsburg's review, *American Journal of Orthopsychiatry* 29 (January 1959): 195.

9. Hollingshead and Redlich, *Social Class and Mental Illness*, p. 19.

10. A. B. Hollingshead and F. C. Redlich, "Social Stratification and Psychiatric Disorders," *American Sociological Review* 18 (April 1953): 167.

11. Hollingshead and Redlich, *Social Class and Mental Illness*, p. 343.

12. Ibid., pp. 265 and 419.

13. In chapter 13 we indicated that information on 19 percent of the Midtown office patients reported to us failed to include the requested home address information needed to classify housing quality as a socioeconomic indicator. To prevent their exclusion from the rates in table 16–1, we arbitrarily assumed they were distributed on the present SES trichotomy as were the 81 percent of reported office patients for whom correct addresses were furnished. However, it seems plausible that office therapists would be more prone to shield the addresses of "top-drawer" people than of others. If so, the indicated correction we have introduced for the address-missing patients would make the office therapy rate of the Midtown upper-SES group an *understatement* of the true rate.

It is impossible to estimate the number of patients altogether unreported by the Manhattan office therapists. If these patients also are predominantly from the top rung of the socioeconomic ladder, then they represent a further error of understatement attached, with magnitude unknown, to the upper-SES rate in table 16–1.

14. The respondent was credited with a "yes" if he answered "no" but volunteered that he had been to a clinical psychologist or some other kind of certified therapist.

15. Such merger of course tends to reduce differences between groups at the extremes of the SES range.

16. Hollingshead and Redlich, *Social Class and Mental Illness*, pp. 335–356.

Steerage by Alfred Stieglitz. Courtesy The Witkin Gallery

"Remember, remember always that all of us . . . are descended from immigrants."—President Franklin D. Roosevelt

CHAPTER 17

IMMIGRANT AND NATIVE GENERATIONS: RURAL–URBAN ORIGINS

LEO SROLE AND THOMAS LANGNER

American history is the epic of a nation hewed out of wilderness by the brawn and wits of diverse peoples gathered from the length and breadth of the Old World. Nationality and religious segments in this patchwork diversity are being held for separate examination in the two chapters that follow.

Here we want to look at the demographic architecture of the Midtown population from another angle, one that delineates a tier of groups arranged in a sequence of generations from the immigrants through successive orders of their lineal descendants. In the foundation group, of course, are all the foreign-born, designated generation I. American-born offspring of immigrants stand as generation II, and grandchildren of the foreign-born as generation III.[1] Midtowners who have four American-born grandparents are placed in generation IV; that is, the nearest immigrant forebears were great-grandparents or even more remote ancestors.[2] It is no surprise, therefore, that this oldest-in U.S. generation group is largely derived from Old American, Anglo-Saxon stock.

On this ordering of the generations, the Midtown age 20 to 59 sample adults are distributed[3] as follows:

Generation	Percent
I	35.8
II	34.5
III	15.9
IV	13.6
Unknown[4]	0.2
Total (N = 1,660)	100.0

What specific relevance to the concerns of the Midtown Study has the seeming genealogical criterion that differentiates these generation levels? In the first place, these are not categories that claim only conceptual identifiability. Rather, they are in varying respects groups that have separate identities and self-images. Certainly, immigrants—within the several nationality divisions—have their own informal associations and accessible formal organizations. So also does the Old American generation IV, as can be seen in the Colonial Dames of America, the Sons of the American Revolution, and the Society of Colonial Wars, among others.

Lerner refers to the persistent effort during the colonial period "to build an aristocracy of prior immigration."[5] Every wave of immigrants from the early English colonists onward tended to look askance on subsequent newcomers as somehow of suspect and inferior character. The invidious implications of the self-styled "patriotic societies" within the Old American group are not likely to be missed by those who are excluded on ancestral criteria. Of course, more than mere implication was involved in the congressional acts of 1921 and 1924, which drastically cut the number of newcomers, above all by discriminating against the newer sources of immigration.

As subsequent professional analyses of school textbooks in American history have shown, the facts about immigrants reported there often "were, to put it politely, uncivic, uncivil, and untrue."[6] Saveth, one of these analysts, refers to such textbooks as "miseducation by insult, whereby American children are systematically exposed to a racist evaluation of—in so many cases—their own parents and grandparents."[7]

Such grading of the generations on an inferior-superior scale was one process among others serving to widen the boundaries between these groups.

THE GENERATION–IN–U.S. HYPOTHESES

Even more important for our research concerns was a chain of other processes that hinge on these facts: Generation IV, in personality and behavior, is "at home" under the roof of American society. By contrast, immigrants on arrival are often at the farthest pole removed as strangers in the land and aliens to the patterns and nuances of American conduct. During his remaining lifetime the immigrant proceeds some distance in acculturation toward the American model; his children proceed considerably farther; and in his adult grandchildren the process is substantially but rather less than completed.

An extensive literature on the experiences accompanying this process has accumulated in the work of novelists, sociologists, and a new generation of historians. Almost without exception they portray the immigrant as one caught in the dilemma of the iron maiden type, impaled by himself when he yielded to environmental pressures on issues of central importance to his integrity and impaled by the environment when he refused to yield to these pressures under the interdictions of his "out of context" personality.

Rarely has this predicament been conveyed with more detailed insight than in Handlin's *The Uprooted*.[8] On the impact of transplantation, Handlin notes that the "shock and the effects of shock persisted for many years."[9] Among these effects,

. . . the immigrants witnessed in themselves a deterioration . . . a marked personal decline and a noticeable wavering of standards. [They] found it difficult, on the basis of past habits, to determine what their own roles should be . . . they had been projected into a situation where every element conspired to force them into deviations. . . . It was significant of such deviations—pauperism, insanity, intemperance, gambling—that they represented a yielding to the disorganizing pressure of the environment. . . . If only a small number actually plunged into [such deviations] many more lived long on the verge.[10]

In short, here was the discontinuity phenomenon, not in one role but in the immigrant's entire complex of roles—as worker, consumer, tenant, neighbor, husband, father, etc. In the light of these multiple points of potential stress, it was hypothesized that on the generation scale mental health conditions would be found most adverse of all in the Midtown immigrant group.

The predicament of the generation II child, although different, was directly chained to that of his parents. The latter saw themselves challenged and disarmed on almost every front of their new lives. However, one salient on which they could defend themselves was in the refuge of their dwelling, where they partially recreated a family regimen rooted in their traditions, perhaps now magnified and idealized.

This was the intrafamily atmosphere in which they often raised their child without serious extrafamily challenges during his preschool years. Thereafter, however, he came under the increasing pressures of peers and school to conform with American ways. Between these crosscurrents of conflicting sets of values and behavior patterns, both of which exerted powerful claims upon his identifications and loyalties, the generation II child was caught.[11] It has been said of this generation that it is their predicament to stand in both cultural worlds but to be completely at home in neither. Complicating the situation further was the unmistakable antiforeigner bias that these children encountered among people perceived as the authentic American type, including the writers of textbooks in American history. Internalizing this attitude led them to rebel with focused hostility against their immigrant parents, seen miscast as incongruous models and overbearing authorities. In culmination, they could reject themselves as well in a form that Lewin has called "self-hatred."[12]

Hypothesizing about generation II adults, on these grounds, we could expect to find their mental health composition tending in a relatively unfavorable direction. However, we also anticipated that it would be less adverse than that of generation I. Our reasoning was twofold: (1) In degrees of discontinuity there was greater disparity for the immigrant between his natal home and the new environment than there was for the generation II individual; (2) in the intergeneration conflict the American environment was openly a supportive ally of the child and an antagonist of his immigrant parent. This would intrinsically tend to tip the balance, in settling the conflict, toward the former and away from the latter. Thus, the blows of the encounter, we observed, were harder on the foreign-born parent than on his American-born child.

In framing predictions for generation III we had in mind the notable essay by historian Marcus Hansen.[13] Contrasting the second generation's conflicted rejection of the parents' traditional way of life, Hansen says of the third generation: "It has none of the bitterness or heartbreaking features of its predecessors. . . . Whenever any immigrant group reaches the third-generation stage of development a spontaneous and almost irresistible impulse arises which forces the thoughts of many people of different professions, different positions in life, and different points of view to interest themselves in that one factor which they have in common: heritage. . . ."

This statement was congruent with our own wide but unsystematic observations that, not being defensive either about their American identification or about their family tradition, generation III children are no longer conflicted in these important dimensions of the self-image. To this extent we could hypothesize that in adulthood they would appear as a group less vulnerable to the blows of life and more skilled in crisis management than would generation II.

Compared to generation IV, in turn, the only situational liability we could discern for generation III during childhood was their generation II parentage and the latter's own embattled personality development. Accordingly, it seemed plausible to advance the consistent general hypothesis that progressively upward on the generation scale, i.e., from I to IV, the group mental health trend would be toward diminishing frequencies of mental pathology.

HOME SURVEY SAMPLE: MENTAL HEALTH DISTRIBUTIONS

Our hypothesis that mental health varies inversely with generation-in-U.S. is here tested for the first time on a community cross-section population. Also for the first time, the generation variable has been refined to go beyond the usual simple dichotomy (foreign versus American birth) to encompass three categories of the native-born.

We turn now to table 17–1 below for distributions of the four Midtown generation groups on the psychiatrists' classification of mental health. Focusing first on the two intermediate mental health categories, i.e., Mild and Moderate symptom formation, we note, as in previous chapters, high consistency of their rates across the generation range. Looking next to Well and Impaired frequencies, we see that generations II and III are identical; relative to these, generation I has a somewhat larger Impaired-Well ratio and generation IV a decidedly smaller one. As cumulative effect, the Well and Impaired frequencies of the immigrants (16.1 and 26.7 percent, respectively) are completely reversed in the fourth-generation group (27.9 and 17.2 percent, respectively).

Except that the anticipated difference between generations II and III does not appear, the Impaired-Well ratios vary in the direction postulated, although hardly to the degree that had been expected. Moreover, before this modest support can be claimed for the hypoth-

TABLE 17–1. HOME SURVEY SAMPLE (AGE 20–59), RESPONDENTS'
DISTRIBUTIONS ON MENTAL HEALTH CLASSIFICATION BY GENERATION-IN-U.S.

Mental health categories	Generation groups			
	I	II	III	IV
Well	16.1%	17.8%	17.4%	27.9%
Mild symptom formation .	36.0	37.8	36.7	32.3
Moderate symptom formation	21.2	21.5	23.9	22.6
Impaired	26.7	22.9	22.0	17.2
Marked symptom formation	14.9	13.6	11.8	8.8
Severe symptom formation	9.4	6.3	7.2	5.8
Incapacitated	2.4	3.0	3.0	2.6
N = 100%*	(593)	(573)	(264)	(226)
Impaired-Well ratio	165	128	126	62

* Four respondents are of unknown U.S.-born generation

esis as tested, we must take the precaution of inquiring about the potential play of other demographic factors.

This inquiry becomes particularly pertinent when we discover age differences among the sample's generation groups.[14] Likewise, there are some marked differences in SES origin. As we have seen in a previous chapter, frequency of impairment varies directly with respondent age and inversely with SES origin. Accordingly, we must analytically parcel out the separate effects of the latter two factors if we are to determine what residual relation remains between the generation variable, in its own right, and mental health. This can be accomplished most expeditiously by the device of "standardizing" the generation groups' populations. By this method, we recompute the mental health distributions that would result if all four groups were identical in age and SES origin with a population accepted as the standard.[15]

On this standardized basis, the mental health distributions in the several generation groups appear as presented in table 17–2. The limited support for our test hypothesis, as read from table 17–1, is here seen to be largely spurious.[16] For all practical purposes, no relation between generation and mental health remains[17] when SES

TABLE 17–2. HOME SURVEY SAMPLE (AGE 20–59), RESPONDENTS'
DISTRIBUTIONS ON MENTAL HEALTH CLASSIFICATION BY GENERATION-IN-U.S.
GROUPS AS STANDARDIZED FOR AGE AND PARENTAL SES

Mental health categories	Standardized generation groups			
	I	II	III	IV
Well	16.5%	18.1%	16.6%	24.3%
Mild symptom formation	36.5	37.9	36.8	26.4
Moderate symptom formation ...	21.7	21.0	23.9	26.3
Impaired	25.3	23.0	22.7	23.0
N = 100%	(593)	(573)	(264)	(226)

origin and respondent age are held constant.[18] This says, in effect,
that there are no mental health divergences among respondents of
different generation levels who are alike in parental SES and age. To
be sure, the latter variables in combination are highly correlated with
respondent mental health. And it may be expecting too much of a
third demographic variable to come through the fine screen of these
two with a separate relationship all its own. Yet, in the light of the
general evidence that prompted our hypotheses about the four generation groups, this is exactly what we *did* expect. In failing this expectation, the findings of table 17–2 seemed to flatly contradict the
nearly unanimous testimony of a large and diverse corps of compe-
tent observers. Accordingly, we regarded our data with special
skepticism and proceeded to probe and dissect them from a number
of possible angles.

DATA AND HYPOTHESES RECONSIDERED

There was the obvious possibility, for example, that the Study
psychiatrists had been influenced by their own observations of the
conflicted predicaments in which both immigrants and their children
were caught. If so, in classifying respondents' mental health they
could have regarded a given set of symptoms more seriously if occurring in generation III or IV individuals than if found in generation I
or II people. In that event, of course, real differences among these

groups could be more or less leveled out. However, inspection of the psychiatrists' Rating I classifications, made without knowledge of respondents' generation level, indicated trends in no way different from those reported in table 17–1. Thereby, the possibility that a judgmental bias intruded at the point of classifying mental health can be confidently rejected.

A second possibility was that the evidence prompting our hypothesis was biased in the sense that it overstated the negative aspects of the immigrant's situation and understated the positive aspects. Lerner seems to imply this view:

The immigrant experience was . . . somber and tragic. Yet it would be a mistake to see it thus without adding that it was also one of excitement and ferment. Millions of the immigrants, after giving their strength to the new country, died with a sense of failure and frustration. But many more millions survived their ordeal, became men of influence in their communities, and lived to see the fulfillment of the American promise in their own lives doubly fulfilled in the lives of their children. "Everything tends to regenerate them," De Crevecoeur wrote of his fellow immigrants, "new laws, a new mode of living, a new social system; here they are become men: in Europe . . . they withered and were mowed down by want, hunger and war; but now by the power of transplantation, like all other plants, they have taken root and flourished!" One doubts whether this lyric description, written at the end of the eighteenth century, would have been accepted as a faithful one a century later; yet it described a process which would have meaning for many through the whole course of the immigrant experience and even more meaning for the second and third generations, who reaped the harvest of the transplanting of their fathers without having had to suffer the ordeal.[19]

This comment of course is well grounded for many immigrants in the later years of life. However, if it does not minimize the earlier ordeal which immigrants survived, it *does* seem to gloss over the turbulent childhood of the second generation. In any event, needless to say, the senior author had taken this view into account in framing the chapter's test hypothesis.

A third possibility is that the test hypothesis would have secured confirming data were the Midtown Study designed differently, i.e., had it sampled generation groups that stood as lineal kin to each other. Although it is difficult in Manhattan to draw a probability sample comprehending pairs of adult respondents who stand to each other as offspring to parent or grandchild to grandparent, there is more to this critical point than we realized when we planned the study. At that time, it was our implicit, unconsidered assumption that the sample's generation I would be more or less representative of the unsampled parents of the generation II respondents, and that the latter, in turn, would be more or less representative of the unsampled parents of the interviewed generation III group, etc. Therefore, we assumed that the sample would permit us to reconstruct the *unbroken* generation-to-generation progression in mental health.

The simplicity of this assumption is revealed when we examine our sample generation II in terms of a hypothetical average member. About 39 years old when we interviewed him (in 1954), "Mr. Two's" year of birth was 1915. His parents were born abroad, probably between 1880 and 1895, and migrated here most likely between 1901 and 1914.

In this connection it is relevant to recall that with a total population in 1900 of 76 million, the United States received in the following 15 years almost 14 million immigrants along with Mr. Two's parents. Involving an arrival rate of almost 1 million per year, this period (1901–1914) marked the flood-tide climax in a century of sustained massive immigration unparalleled in history. Dependence on the economic "crumbs" of the natives, the sheer enormity of the influx, and accelerating political disorganization of the receiving cities probably made these fifteen years the century's high point also in the survival difficulties faced by "green" immigrants.[20]

Our key question now is this: With the sample's generation II originating from immigrant parents who arrived in the climactic period 1901 to 1914, how comparable to these parents are the sample's generation I? In answer, we note that the average member of the latter group was born in 1908. In time of arrival he belongs on the whole to another chapter of American immigration history, namely, the period after congressional passage of the acts of 1921 and 1924 that ended relatively free immigration from the Western Hemisphere.

With admissions sharply reduced (to a token number of about 150,000 annually) there came a change in the make-up of the immigrants. In the first years of the twentieth century males outnumbered females by about 7:3; in the late twenties the sex ratio had changed to 5:5; and in the thirties, to 4:6. During the earlier (pre-1921) period of mass immigration the overwhelming majority of those reporting occupation had been relatively unschooled laborers from farm, village, or town. Federal sources[21] document the rapid relative increase, during the "new" period, of professional, semiprofessional, and other white-collar workers, a fact reflected in our sample generation I. Also, of this sample group only about one-third were from a farm or village. An additional 15 percent were from towns, 25 percent from small or middle-size cities, and 25 percent from big cities.[22] Finally, many of these sample immigrants were offspring of fathers who in their homeland occupations were skilled blue-collar or white-collar workers.

These and other characteristics convey a picture of decided change in make-up of the shrunken post-1921 immigration as compared with the massive immigration waves at the turn of the century that drained large rural stretches in Europe of their young people.

Certain of the known attributes of the "new" immigrants were of a nature that would probably make for an easier and faster[23] adaptation to the American metropolis than had been the case for their predecessors. Moreover, in the interim the metropolis had itself changed—from a "vast jungle" that Lincoln Steffens stamped as "the shame of the cities"—to something more nearly approaching "community." In particular, between 1910 and 1930 Manhattan reduced its impossibly engorged resident population by almost 500,000. On both counts, therefore, it doubtless could more easily and humanely accommodate the smaller company of newcomers than had been possible for the hordes who had come earlier.

All told, therefore, the *Sturm und Drang* ordeal of exile we have come to associate with the pre-1921 immigrants appears likely to have diminished for their post-1921 successors. Better equipped for metropolitan life and probably better received, our sample generation I group could plausibly be expected to appear with less wear and tear of mental health than had their predecessors by two decades at the same stage of life.

Thus, if in table 17–2 above we find no difference in mental health composition between the sample's generations II and I we can infer that were comparison possible between group II and their own parents, such a difference would likely have been found in the direction suggested by this chapter's test hypothesis.

IMMIGRANTS' PARENTAL SES, RURAL–URBAN ORIGIN, AND MENTAL HEALTH

This line of reviewing the overlooked implications of historical changes in the immigration stream led us to reexamine the generation I group. There we conducted an analytical search for respondents who would most closely exemplify the old and the new immigrant populations. From this dissection we were able to isolate two extreme types. Type O is the nearest approximation in two respects to the kind of individual who dominated the older, pre-1921 immigration; that is, these respondents are from Europe's farms, villages, or small urban places and derived from parents who were low (E–F) in our SES-origin scale. Type N, on the other hand, represents in two respects the newer element appearing in the post-1921 immigration, namely, those who came from Europe's big or medium-size cities and out of families who stood in the higher strata (A–D) of our SES-origin ranking. In table 17–3 these two types and the totality of generation I, standardized for age, are seen in their distributions according to the psychiatrists' classification of mental health.

TABLE 17–3. HOME SURVEY SAMPLE (AGE 20–59), RESPONDENTS' DISTRIBUTIONS ON MENTAL HEALTH CLASSIFICATION BY TYPES OF IMMIGRANTS AS STANDARDIZED FOR AGE

Mental health categories	Type O	Type N	Total generation I
Well	10.2%	17.9%	16.0%
Mild symptom formation	30.8	40.5	37.2
Moderate symptom formation ...	24.7	23.1	21.2
Impaired	34.3*	18.5*	25.6
N = 100%	(163)	(185)	(593)
Impaired-Well ratio	336	103	160

* $t = 3.4$ (.001 level of confidence).

Thus, had type O been predominant in our sample generation I group (as it had in the earlier period of immigration), it seems clear that the mental health difference we originally hypothesized for generations I and II would likely have received the support of the Midtown data.

The pronounced difference we see above in types O and N suggests that what is decisive among immigrants is *not* transplantation to the American metropolis per se, but resettlement in the American metropolis from a *particular kind* of overseas milieu, namely, from the low socioeconomic strata in farm, village, or town. In this perspective, "foreignness," in the nationality and linguistic sense alone, may involve certain initial difficulties for the immigrant from the middle- or near middle-class strata of European cities. But these difficulties in themselves probably are minor in significance and relatively brief in duration, at least compared to the situational and adaptational burdens that descend when the immigrant combines this foreignness of nationality with other special dimensions or meanings of the word *foreign*. Those dimensions hinge on the contrast between the involuted complexities of Manhattan and the simple way of life in Europe's rural places as delineated with great artistry in a novel like Reymont's *Peasants*[24] or in Gavin Maxwell's book[25] portraying an economically depressed Sicilian village. The contrast stretches in time from the somnolent agrarian, preindustrial order characterizing the early-nineteenth-century hamlet to the twentieth century's summit point in the industrial cosmopolis. To compress the profound historical changes of a revolutionizing century into a few adult years of an individual life cycle may exact a high price in psychological wellbeing, such as is intimated in the mental health distribution of type O immigrants seen in table 17–3.

If this formulation accounts, at least in part, for the mental health differences between types O and N, perhaps primarily responsible is not the character of the environment at the immigrant's point of origin in itself, but its distance in "social time" from New York and the rush with which the O-type immigrant had to accomplish his sociopsychological vault from one to the other. Thus, divergence between O and N immigrants in their Impaired-Well balance may reflect different magnitudes of role discontinuity bridged in the transition from their respective native environments.

Within the framework of the generation-in-U.S. variable, immigration from abroad, at least on the part of adults, is usually a motivated act; as such, personality differences may be associated with the distinction between the self-chosen migrants and their nonmigrant townspeople. We can assume that *self-choice* was maximally involved among generation I respondents who migrated "on their own steam" as isolated adult individuals, involved to a lesser degree among adults who migrated with family or settled with kin, and involved negligibly among those who, as children, were brought to this country by their parents. On the criterion of their present mental health composition, at least, these three subgroups of immigrants emerge without any significant differences.

This bit of evidence is suggestive but hardly conclusive on the issue, since the three subgroups may deviate psychologically in similar fashion from the nonmigrants. In part they could deviate not only by the processes of subjective selection,[26] but also as a consequence of the objective selection engineered through the screening apparatus of the United States government. By way of explanation: "The visa requirement established by the Immigration Act of 1924 is in itself an important regulative device. . . . In order to secure a visa an immigrant must have established his eligibility to enter the United States, a process requiring many documents with respect to the identity, character and financial standing of the applicant. The overseas issuance of visas has proved an effective means . . . of screening immigrants prior to entry."[27] According to an official document, beyond rejecting those "likely to become a public charge," such screening also rejects individuals who "are not mentally sound and physically fit, [or are] drug addicts and chronic alcoholics, [or are] over 16 years of age [and] cannot read and understand some language, [or] have committed a crime. . . . In short, an alien who does not measure up to the moral, mental, physical and other standards fixed by law is subject to exclusion, or [after admission] may be deported to the country from which he came."[28]

This is a formidable screen, especially for personality deviants of all kinds, both as it is directly applied to visa applicants by American overseas consulates and as an indirect restraint in discouraging applications.[29] The threat of rejection, or of acceptance and subsequent deportation, was known to be taken into grim account by potential applicants.

Under such screening, direct and indirect, this seems certain: Winnowed of those already impaired in mind or body and probably of many others representing gross risks in such directions, immigrants in the years 1924–1954 were a more selected, and more homogeneous population in mental health respects as compared to their nonmigrant fellow townspeople.

Moreover, the steady stream of returnees to the homeland[30] is evidence suggesting that the nonreturnees have been further sifted of those who could not adjust to the difficult demands placed upon the immigrant new to America and to the metropolis.

These points have been developed here on the same rationale that prompted a parallel discussion of marital status in chapter 12 (Book One), that is, to underscore the probability that the sample immigrant group, including type O itself, being largely post-1921 in arrival date, is a residue of multiple winnowing processes.

On the one hand, this may shed light on a fact previously unattended in table 17–1, that among its four groups the incapacitation rate of generation I is no greater than that of the rest. On the other hand, it leads us to a reconsideration of the earlier immigrants who were the parents of our generation II respondents.

A decisive fact is that this earlier wave of immigrants arrived before establishment of the United States visa-screening apparatus. Thus, it is almost certain that they had a substantially greater representation of mental disorder risks than did the later immigrants. Also more numerous in the earlier wave of immigrants was the type O background that we now know, from our post-1921 sample immigrant group, to be particularly associated in Midtown with a high mental morbidity rate.

On both of these counts, there are ample grounds for the expectation that our generation I respondents, as an aggregate, are better off in mental health respects than the immigrant parents of our generation II had been at the same age. Second, according to our original test hypothesis, we expect that our generation II respondents are also in better mental health composition than their parents had been at the same age. Third, if indeed both sample generation I and sample generation II are healthier than the latter's unstudied immigrant parents had been, then it could have been hypothetically predicted that these two sample groups would not be far apart from each other in this respect. Of course, table 17–2 offers evidence that when respondent age and SES origin are held constant, these two generation groups are almost identical in their mental health distributions.

All in all, reconstruction in terms of the probable differential effects of selection processes on the earlier and more recent waves of immigrants, together with the direct evidence from immigrant types O and N appearing in table 17–3, represent separate lines of analysis that lead to the same conclusion: Far from rejecting the test hypothesis predicting mental health differences between immigrants and their native-born children, the data in table 17–2, historically interpreted, seem to stand in support of that hypothesis.

PARENTAL SES, THE URBAN–ORIGIN VARIABLE, AND MENTAL HEALTH AMONG THE U.S.–BORN

In table 17–2 generations II and III also appear to contradict our original hypothesized predictions for these groups. Here again, processes of self-selection may have unexpectedly intruded to complicate the picture.

Although we had always seen generation I as open to self-selection processes, we had viewed a position in generation II, III, or IV as a matter of descent and therefore independent of individual influence or choice. We had also been aware of the fact that about half of the U.S.-born people in Midtown were themselves in-migrants from birth places reaching to the four corners of the nation. To be sure, like immigration of the foreign-born, in-migration of the native-born is a motivated act, usually self-determined, and therefore amenable to the influences of subjective selectivity.

However, in the absence of census data on this point, we had simply assumed that the weightings of in-migrants among generations II, III, and IV would not be grossly different. When the Midtown sample data were in and analyzed, however, we found that this assumption had been erroneous.

Figure 7 below reveals that in generation II a minority of 30 percent are in-migrants from the rest of the country, i.e., 70 percent are native New Yorkers. On the other hand, in generation III the in-migrant proportion rises to 47 percent and in generation IV it jumps to a commanding majority of 72 percent, i.e., only 28 percent are native to the City. In short, the seemingly independent variable of generation differences among the U.S.-born respondents proves to be entwined with the reciprocal variable of in-migration from communities large and small on the continuum of American rural-urban places.

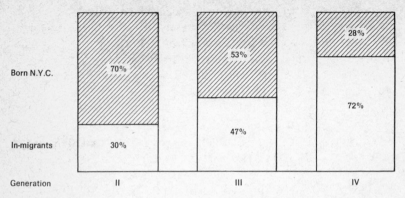

FIGURE 7. THREE MIDTOWN AMERICAN-BORN GENERATIONS (AGE 20–59), PROPORTIONS OF IN-MIGRANTS AND NEW YORK CITY–BORN

It is possible that mental health differences selectively associated with in-migration tend to obscure the expected decrease in the impairment rate from generation II through IV. This possibility can be checked, although under some handicaps. First, generations III and IV, each with about 250 respondents, are too small to sustain analysis of the in-migration factor while also controlling for both parental SES and age. Accordingly, for this purpose we have no choice except to combine the two generations in one group. This is unfortunate because it will blur the close comparison of generations II and III that we seek to make. Even so, the merged group, i.e., III–IV, has too few respondents of low SES origin for reliable treatment of the latter.

Confining ourselves to the middle (C–D) and upper (A–B) strata, we find these countertrends in both SES-origin classes: (1) among the native New Yorkers, generation II emerges with a higher Impaired-Well ratio than does group III–IV (with age standardized in all instances); (2) among the in-migrants the reverse obtains; i.e., here generation II has a smaller Impaired-Well imbalance than do the group III–IV respondents. As illustration, we offer the Impaired-Well ratios in the four subgroup cells representing the middle SES-origin stratum in table 17–4.

If we focus only on the native New Yorkers in the left-hand column of the table, the generation difference in balances of Impaired and Well people is in the direction originally hypothesized. However, the

TABLE 17–4. HOME SURVEY SAMPLE (AGE 20–59, SES C–D), IMPAIRED-WELL RATIOS AMONG U.S.–BORN GENERATIONS BY PLACE OF ORIGIN

	Native New Yorkers	In-migrants
Generation II	140 (N = 178)	63 (N = 90)
Generations III–IV	99 (N = 68)	90 (N = 82)

in-migrant generation II respondents are the healthiest of the four subgroups, and their weight is sufficient to counterbalance the generation difference observed among the New York–born.

That the intergeneration difference among in-migrants (right-hand column above) is not in the hypothesized direction may be largely a function of differential subjective selectivity for movement to New York, operating in ways we cannot document or reconstruct as yet.[31] On this open-ended note we can at least draw this inference: Table 17–4 offers no warrant to reject the original hypothesis positing that mental health composition would be less favorable in generation II than in III.

The identification of types O and N among immigrants hinged on the factor of rural-urban community settings during childhood abroad. To round out this exploration, we can next apply the same variable[32] to the U.S.-born respondents (generations II to IV inclusive).

There are too few of these respondents reared in a farm or village community to be included while controlling for SES origin and age. Accordingly, the categories examined can cover only the broad urban range and include (1) town or small city, to be abbreviated as *town*, (2) medium or big city (excluding New York City), designated *city*, and (3) *New York City*.

Among American-born adults of low (E–F) parental-SES, mental morbidity rates, with age standardized, do not vary with the urban-origin factor so categorized. Along the remainder of the SES-origin range, however, there are noteworthy mental health differences. These are reported in table 17–5 below.

Although the relationship of impairment rates to urban origin here verges on statistical significance (slightly below the .05 level of con-

TABLE 17-5.   HOME SURVEY SAMPLE (AGE 20-59), DISTRIBUTIONS ON MENTAL HEALTH CLASSIFICATION OF U.S.-BORN RESPONDENTS BY URBAN-ORIGIN TYPES AS STANDARDIZED FOR AGE AND PARENTAL SES (INCLUSIVE OF SES STRATA A-D ONLY)

Mental health categories	Urban-origin type		
	Town	City	N.Y.C.
Well	26.6%	24.7%	19.2%
Mild symptom formation	34.3	40.3	36.8
Moderate symptom formation ..	26.0	16.2	22.5
Impaired*	13.1	18.8	21.5
N = 100%	(173)	(170)	(386)
Impaired-Well ratio	49	76	112

* $x^2 = 5.51$, $2df$, $p > .05$.

fidence), the trends in both Impaired and Well frequencies are consistent in their respective directions.[33] Here we see a reversal of the trend previously observed in generation I. Among the latter, Impaired-Well values of *greatest* magnitude were isolated in low SES-origin immigrants from the smaller, principally rural, communities abroad. In table 17-5 the Impaired-Well ratios of *least* magnitude are noted in Midtown respondents from the nation's smaller urban places. The facts that their childhood communities were American and urban and that their parental-SES derivations were in the upper two-thirds of our SES-origin range together offer the reasonable inference that no adaptive problems of sharp change in environment had here been involved.

Instead, we are left with two alternative explanations for this discerned mental health trend on the American urban-origin variable. The first is that the three urban-origin types living in Midtown more or less accurately reflect mental health differences in the like-age-and-SES segment of their parent American communities. Under this assumption, then, the smaller the urban community in which American middle- and upper-status children grow up, the better are their mental health chances when they reach adulthood. If this should be the case, New York City would appear to be the least favorable place to rear such children.

The second possible interpretation proceeds from a far more complicated framework. To begin with, it asserts that in most American communities the indigenous *permanent* residents as a rule far out-number the native-son *emigrants* who settle elsewhere. On this ground of much greater numerical strength, the indigenous residents are likely to be more representative or reflective of the community's mental health productivity than are the minority of native-son-and-daughter emigrants.

By this line of reasoning, the native New Yorkers in table 17–5 probably are not far different in mental health make-up from the population universe of New York–bred adults of the specified age and parental SES. On the other hand, the in-migrants seen in table 17–5 are less likely to be representative of mental health conditions among like-age-and-SES people in their *home* communities.

Third, this approach also takes into account the fact that emigrants from a given community, in moving to their adopted places, travel varying "distances" in the social dimensions of the rural-urban con-tinuum.[34] In this sense, the town group appearing in table 17–5 has "traveled farther" to settle New York than has the city type. Next we can posit as a consequence of subjective selectivity that personality and mental health differences divide those who in this sense travel near ("hoppers") from those who move far ("broad jumpers"); specifically, of these two categories of emigrants from the same child-hood community, the jumpers may deviate farther from the mental health composition of their common population of origin than do the hoppers.

As to how representative the three groups in table 17–5 are of their respective parent populations, by this formulation the New York–born respondents are the most representative and the town in-migrants are the least. Since we have reason to believe that such town-to-metropolis traffic[35] is an important facet of upward SES mobility, as discussed in chapter 14, it seems likely that both types of Midtown in-migrants were actually more favorable in mental health composi-tion than were their respective back-home populations of like-age-and SES origin. Accordingly, from the town and city groups in table 17–5 we cannot generalize that the smaller the urban community in which middle- and upper-class American children live, the better are their mental health chances as adults.

In chapter 20, the senior author presents recently emerging evi-dence that suggests what we *can* generalize about the links between indices of community well-being and rural-urban-metropolitan differences.

TREATMENT CENSUS FINDINGS

In the Midtown Study the factor of treatment was covered, although in very different ways, by both of our major research operations. One was the Treatment Census, with its goal of enumerating all Midtown residents in the care of hospitals, clinics or office therapists at a given point of time. The other was the Home Interview Survey, in which we asked each sample respondent whether he had ever been to a psychotherapist, and if so, when. (For characteristics differentiating the Home Survey operation from the Treatment Census see Book One, chapter 10, p. 191.)

It has been our consistent effort to relate Midtown data bearing on the demographic factors to published studies that are substantively or technically relevant and challenging to the present investigation. Pertinent to this chapter is a monograph that appeared under the sponsorship and imprint of the Social Science Research Council (SSRC) and its Committee on Migrant Differentials. Entitled *Migration and Mental Disease,*[36] the monograph includes an introductory chapter by Dorothy S. Thomas, chairman of the stated SSRC committee.

Since this work presented expert views on the migration factor (both immigration and in-migration) and its links to *treated* mental disorder, we are called upon to take it into serious account by way of providing a backdrop for the Midtown treatment data.

The general mandate of the SSRC committee had been to consider in what respects migrants are different from nonmigrants. The monograph reports its examination of mental illness as one of the possible differentials. Reviewing the relevant literature up to 1953, Thomas in her introductory chapter considers that the most rounded work in this field had been done by Odegaard, the Norwegian psychiatrist, and Malzberg, the American statistician. Both of these investigators took first-admission patients of mental hospitals as their criterion of the frequency of mental illness.[37]

As indicated in the Thomas chapter, Odegaard's study[38] is probably unparalleled. He compared the public hospital rates over a forty-year span (1889–1929) of Norwegian-born immigrants in Minnesota with those (1) of the total native-born population of Minnesota and (2) of the total population of Norway, with standardization for age and sex differences. Odegaard found the Norwegian-born Minnesotans to have patient rates higher than those of U.S.-born Minnesotans; the latter, in turn, had rates higher than those of the population in Norway. In short, *both* U.S.-born and Norwegian-born Minnesotans had higher hospitalization rates than did the population of Norway. Odegaard notes that differences in

. . . the hospital facilities of the two countries may to some extent explain this, but of course nothing definite can be known about them. . . .[39] The discrepancies [between hospital patient rates in Minnesota and Norway] seem too large for such an explanation to be entirely satisfactory, and it is probably safe to assume that there is actually more insanity among native-born Minnesotans than in the population of Norway. This is in fact very natural, if, as we have some right to believe, there is a connection between immigration and mental disorders. During [1890–1900] about 33 percent of the native-born [Minnesotans] were actually [in-migrants] from other states in the Union, mostly the East. . . . The factors which tend to increase the incidence of mental disease in the Norwegian immigrants [to Minnesota] will therefore probably to some extent be at work in one-third of the native-born [i.e., in the U.S.-born in-migrants to Minnesota] also.

Odegaard sees two main factors as explaining "the natural . . . connection between immigration and mental disorders." One is the "mental and physical strain" of resettlement; and this, for him, applies both to the Norwegian and Yankee settlers of Minnesota. The other, more heavily emphasized element is the "prevalence of certain psychopathic tendencies in the constitution of those who emigrate. Emigration is frequently a result of the restlessness and difficulties of adaptation which may at times be a basis for a later psychotic development."

For our present purposes, the principal difficulties in Odegaard's investigation lie not in the sweeping generality of its etiological conclusions, but in the inadequacy of its data to support etiological inferences of any kind. The root difficulty is the author's assumption that variations in hospitalization rates among the three population groups under study adequately reflect differences in their overall frequencies of severe mental disorder. This assumption may perhaps be valid in some places and not in others and at some points of time and not at others. Accordingly, there is no warrant to impute varying characteristics to diverse groups on the basis of intergroup differences in hospital rates, if the validity of this assumption at the particular places studied is unknown. This precaution is especially indicated by the simple fact that variations in the bed capacities of mental hospitals and the latter's spatial distance from large population centers rather than a presumed "constitutional" etiology tend to determine the number that can be institutionalized.[40]

In a subsequent paper[41] Odegaard takes note of such criticisms. He suggests that the goal of such research is "not to obtain a higher degree of completeness by extending the concept of mental disease, but to establish some definite limitation to make it possible for various authors to compare results." For this purpose,

. . . hospital admission is, in borderline cases, the only distinctive landmark; and besides, it is not at all without clinical meaning. Practically all psychoses with definite clinical symptoms will at some time necessitate admission. At least this is so for schizophrenic and allied disorders and for general paresis, although for the depressive psychoses it may be more doubtful. For senile psychoses, and for psychoses with mental deficiency and epilepsy, on the other hand, hospitalization will frequently be dependent more upon social than upon clinical factors; and admissions for those diagnostic groups do not allow any safe conclusions as to the incidence of the disease.

To round out, if hardly to close this debate, several observations can be addressed to Odegaard's comments. First, as reported earlier (chapter 10), the Midtown Treatment Census found that in *ambulatory* care were 36 percent of all reported nonparanoid schizophrenic patients and 14 percent of all paranoid schizophrenic patients. Second, from other studies there is evidence indicating that when hospitalization does eventuate it often does so long after psychotic symptoms first appeared.[42] Furthermore, the effort to secure psychiatric treatment of any kind often depends upon social factors like a break in family or local tolerance of the symptoms, precipitating, if not a first recognition of "illness," at least a change in the previous view that the condition is "harmless."

Finally, in the whole battery of possible social elements impeding the family from committing a member to a hospital, one potentially affecting immigrants in particular is noted by Malzberg and Lee: "It is claimed that recent immigrants may sometimes be sent to hospitals for mental disease with reluctance because of the possibility of deportation on the ground that the disease was contracted before entry into the United States."[43]

All in all, there are ample grounds for questioning confidence in the inevitability that any of the more frequent psychotic disorders "will at some time necessitate admission to a mental hospital."

Also worthy of attention is Odegaard's claim that immigration tends to recruit people predisposed to mental disorder, with the obverse implication that nonmigrants tend to be selectively less predisposed. That migrants and nonmigrants are selectively different in such characteristics as mental health seems to be a plausible hypothesis. But that such selection operates in the direction suggested by Odegaard has yet to be established.

As mentioned earlier in the present chapter, we can test this hypothesis in the Midtown sample's immigrant group by dividing it into three subgroups: (1) those who came to the United States as children and therefore are not self-selected migrants; (2) those who came as youths in the company of parents or kin, with the element of self-determination of the migratory act somewhat ambiguous; and (3) those who came unaccompanied, as youths or later, most probably a self-selected group. To corroborate Odegaard's postulate, group 3 should have the highest impairment rate and group 1 the lowest. However, the data for these three subgroups show no differences in their Impaired or Well frequencies. There is no endorsement in these Midtown data for the view that the self-recruited newcomers who initiated their own immigration to the United States have a higher rate of mental morbidity than the less selected who were brought on the initiative of others.

The main body of the SSRC monograph is the study report contributed by Malzberg and Lee. In their own opening chapter, these authors take note that from

. . . the literature on this subject, it is generally concluded that the incidence of mental disease is higher among migrants than among nonmigrants, and that the difference is attributable either to selection of poorer risks at places of [migrants'] origin or to stresses of migration and adjustment at places of destination. Most of these differences have been based on scanty or otherwise inadequate data, and even the fact of higher incidence of mental disease among migrants is not firmly established, much less the theories as to cause.[44]

Their study covered all residents of New York State who were first-admission patients in hospitals supported by the state or federal government (VA) and in state-licensed private hospitals during the three fiscal years ending June 30, 1941.[45] For the white population only, Malzberg and Lee report these average annual rates of hospital first admissions (per 100,000 population), as standardized for age:

> Foreign-born males 156
> Native-born males 140
> Foreign-born females 143
> Native-born females 118

Thus, among these four groups only the U.S.-born females deviate in their rate to any extent. Moreover, most of their deviation from the other three groups is traceable to the age range above the 60-year line.[46] There is the definite impression that many senile U.S.-born women in the pre-World War II years were placed for custodial care in nursing homes rather than in psychiatric hospitals.

With this evidence suggesting little difference in hospitalizations between immigrants and U.S.-born in the white population of New York State, Malzberg and Lee concede that

. . . rates of first admission are far from ideal indicators of the incidence of mental disease, but for our purposes they are the best available. It is impossible to determine the number of persons who each year become psychotic because many persons with psychoses may not be included in the statistics of mental disease. There are persons who would be considered psychotic by psychiatrists but who are never treated or diagnosed. Others are treated privately but never hospitalized, and their cases are not reported. [Later they elaborate that] comparisons of migrant and nonmigrant populations are affected to an unknown extent by differential ability or willingness to care for mentally ill persons at home.[47]

The reservations placed by Malzberg and Lee on hospital patients as study populations are shared by the present authors. However, to the view that such patients are "the best available" indicators of the frequency of mental illness we must counter that *best available* does not necessarily imply *good enough* for the kinds of generalizations drawn from them.

A more recent work that concentrates on the migrant-nonmigrant dichotomy straddles both horns of the dilemma posed by patient aggregates and general populations as appropriate bases for etiological generalizations.[48]

In the New Haven study alluded to in previous chapters, the scope of coverage for the first time encompassed ambulatory as well as hospital patients and used prevalence instead of incidence as the measure of frequency. For the demographic factor of concern to this chapter, the New Haven investigators report only for foreign-born and native-born above the age of 20.[49] From distribution data published, we calculate New Haven Total Patients rates of 1,169 per 100,000 immigrants and 1,005 per 100,000 of the American-born population. However, even within the adult age range immigrants are decidedly the older of the two groups, and therefore standardization for age is indispensable. Such standardized rates have not yet been reported. However, the effect of such standardization can be anticipated from the results secured when we remove cases diagnosed as disorders of senescence[50] from the patients of both New Haven generation groups. When this is accomplished, the rates per 100,000 among adult immigrants and natives are reduced to practical identity. We might note in passing that this "no difference" parallels the New York State findings.

We turn now to the Midtown Treatment Census. On the basis of institutional records, hospital and clinic patients could be classified into three generation-in-U.S. groups paralleling the Home Survey sample's I, II, and III–IV. On the patients of office therapists no data identifying generation level were secured. We are therefore extrapolating estimates of office patients from the current patients[51] identified in the Home Survey sample. Because these estimates relate to the 20 to 59 age range, in table 17–6 below we are including only hospital and clinic patients who are within this age span.

To what ends can tables like this be put? In concrete terms, they serve to map the patient traffic in terms of (1) its volume, (2) its differential group origins in the community population, and (3) its flow toward different destinations among the various types of available treatment facilities. Such information, in turn, can have important implications for policy decisions in planning service programs. By way of a single example, we know office therapists are treating psychotics in considerable numbers, diverting them from hospitalization—especially, we now discover, in generation group III–IV. Ambulatory treatment in clinics could probably serve the same pur-

TABLE 17–6.   TREATMENT CENSUS (AGE 20–59 ONLY), PREVALENCE RATES (PER 100,000 POPULATION) OF MIDTOWN PATIENTS BY TREATMENT SITE AND GENERATION-IN-U.S.

Treatment sites	Generation groups		
	I	II	III–IV
Hospitals	504	829	298
Clinics	76	210	89
Office therapy*	430	2,058	4,811
Total Patients rate*	1,010	3,097	5,198

* Estimated.

pose for generation I and II people who cannot afford high-cost private therapy. But, table 17–6 indicates that those clinics available to Midtowners served *adults* of *all* generations to a negligible degree. Clearly, such knowledge can guide plans for the expansion of treatment facilities that will inevitably come.*

There is one function table 17–6 clearly cannot serve: It cannot offer any ground for proceeding from known demographic differences in frequencies of *treatment* to inferences about frequencies of *illnesses* untreated. To fix the point, we might compare tables 17–1 and 17–6 in this chapter, both having reference to the age 20 to 59 Midtown population. Among the three generation groups in table 17–6 the hospital rate of generation II is substantially highest and of III–IV the lowest. In table 17–1, Incapacitated is a category in Rennie's classification scheme that is the closest available approximation to the criterion of *hospitalizable*. According to that table there are *no* significant generation differences in the proportions of these noninstitutionalized Incapacitated people. The generation trends of the Incapacitated and of the Hospitalized bear no resemblance to each other.

Or, in table 17–6, let us take the clinic *and* estimated office treatment rates which, together, *rise* from 506 (per 100,000 population) in generation I to 4,900 in group III–IV. In table 17–1, the mental health categories designated Impaired-Severe and Impaired-Marked

* This sentence stands as written in 1961. Chapter 1 (Book One, p. 13) gives a summary account of just such developments that followed between 1963 and 1974.

could be expected to delineate the reservoir of potential eligibility for ambulatory treatment. The joint frequency of these two categories *declines* from 24.3 percent in generation I to 19 percent in group III and 14.6 percent in group IV. In short, the two trends on the generation variable move in opposite directions.

The objection may be made that these cross-directional findings on the generation pyramid are chance or freak incongruences that are of no general significance. In rejoinder, it should be noted first that a similar phenomenon has already been reported in previous chapters for the age and socioeconomic status factors and will be encountered again in the chapter on religious groups.

Second, that treatment rates may vary in ways different from morbidity rates can be demonstrated if a criterion group of known mental morbidity cases are circumscribed and treatment rates then are shown to vary among them with differences in demographic characteristics. Equally important is that this will bring to bear data on that part of our key question which asked: What kinds of impaired people do *not* get treatment?

HOME SURVEY SAMPLE: HELP–NEED AND THE PATIENT–HISTORY VARIABLE

Toward these ends, we would now return to our age 20 to 59 Home Survey sample, where the Study psychiatrists have placed 389 respondents in the Impaired category of mental health. Despite apparent limitations, this category in the sample has served as our working criterion of potential need for professional help.

It will also be remembered that on the basis of interview material we were able to classify all sample respondents on a variable we call *patient history*. Those who had never been in one or more professional sessions with a psychotherapist are never-patients; those who had been in such a session during the previous month are designated current patients; and the remainder who had ever been to a therapist are ranked as ex-patients.

In table 17–7 below, only the Impaired in each generation group are shown in their distribution on the patient-history variable. Because of their small numbers the Impaired of generations III and IV are here combined.

TABLE 17-7. HOME SURVEY SAMPLE (AGE 20-59), DISTRIBUTIONS OF IMPAIRED RESPONDENTS ON PATIENT-HISTORY CLASSIFICATION BY GENERATION-IN-U.S.

Patient history	Generation groups		
	I	II	III-IV
Current patients	0.6%	4.6%	14.3%
Ex-patients	16.5	24.4	25.5
Ever-patients	17.1	29.0	39.8
Never-patients	82.9	71.0	60.2
N = 100%*	(158)	(131)	(97)

* Three Impaired respondents are of unknown generation.

Table 17-7 indicates that among Impaired respondents the ever-patient rates increase in regular progression up the generation scale. If the increase is far sharper for current patients than for ex-patients, we can assume that among the latter are mixed the formerly hospitalized, whose rates by generation vary in a direction opposite to the probable trend in the ambulatory ex-patients.[52]

Two important questions remain open: Do these patient-history differences genuinely adhere to the generation factor independently of other demographic factors? Or are these differences largely the indirect reflection of more powerful demographic variables that are concealed in the generation factor? That these questions are decidedly in order is indicated by the facts revealed in previous chapters that ever-patient rates among the Impaired are largest in the younger and higher own-SES segments of the Midtown sample population. The latter are of course underrepresented in generation I.

To answer these questions we shall convert the data in table 17-7 by standardizing the Impaired category in each generation group to a hypothetical ideal population.[53] The results appear in table 17-8.

In this table we discern that the marked difference in current-patient rates previously observed between II and III-IV is erased. The conclusion seemingly to be drawn is that when age and own SES are controlled, the tendency of the Impaired to be treated in an ambulatory setting splits rather sharply on the line dividing the immigrants from the American-born generations. That is, among the Impaired those with the highest ever-patient rates are U.S.-born younger

TABLE 17–8. HOME SURVEY SAMPLE (AGE 20–59), DISTRIBUTIONS OF
IMPAIRED RESPONDENTS ON PATIENT-HISTORY CLASSIFICATION BY
GENERATION-IN-U.S. AS STANDARDIZED FOR OWN SES AND AGE

Patient history	Generation groups among impaired		
	I	II	III–IV
Current patients	1.1%	11.0%	13.4%
Ex-patients	13.8	25.5	22.4
Ever-patients	14.9	36.5	35.8
Never-patients	85.1	63.5	64.2
N = 100%	(158)	(131)	(97)

adults (age 20 to 39) of higher socioeconomic status. Whereas lagging far behind in such rates are the older adults (40 to 59) of lower
SES and foreign birth.

HELP–NEED AND PROFESSIONAL ORIENTATION

We have seen earlier in this chapter that among Midtown sample
adults mental health distributions do not vary with generation-in-U.S.
level when parental SES and respondent age are controlled. Furthermore, we have just observed that within the criterion Impaired category, when own SES and age are controlled, ever-patient rates are at
the same relatively high point in generations II and III–IV and substantially lower only in the immigrant group.

The question is now raised about the relative extent of *effective*
demand for professional help that exists among Impaired respondents
in the several generation groups. To this end, the effective demand
can be judged by their replies to two interview questions that were
put to all respondents. The questions inquired about the nature of the
advice the respondent would give if such counsel were solicited by a
friend concerned about "what to do" (1) with a problem child and
(2) with a problem spouse. Respondents were classified according to
the most specialized kind of professional help they would recommend
for either or both problem situations. In so doing we can assume they
reveal, by indirection, what kind of professional help they are themselves aware of and disposed to seek. In table 17–9, the Impaired

respondents in each generation group, as first sorted by own-SES class, are shown with the proportion who recommended psychotherapy in their replies.

TABLE 17–9. HOME SURVEY SAMPLE (AGE 20–59), PROPORTION RECOMMENDING PSYCHOTHERAPY AMONG IMPAIRED RESPONDENTS BY GENERATION-IN-U.S. AND OWN SES

Own-SES classes	Generation groups among Impaired		
	I	II	III–IV
Lower (E–F) .... N = 100%	12.4% (97)	13.1% (61)	10.7% (27)
Middle (C–D) .... N = 100%	9.8% (51)	32.7% (52)	40.0% (30)
Upper (A–B) .... N = 100%	—* (10)	55.5% (18)	60.0% (40)

* These cases are too few to present a meaningful percentage.

In positive orientation to or awareness of psychotherapy among Impaired respondents, lower-SES respondents in the U. S-born generation subgroups are as often remote as are the foreign-born. Among the upper-status respondents the pro-therapy proportions are far higher but again more or less uniform among the generations. With the middle-stratum Impaired cases, the pro-therapy rates split sharply on the line dividing the foreign-born from the natives. Stated differently, higher frequencies of potential demand for psychiatric care seem to be localized among the American-born Impaired people of the upper two-thirds of the own-SES range.

SUMMARY

We might now briefly retrace the new ground we have traversed in this chapter's coverage of the generation-in-U.S. variable.

1. On the foundations of the large literature reporting observations of American immigrants and their children, it was hypothesized that mental health would be most unfavorable in generation I and would

be progressively more favorable in successive generation groups from II through IV.

2. As distributed on the psychiatrists' mental health scale, the four generation groups in the Midtown sample emerged with Impaired and Well differences that leaned in the hypothesized direction. However, these differences were relatively small in magnitude except between the two anchoring groups—I and IV.

3. When the age and SES-origin factors entangled with the generation variable were controlled by standardizing, the original Impaired-Well differences observed were practically erased. With no evidence of mental health differences specifically attributable to the generation variable apart from the age and SES-origin factors, rejection of the tested hypothesis was indicated.

4. The face implausibility of this "no relationship" finding prompted a critical reexamination of our assumptions and methods. A number of these were seen to be grossly simplistic. However, re-analysis of the data in the light of the overlooked complexities suggested that (a) at the very least, the data do not warrant rejection of the chapter's major hypotheses; and (b) with considerable probability, the data seem to support these hypotheses.

5. In the course of this dissection we discovered in the sample's immigrant group that relatively frequent prevalence of mental morbidity was associated with the combination of lower parental SES and a rural-town childhood background. Conducting a similar exploration among the sample's American-born respondents (generations II to IV), we found urban-origin differences in mental health only within the middle and upper brackets of parental SES. With the urban-origin variable classifying Midtown respondents according to town, city, or New York derivation, mental health composition was most favorable in the town category and least favorable among the native New Yorkers. Two contradictory interpretations of this trend were discussed.

6. Turning to the factor of psychiatric treatment, we reviewed three studies that focused on immigrants and the native-born among psychiatric patients. Noted were differences in the findings and inferences they generated. Also brought to bear were the generation data yielded by the Midtown Treatment Census, with emphasis on their special utility and their specific limitations.

7. Returning to the Midtown Home Survey, those in the sample's

Impaired category, taken as criterion of professional help-need, were analyzed by generation groups for differences in patient history. Upward on the generation scale the ever-patient rates increased and the never-patient rates diminished. However, with standardization for own SES and age, the trend changed to a dichotomy that broke sharply on the line dividing the Impaired immigrants from the Impaired native-born groups. Compared to the latter of like age and socioeconomic status, the foreign-born Impaired people get to a psychotherapist to a considerably lesser extent.

8. On an indirect test of awareness of and disposition to seek psychotherapy among Impaired respondents, again the U.S.-born of middle and upper own-SES strata were far ahead in their pro-therapy frequencies. This roughly delineated the locus of effective demand for professional intervention among Midtown's help-needy adult residents.

NOTES

1. Placement in a generation group was made not on the judgment of the respondent but on that of the interviewer and was subsequently checked by office staff.

In classifying the Midtown sample, all U.S.-born respondents who had one foreign-born parent and the other of American birth were arbitrarily placed in generation II. This mixed subgroup numbered about one-fourth of all sample respondents assigned to generation II. Similarly, all U.S.-born respondents with both parents of native birth were placed in generation III if one to four grandparents were foreign-born. Approximately half of all sample respondents classified as generation III had from one to three U.S.-born grandparents. Because the mixed subgroups of generations II and III are not significantly different in their mental health composition from their unmixed generation peers, they will not be differentiated in the data analysis that follows.

2. In the interest of conserving interview time, the identification of such respondents' immigrant forebears was not pursued beyond the question, "About how many generations before your father's parents did his family come to the United States?" With an identical question for mother's family, the answers ranged from respondent's great-grandparents to ancestors dating back to the eighteenth century. Thus, the category of generation IV for a respondent should be understood as referring to four or more generations in the United States on *both* father's and mother's side.

3. By sample design only one age-eligible occupant was drawn from each randomly selected dwelling. Furthermore, in a metropolitan area like Midtown the chances are slight of drawing two linear kin from separate households. To our knowledge no generation II respondent is either offspring of a generation I respondent or parent of a generation III respondent.

4. Four U.S.-born respondents terminated the interview before the generation section was reached. However, the symptom coverage was sufficient in scope for mental health evaluation, permitting their retention in the interviewed sample.

5. M. Lerner, *America as a Civilization*, 1957, p. 476.

6. E. N. Saveth, "Good Stocks and Lesser Breeds: The Immigrant in American Textbooks," *Commentary*, May 1949, pp. 494–498.

7. Ibid., p. 498.

8. Oscar Handlin, *The Uprooted*, Boston, 1951. For a recent critique of the Handlin work see C. Greer, *Divided Society*, 1974, pp. 1–35, 331–333. See also T. C. Wheeler, ed., *The Immigrant Experience: The Anguish of Becoming American*, 1971.

9. Handlin, *The Uprooted*, p. 6.

10. Ibid., pp. 155–164.

11. For a field study of variations in these conflict situations among eight different immigrant groups, cf. W. L. Warner and L. Srole, *The Social Systems of American Ethnic Groups*, 1945, pp. 124–155. Cf. also I. L. Child, *Italian or American? The Second Generation Conflict*, 1943; O. Handlin, ed., *Children of the Uprooted*, 1966; J. Lopreato, *Italian Americans*, 1970.

12. K. Lewin, *Resolving Social Conflicts*, 1948, pp. 186–200.

13. M. Hansen, "The Third Generation in America," in his *The Immigrant in American History*, 1940. See also S. Koenig, "Second and Third Generation Americans," in F. J. Brown and J. S. Roucek, eds., *One America*, 1952.

14. Average age in generations I and II is 46 and 39, respectively; in both III and IV it is 36.

15. Since we shall use this device in subsequent chapters, considerations of interchapter comparability suggest that the same kind of standard population be applied throughout. To this end, it is necessary to construct a hypothetical ideal standard. In the present instance, the standard generation group is one constructed to be equally distributed among the six cells (i.e., with 16.7 percent of the group's population in each cell) that are produced when parental SES is trichotomized (lower, middle, upper) and respondent age in each SES stratum is dichotomized (20 to 39 versus 40 to 59). Calculations are then made of the mental health distributions that would have emerged from the four generations so identically constituted.

16. For the record, we would note also that no significant differences in mental health composition emerge when we sort out and compare males and females in each of the four generation groups.

17. To be sure, generation IV splits 2:2 on the Well-Mild line, whereas the other generations split roughly 1:2. Plausible explanations for this difference, at the better end of the mental health range only, do not suggest themselves. In any case, this localized deviation is hardly sufficient to revise the comprehensive "no difference" judgment.

18. As a corollary, the relationships of SES origin and age to mental health are negligibly altered when the generation variable is analytically controlled.

19. Lerner, *America as a Civilization*, pp. 87–88.

20. See the remarkable novel *Christ in Concrete* by Pietro Di Donato, 1937.

21. U.S. Immigration and Naturalization Service, *Annual Reports*.

22. Population of 500,000 or over.

23. On the average, the sample's immigrants, when interviewed, had been in the United States about twenty-five years.

24. P. Reymont, 1924.

25. *The Ten Pains of Death*, 1959.

26. The psychological processes that carry the individual toward considering and applying for emigration we shall hereafter refer to as *subjective selectivity*. The qualities distinguishing those accepted for migration (by the screening of external processes) from those rejected we shall refer to as *objective selectivity*.

Where we refer to selectivity without such specifications, we have in mind the special characteristics of migrants that are the *joint* consequences of both kinds of selection processes.

27. W. S. Bernard, *American Immigration Policy*, 1950, p. 30.

28. U.S. Department of Justice, *United States Immigration Laws*, M-50, rev. 1958, p. 2.

29. For a travel visa to the U.S., the prosecutor's stance and guilty-until-proved-innocent attitude of American consulate personnel toward applicants had come to be epitomized abroad in the cryptic phrase: "Even Columbus couldn't get a visa." For those seeking an immigrant's visa "the bureaucratic barrier and curtain of red tape" were a far more forbidding gauntlet. How this gauntlet was experienced by refugees fleeing persecution has been poignantly conveyed in Menotti's stirring opera *The Consul*.

30. In the years 1921 to 1940, some 4.6 million immigrants entered the country; in the same period 1.5 million departed, principally returnees to native lands.

31. The literature based on investigations of mental hospital patients has offered discussion of the "drift theory." The latter is addressed to the finding that the institutionalized schizophrenic rate is highest in residential areas nearest the city's central business district (R. Faris and H. W. Dunham, *Mental Disorders in Urban Areas*, 1939). The theory assumes that such concentration is the result of movement into these sections of prodromal schizophrenics from other areas.

With group balances of Impairment and Wellness as our particular criterion, the data just presented suggest that U.S.-born migrants to Midtown on the whole are healthier in mental health composition than are the area's native New Yorkers.

This, of course, does not necessarily invalidate the drift theory as an explanation for the high mental *hospitalization* rates in core-of-city residential areas.

Focusing on the psychotics who are in-migrants and probably detached from kin, as compared with those who are natives of the city and are more likely to have protective kin nearby, it is a plausible hypothesis that the former, lacking such protection, are more likely than the natives to be surrendered to institutionalization. Here again, patient rates should be pointed not to questions of etiology, but rather to forces blocking or facilitating paths to different kinds of help.

32. Rural-urban origin for all respondents was derived from replies to an interview question about size of place where "you spent most of your childhood up to the age of 16."

33. In the upper parental-SES class (A–B) the left-to-right urban-origin Impaired-Well values are 44, 66, and 97, respectively. In the middle class (C–D), the corresponding values are 56, 84, and 130, respectively.

34. By the latter criterion, a change from Boston to New York, i.e., from a smaller metropolis to a larger one, is minimal in magnitude, whereas removal from Roxborough (Vermont) to Boston, i.e., from a village to a metropolis, is assumed to be a near maximal change.

35. Sociologists have emphasized the significance of intercommunity movements as an American phenomenon. In its general outlines this formulation is indebted to S. A. Stouffer, "Intervening Opportunities: A Theory Relating Mobility and Distance," *American Sociological Review* 5 (December 1940): 845–867; and A. M. Rose, "Distance of Migration and Socio-economic Status of

Migrants," *American Sociological Review* 23 (August 1958): 420–423; G. W. Pierson, *The Moving Americans*, 1972.

36. B. Malzberg and E. S. Lee, *Migration and Mental Disease*, 1956.

37. Here we shall not be at all concerned with the controversial issues centering on the relative merits and limitations of incidence (first admissions over a span of time) and prevalence (total patients at a given point of time) as alternative measures of patient frequency when applied to hospital populations (see Appendix C).

38. O. Odegaard, "Emigration and Insanity," *Acta Psychiatrica Neurologica*, Suppl. 4, 1932. All citations here drawn from this work are as quoted in Dorothy S. Thomas's chapter in the SSRC monograph.

39. The reference here is to the bed capacities of tax-supported hospitals in Minnesota and Norway, facts known from the public records at both places.

40. Goldhamer and Marshall refer to the " 'law of distance,' whereby the frequency of [mental hospital] admissions tends to be inverse to the distance from a hospital." (H. Goldhamer and A. Marshall, *Psychosis and Civilization*, 1949, p. 63). The element of spatial accessibility seems to uncover one of many possible considerations taken into account by the prospective patient and his family in deciding whether or not to accept hospitalization when both the need is indicated and the bed space is believed to be available.

41. O. Odegaard, "A Statistical Investigation of the Incidence of Mental Disorder in Norway," *Psychiatric Quarterly* 20 (July 1946): 382–383.

42. J. A. Clausen and M. R. Yarrow, "Paths to the Mental Hospital," *Journal of Social Issues* 11, no. 4 (1955): 25–32.

43. Malzberg and Lee, *Migration and Mental Disease*, p. 47.

44. Ibid., p. 43.

45. Not covered were patients in out-of-state private hospitals or patients at in-state municipal psychiatric hospitals offering short-term treatment.

46. Cf. Malzberg and Lee, *Migration and Mental Disease*, pp. 70–71.

47. Ibid., p. 123.

48. M. B. Kantor, ed., *Mobility and Mental Health*, 1965.

49. B. H. Roberts and J. K. Myers, "Religion, National Origin, Immigration and Mental Illness," *American Journal of Psychiatry* 110 (April 1954): 761.

50. Of course, these occur largely beyond the age of 60, where adult immigrants are now far more concentrated than are the native-born.

51. The sample's current patients encompass both clinic and office cases without differentiation between the two; but since a group's clinic rate is known from the Treatment Census, by subtraction of the latter rate an estimate of the office patient rate is possible. Two limitations beset these estimates: (1) Current patients among sample respondents may be a close but not exact equivalent of the one-day prevalence measure used in the Treatment Census; and (2) such estimates are always subject to sampling variance and therefore lack assurance of precision. Nonetheless, with due caution they can serve the purpose of filling a gap in our Treatment Census data.

52. The latter, we can assume, follow the generation trend observed in the ambulatory current patients.

53. This population is equally distributed among the six cells produced by trichotomizing respondents' own-SES range and dichotomizing the age range.

Photograph by Ira Srole

"New York is a prism that refracts the spectrum of nationality groups from the entire face of our earth."

CHAPTER 18

EIGHT NATIONAL–ORIGIN GROUPS

THOMAS LANGNER AND LEO SROLE

Having probed the generation-in-U.S. levels for their connections with mental health, we can take the next step of examining the main national-origin or ethnic groups that subdivide Midtown's immigrant, second and third generations.

In the description of the Study area's population presented in chapter 4, a number of key facts about these groups were indicated. Here we can enlarge the picture somewhat by sketching in several salient background details in space and time.

It will be remembered that at the time of our field work, immigrants accounted for about one-third of Midtown's residents. According to the United States census, Germans and Irish were then the two largest nationality segments of Midtown's immigrant population, comprising 21.7 and 16.9 percent of the latter, respectively.

Next in size within this generation (I) were people born in Czechoslovakia (9.2 percent of Midtown's immigrants), in Hungary (8 percent), in Italy (7 percent), and in the United Kingdom (6.9 percent). Among the still smaller groups were immigrants from Austria, who constituted 5.9 percent of the foreign-born population. Because they were few, and of identical language, they will here be merged with the German group.

There were also people from Poland, Russia, and Lithuania who were predominantly Jewish and together added up to 5.6 percent of Midtown's immigrants. In view of their heterogeneity of national origin and small numbers, they are being held for separate analysis, with Jews of other nationalities, in the chapter on religious groups that follows.

Puerto Ricans, although few in the Study area, presented special problems. On their home island they are citizens of the United States; therefore, on arrival in New York they are citizen in-migrants rather than alien immigrants. Nonetheless, sociological students of Puerto Ricans have observed: "As established by law, the Puerto Rican is an American, but the contrast between his rural island with its Spanish heritage and the American metropolis makes him in psychological and cultural reality a foreigner in the city."[1] In this sense, we regard Puerto Ricans as an ethnic group differentiated on the same psycho-social plane as other nationality elements in the Study area. To judge from the Home Survey sample, Puerto Rican–born residents comprised about 4 percent of Midtown's generation I group in the age 20 to 59 range.[2]

Still unaccounted for by Census Bureau reckoning were people from many other countries abroad—each group too small to be handled statistically here. These "all others" plus Russians, Poles, and Lithuanians with whom they are merged in this chapter, together add to about 25 percent of the age-inclusive Midtown immigrants.

By way of brief historical perspective, between 1910 and the time of this Study the total population of the Midtown area contracted about 15 percent. Seen in terms of the generations, the immigrants diminished in absolute numbers by one-third and the second generation by about 20 percent; whereas levels III and IV (not differentiated by the Census Bureau) actually expanded by nearly one-third. Also noteworthy is that in that period the number of resident foreign-born from Germany, Austria, Ireland, Italy, Hungary, and Russia fell in each case by roughly one-half. On the other hand, in the same years people from the United Kingdom increased by 12 percent, and those from all other countries combined multiplied by about four times. Populated once by a relatively small number of large nationality groups, the Midtown scene became ethnically diversified to a far greater degree, i.e., characterized by a large number of smaller groups. When such a fractionated population must be studied in miniature cross section through a sample, analysis of ethnicity as a demographic variable presents refractory technical problems that we shall return to presently.

It is obvious that in focusing on the factor of national origin our interest is not in political entities per se. Historically, each immigrant-contributing nation-state had usually emerged from a people with an underlying communality in linguistic and other cultural traditions. Thus, nationality is a convenient, if rough, operational index of cultural differences within the broad tapestry of European civilization. Furthermore, at least for the larger of Midtown's ethnic groups, the element of common national background exerts a gravitational pull toward knitting local families into institutions and varying approximations of "community."

Social scientists are known to divide on several issues touching on the mental health implications of these national differences in what we shall call the immigrant's *ancestral culture*.[3] One view tends to see the ancestral culture as a single, more or less homogeneous whole, which is significantly different from the cultures of other European nations in two (among other) respects: (1) in the character of the built-in mechanisms that tend to generate stress—mechanisms seen as largely rooted in the culturally conditioned emotional economy of the several intrafamilial roles during childhood, and (2) in the nature of the culturally approved cathartic outlets for stress.

Relative to the ancestral cultures of the main ethnic groups represented in Midtown, there was no systematic knowledge available to us bearing on their differences in culturally patterned stress-generating and stress-ventilating mechanisms.[4] Furthermore, procurement of such knowledge was beyond reach of the methods employed in either the Home Survey or Treatment Census operations.

The literature of psychology and common observation bear out the pronounced tendency of outsiders to characterize the members of a minority group in stereotyped terms. The common-stamp attribution takes a more sophisticated form among those students who seem to assume a given people to be essentially homogeneous in their most significant cultural features.[5]

Relative sociocultural homogeneity within an ethnic group is an empirical issue that cannot be swept under the research carpet in the guise of a self-validating axiom. To be sure, this would make for seemingly tidy convenience in the research operation, but it also delays the day of full reckoning.

The Midtown ethnic groups revealed in our sample population are excellent cases in point. Approximations of complete homogeneity, at least in the sphere of religious origin, are found among local Italians[6] and Irish, who are 95 percent of Catholic background, and among Puerto Ricans, who are 89 percent Catholic. On the other hand, the ratio of Catholics to Protestants to Jews among Hungarians is roughly 6:1:3 and among German-Austrians 4:4:2.

The closest approximation to homogeneity in educational background is traced to the sample Puerto Ricans, 70 percent of whom did not go beyond primary school, and only 4 percent reached college. At the other extreme, in Midtown's sample British group[7] the corresponding proportions are 27 and 36 percent, respectively.

Or, consider generation composition itself. In the Midtown sample, representation of generation I ranges from 85 percent of the Puerto Ricans and 61 percent of the Hungarians to only 28 percent among Italians. Conversely, few or no generation III people appear among sample Puerto Ricans and Hungarians, in contrast with 33 percent among both Irish and British and 20 percent among German-Austrians.

The generation III element is itself interesting, if we dichotomize it into (1) those whose four grandparents were of like transoceanic national origin and (2) those whose grandparents were of two or more different national backgrounds, Old American included. The ratio of people in these two subgroups is about 1:2 among both Irish and German-Austrians and 1:9 among the British third generation. If the criterion is intermixing of nationality stocks, the American "melting pot" is here seen in slow but inexorable operation.[8]

If we narrow the focus to the immigrant segment in each nationality group, we find important intergroup demographic differences bearing on mental morbidity rates. For example, sample generation I Germans show only 12 percent of their members to be in the 20 to 39 age range, whereas of Puerto Rican immigrants fully 75 percent are in that age bracket. In other ethnic groups, the immigrants are more evenly balanced in age distribution.

Among the several groups of immigrants we also find differences in SES origin, i.e., parental socioeconomic status. It will be remembered that the sample's range in parental socioeconomic distribution, when its analytical control becomes necessary, is cut into three equally populated categories, designated low, middle, and high. On this criterion, generation I Irish, Italians, and Czechs are each predominantly (over 50 percent) from low-SES families; whereas German-Austrian, British, and Hungarian immigrants are in each instance more heavily derived from middle-SES parents. Of these two sets of immigrant groups, the Irish, Italians, and Czechs were in greater numbers drawn from farm, village, or town communities and the German-Austrians, British, and Hungarians from more urbanized places.

Speaking of immigrant groups in America generally, Mills, Senior, and Goldsen observe that each "is accused of 'clannishness.' Yet the immigrant group itself is almost never cohesive, but is criss-crossed by economic cleavages, intervillage rivalries, rural-urban lines, and sometimes by religious differences, educational rank, and vocation. But if the group as a whole has one visibly distinguishing characteristic, it is that all members are usually lumped together by the 'natives.' "[9]

GROUP ATTACHMENTS

One of our concerns in designing the Study was to take the question of relative cohesiveness within ethnic groups out of the realm of impression and onto an empirical footing for comparative analysis. Stereotypes aside, one could uncritically observe the impressive institutional apparatus of a given ethnic group on the metropolitan scene and conclude that it is a broadly based, effectively functioning community, with its people rocklike in their attachment to their nationality origins and traditions. Yet more complete investigation might well reveal facts of a different nature.

To meet this empirical problem in the context of the Home Survey interviews, an operational scale was devised according to which one could measure an individual's relative behavioral attachment to or detachment from his national traditions, his country of origin, and his local ethnic group. The scale consisted of a sampling of five component indicators: (1) whether or not the individual prefers his native culinary tradition; (2) whether or not he observes native secular or religious holidays, e.g., St. Patrick's day among the Irish; (3) whether or not he retains any interest in the "old country"; (4) whether or not he participates in the secular affairs of his local ethnic group; and (5) whether or not he is opposed to young people marrying out from his nationality group.

The interview questions constructed to represent these components were uniformly worded for all groups, adapted only to refer to the specific national origin of the respondent. As read, for example, to generation I, II, and III respondents of Italian descent, the questions were as follows:

1. Comparing Italian style cooking and regular American style cooking, do you like Italian style cooking (*a*) better, (*b*) just as much, or (*c*) not as much?

2. During the last year or so did you do anything at all special about *any* of the Italian holidays?

3. Are you interested at all in what's going on today in Italy?

4. Do you attend Italian-American meetings or social affairs often, occasionally, or not at all?

5. Some Italian parents feel that it is all right if a son or daughter wants to marry someone who is not Italian. Other Italian parents don't feel that way at all. How do you feel about it: is it all right or *not* all right?

Each respondent was scored from 0 to 5 according to the number of yes or "attached" replies he gave. For convenience in reporting, we will here designate respondents as *attached* if their score was 2 to 5 and *detached* if the score was either 0 or 1.[10]

The nationality attachment-detachment scale was devised in order to compare the several ethnic populations in the sample according to extent of group cohesion within each. If the scale *actually* measures what was intended, differences must appear among the generation-in-U.S. levels in only one possible direction, namely, most attachment in generation I and least in generation III. Moreover, within generation I greatest attachment must appear among those who arrived in this country as mature adults (age over 24) and least attachment among those who arrived as children (age 17 or under). The line-up of attached and detached, classified as indicated above, in the several inclusive generation segments is seen in table 18–1.

The differences in attachment rates fall into the rank order expected by our formulation.[11] With this internal evidence as a form of validation for the scale, we can determine its results when applied first to the immigrant segment (generation I) in each of the seven ethnic groups presented in table 18–2.

The number of cases in several of these immigrant groups is small. This suggests caution against drawing inferences from small differences and also prevents control for other relevant factors, namely, age at immigration, sex, years in the United States, etc. Nonetheless,

TABLE 18–1. HOME SURVEY SAMPLE (AGE 20–59), NATIONALITY ATTACHMENT-DETACHMENT RATES BY GENERATION LEVEL

Generation level	Attached	Detached	Total
Generation I arrived as:			
Mature adults (over 24)	51.1%	48.9%	100%
Young adults (18–24)	41.4	58.6	100
Children (under 18)	33.4	66.6	100
Generation I: Total	43.2	56.8	100
Generation II: Total	23.8	76.2	100
Generation III: Total	16.7	83.3	100

we can take note that in general the lowest attachment rates are found among the British and German-Austrian immigrants, the only two ethnic groups that are in combination (1) West European (2) predominantly Protestant,[12] and (3) more heavily of urban than of rural origin. Substantially higher in attachment rates are the Czechoslovakian and Hungarian immigrants, who of course are (1) East European in language stock, (2) predominantly Catholic,[13] and (3) in the former group, at least, predominantly rural in origin.

The highest attachment frequency is found among the Puerto Ricans, probably in part a function of a circumstance that does not apply to any of the other groups; namely, they were of very recent arrival compared to the average of twenty-three years of residence in this country for generation I as a whole.

With the Puerto Ricans seemingly a special case, the immigrant groups in table 18–2 rank themselves according to their nationality detachment rates in an order roughly corresponding to the degree of sociocultural congruity between their backgrounds and the basically

TABLE 18–2. HOME SURVEY SAMPLE (AGE 20–59), ATTACHMENT-DETACHMENT RATES IN GENERATION I BY ETHNIC GROUP

Ethnic group	Attached	Detached	N = 100%
Puerto Ricans	65.1%	34.9%	(23)
Czechoslovakians	53.3	46.7	(60)
Hungarians	53.3	46.7	(45)
Irish	46.8	53.2	(79)
Italians	43.5	56.5	(40)
German-Austrians	34.7	65.3	(164)
British	27.0	73.0	(37)

Anglo-Saxon, urban, industrial, and Protestant trends that are the dominant figures in the cultural fabric of contemporary America.

Although deculturation from the old society and acculturation to the new do not necessarily move in a 1:1 relationship, we can find in table 18–2 confirmation for a generalization advanced in an earlier study,[14] that intergroup differences in acculturation tempo of immigrants depend in part on the degree of native sociocultural congruity with salient aspects of the American environment.[15]

Remaining open is the question whether the data for the generation II segments of the several ethnic groups will also fit the culture congruency postulate. In table 18–3 we present their detachment frequencies only, alongside the corresponding rates for each group's immigrant generation. Appearing with only four generation II people in the sample, the Puerto Ricans cannot be represented in the table.

Of course, in the generation II column, the range of differences

TABLE 18–3. HOME SURVEY SAMPLE (AGE 20–59), DETACHMENT RATES IN GENERATIONS II AND I BY ETHNIC GROUP

Ethnic group	Generation II	N = 100%	Generation I	N = 100%
Czechoslovakians	75.9%	(54)	46.7%	(60)
Hungarians	69.3	(26)	46.7	(45)
Irish	74.0	(92)	53.2	(79)
Italians	74.2	(93)	56.5	(40)
German-Austrians ...	84.4	(109)	65.3	(164)
British	84.4	(32)	73.0	(37)
Total for generation ..	76.2		56.8	

quantitatively possible for the detachment rates is far narrower than among the immigrants. Nonetheless, we see that British and German-Austrians again stand out with high rates among their generation II peers. In this particular sense, we can discern that the factor of cultural congruence continues to be reflected in the deculturation-acculturation tempo of generation II ethnic groups, although with considerably diminished magnitude.

The above discussion has been intended to illuminate, however briefly, something of the intragroup heterogeneity in most Midtown nationality segments and the intergroup differences in tempo of transformation from the old-country to the new-American model of man.

From the specifically Italian, or German, or Irish line of ancestral culture, for example, there was no ground for framing hypotheses relating to the expected mental health composition of corresponding nationality groups in the Midtown sample—especially as these ancestral cultures were all kindred variants of the millennial-old European civilization. Nevertheless, recommending itself was the criterion of relative congruity between the several ancestral cultures in their major contours and the overall cultural fabric of urban America. Accordingly, one of the early hypotheses entertained by the Midtown research team was this: The greater the degree of such congruity among local ethnic groups, the less would be the adaptive stresses and the better correspondingly would be the resulting mental health. An alternative hypothesis was also proposed: The faster the tempo of change among ethnic groups, with respect to shifting attachments from the old to the new cultural foundations, the greater the strain and the less propitious the mental health consequences. Under the "congruity" hypothesis, the British and German-Austrian groups, by way of illustration, would expectedly turn up with the most favorable mental health composition. Under the "tempo" hypothesis, on the other hand, these two groups would foreseeably present the least favorable mental health picture. How the data fall between these two alternatives is examined in the next section of this chapter.

HOME SURVEY SAMPLE: MENTAL HEALTH DISTRIBUTIONS

The ethnic factor is not unknown to studies in medical epidemiology. Among nationality groups resident in the United States, mortality differences have been found for such causes of death as pneumonia, tuberculosis, diabetes, and heart disease.[16] Also reported among these groups are differences in the frequency of cancer at particular sites.[17]

Previous investigations that focused on nationality background and its relation to mental disorder have been exceedingly few in number. The only one known to us that employed a general population is that of Hyde and Chisholm.[18] This study involved 60,000 consecutive selectees from homes in eastern Massachusetts, who were examined in 1941–1942 at the Boston Induction Station. The criterion was rejection for psychiatric reasons. As reported, the rejection rates for three nationality groups also covered in the Midtown Study are given in table 18–4 below.

TABLE 18–4.   SELECTIVE SERVICE PSYCHIATRIC REJECTION RATES IN THREE NATIONAL-ORIGIN GROUPS

	Italian	Irish	Old American
Percent rejected	13.7	12.8	5.7
Percent accepted	86.3	87.2	94.3
N = 100%	(3,472)	(2,440)	(1,640)

Hyde and Chisholm indicate that the Old-American men were from communities[19] that were graded on the whole as high (B) in socioeconomic level, whereas the Italians and Irish were from communities rated as low in SES (E and F, respectively). The authors provide this information so that "corrections can be made for [nationality] differences that may be traceable to [SES]." Although they did not make such corrections, they report elsewhere that overall rejection rates for communities of B, E, and F socioeconomic levels were 9.2, 12.7, and 16.6 percent respectively. In the light of the latter, it appears offhand that if SES differences could be standardized, the Irish would have the highest rejection rate by a small margin and the Old American the lowest rate by a smaller margin than that reported. However, there are reasons for viewing these findings with serious reservations.[20]

We must now turn to the seven nationality groups represented in the Midtown sample population. For the record, we are presenting in table 18–5 the distribution of each group on the psychiatrists' classification of mental health. Covered in each group are its three generation segments, I, II, and III.

A first consideration is that if different national backgrounds exert varying impacts on mental health, they must manifest this power most clearly among people born in and shaped by these overseas societies, i.e., among the immigrant element in the several ethnic groups.

In the light of this overriding consideration, we have no choice except to narrow our comparison directly to the ethnic groupings within the immigrant generation. Although left with relatively few people in these groups, we accept the sacrifice of statistical viability in the interest of substantive insights suggested, if any.

In table 18–6 below, the several identified immigrant groups are arranged in the order of diminishing detachment frequencies as

TABLE 18–5. HOME SURVEY SAMPLE (AGE 20–59), RESPONDENTS'
DISTRIBUTIONS ON MENTAL HEALTH CLASSIFICATION BY NATIONAL ORIGIN
(GENERATIONS I, II, AND III COMBINED)

National origin	Mental health categories							
	Well	Mild symptom formation	Moderate symptom formation	Impaired	Marked* symptom formation	Severe* symptom formation	Incapacitated*	N = 100%
British	22.0%	33.0%	15.0%	30.0%	17.0%	9.0%	4.0%	(100)
German-Austrians	18.6	37.3	21.0	23.1	11.2	9.5	2.4	(338)
Irish	17.5	33.4	27.2	21.9	12.6	7.3	2.0	(246)
Italians	14.0	34.2	24.5	27.3	15.4	9.8	2.1	(143)
Hungarians	13.5	35.1	24.3	27.1	20.3	4.1	2.7	(74)
Czechoslovakians .	10.5	41.1	21.0	27.4	12.9	9.7	4.8	(124)
Puerto Ricans ...	3.7	44.5	7.4	44.4	18.5	25.9	0.0	(27)
All others	18.8	39.4	20.4	21.4	14.1	4.4	2.9	(382)
Old Americans (Generation IV)	28.0	32.0	22.2	17.8	9.3	5.8	2.7	(226)
Sample total	18.5%	36.3%	21.8%	23.4%	13.2%	7.5%	2.7%	(1,660)

* These values are subtotals of the Impaired figure.

previously seen in table 18–2. It is first observed that the British and German-Austrians, who stood highest on the detachment scale, here have the largest Well rates; whereas the most strongly attached group, the Puerto Ricans, are altogether absent from the Well ranks. Seemingly intimated here is the existence of some sort of relationship between ethnic detachment and wellness.

Beyond the category of the Well, however, there seems to be no consistent connection between mental health composition and rank order of detachment from the national-origin group. This applies to the Impaired rates as well as to frequencies of the Moderate and Mild categories of symptom formation. On the whole, therefore, these data from Midtown's immigrant generation fail to lend support to either the congruity or the tempo hypotheses defined above.

Hypotheses aside, our attention is drawn to three groups that stand out as potential deviants in this population of immigrants. We note impairment rates of 37.5 and 18.2 percent among the Italian and Hungarian immigrants respectively, with an accompanying reversal in their Moderate category frequencies, i.e., 15.0 and 31.8 percent. Before interpreting these divergences as reflecting unspecified

TABLE 18–6. HOME SURVEY SAMPLE (AGE 20–59), DISTRIBUTIONS ON
MENTAL HEALTH CLASSIFICATION OF IMMIGRANT RESPONDENTS
(GENERATION I) BY NATIONAL ORIGIN

National Origin	Mental health categories				
	Well	Mild symptom formation	Moderate symptom formation	Impaired	N = 100%
Total generation I .	16.1%	36.0%	21.2%	26.7%	(593)
British	21.6	39.7	19.0	29.7	(37)
German-Austrians .	18.3	32.9	24.4	24.4	(164)
Irish	12.5	35.0	22.5	30.0	(79)
Italians	15.0	32.5	15.0	37.5	(40)
Hungarians	13.6	36.4	31.8	18.2	(45)
Czechoslovakians .	13.3	41.7	18.3	26.7	(60)
Puerto Ricans	0.0	39.1	8.7	52.2	(23)
All others	19.2	39.7	19.2	21.9	(145)

national differences in the culture patterns of Italy and Hungary, a
specifiable fact must first be taken into account.

It will be recalled that the sample respondents were stratified by
socioeconomic status of parents, with the sample's distribution of
parental-SES scores divided, when their analytical control was necessary, into three more or less equally populated SES-origin groups. We
know that there is a link between parental SES, so classified, and the
Impaired-Well mental health ratio, and that the link has survived our
efforts to shake out possible spurious effects of other demographic
variables.

How the populations of Italy and Hungary, at the time our respondents departed these lands, would have distributed themselves on this
SES-origin continuum is of course unknown to us. But we do know
how *these* foreign-born respondents were distributed (table 18–7).

TABLE 18–7. HOME SURVEY SAMPLE (AGE 20–59), PARENTAL-SES
DISTRIBUTIONS OF IMMIGRANT ITALIANS AND HUNGARIANS

Parental SES	Generation I	
	Italians	Hungarians
Lower (E–F)	50.0%	22.2%
Middle (C–D)	32.5	48.9
Upper (A–B)	17.5	28.9
N = 100%	(40)	(45)

The number of people in each ethnic group is too small to permit control of these SES-origin differences by standardization. But knowing that the lower stratum contributes disproportionately to the Impaired category of mental health, we can be sure that were such standardization possible the effect would be to substantially narrow the 2:1 divergence in impairment rates seen between Italian and Hungarian immigrants. Similarly, in place of origin the Italians are predominantly rural and the Hungarians more largely urban. In short, the above divergence in morbidity rates principally reflects the facts that the Italians are mainly type O immigrants and the Hungarians type N. It will be remembered that for *all* type O and type N immigrants in the Midtown sample, the morbidity rates were 34.3 and 18.5 percent, respectively.

The third group warranting special attention in table 18–6 are the Puerto Rican immigrants, half (52.2 percent) of whom appear in the Impaired ranks—or double the rate (26.7 percent) for generation I as a whole—a difference appearing to be statistically significant at the .01 level of confidence. With a mean age of 35, these Puerto Ricans are eleven years younger, on the average, than the sample generation I as a whole. About half of them qualify as type O immigrants. Only a few are type N. The remainder are of low parental SES and town-city origin and seem to define an "urban proletariat" type, which is relatively rare in our sample of immigrants.

Testing the assumption that the current poverty of these Puerto Ricans might be a specific source of stress contributing to their deviant mental health picture, we isolated a subsample of 252 European immigrants with family incomes identical to that of the 18 Puerto Ricans in the lowest income bracket. The morbidity rate of the former aggregate was just half (31 percent) that of the latter (61 percent).

Compared to other immigrants, who found in Midtown a main residential concentration and institutional center for their fellow nationals, the Puerto Ricans in the Study area are, geographically speaking, isolated outriders from the main body of their fellow islanders gathered elsewhere in New York City.[21] We do not know whether subjective selection factors related to mental health have operated to determine this residential self-separation from their cultural group.

Differential selection may also be involved for Puerto Rican immigrants generally. As indicated in the previous chapter, alien immigrants, before receiving an American visa, had to pass the screen of Federal statutes "barring mentally, physically and morally undesirable classes and persons likely to become a public charge."[22] Compared with this severe kind of governmental screening, the Puerto Ricans, as citizen in-migrants, are limited only by the same kinds of spontaneous self-selection as are migrants to New York from the other 49 states. The variable sifting effects on the mental health characteristics of the two forms of migratory movements also remain largely unknown.

Nor can events in Puerto Rico itself be overlooked. That island has rapidly moved from an agrarian to an urban, industrial stage of development. We are not yet informed whether such movement has there had the early unsettling psychological consequences reported from other fast-changing agrarian areas.[23]

Finally, and of particular importance for appropriate perspective, is the fact that the Puerto Ricans in New York are recent arrivals from their home island. They betray signs of the initial, transient stage of uprooted instability that marked most previous nationality groups in the decades immediately following their settlement here.[24]

Although Puerto Ricans in the Midtown sample are few in number, and perhaps atypical, they may give us a brief glimpse into an extremely complicated tangle of factors. This complex of exogenous sociocultural forces and pressures, converging with endogenous selection processes, may have created turbulent effects overtly visible in the problems of the City's Puerto Rican people. It is hoped that more specifically focused research might soon answer these speculations.[25]

In the previous chapter we found little difference in mental morbidity rates between generations I, II, and III of like age and SES origin. When we now compare generation levels within each ethnic group, generation III is represented by sufficient individuals only among the British, German-Austrians, and Irish, and their mental health distributions are uniformly like that of their generation II juniors in the same nationality group. This likewise applies when generations II and I are compared in the British, German-Austrian, and Czech groups. However, we must report that this is not the case among the Irish, Italians, and Hungarians whose mental health distributions are presented in table 18–8.

Here we see that in both the Irish and Italian groups the immigrants have impairment rates significantly higher than those of the

TABLE 18–8. HOME SURVEY SAMPLE (AGE 20–59), MENTAL HEALTH
DISTRIBUTIONS OF IRISH AND ITALIAN GENERATIONS I AND II

Mental health categories	Irish		Italians	
	Generation I	Generation II	Generation I	Generation II
Well	12.5%	18.6%	15.0%	15.1%
Mild symptom formation	35.0	37.4	32.5	35.3
Moderate symptom formation	22.5	27.5	15.0	27.0
Impaired	30.0	16.5	37.5	22.6
N = 100%	(79)	(92)	(40)	(93)

second generation. However, there are intergeneration age and SES-
origin differences in each ethnic group. Standardization for these
differences is not possible among the Italians[26] but is possible among
the Irish, where we shall now merge generations II and III. The Irish
mental health distributions, so standardized, are as follows (table
18–9):

TABLE 18–9. HOME SURVEY SAMPLE (AGE 20–59), MENTAL HEALTH
DISTRIBUTIONS OF IRISH GENERATIONS I AND II (STANDARDIZED FOR AGE AND
SES ORIGIN)

Mental health categories	Irish	
	Generation I	Generations II–III
Well	11.2%	18.0%
Mild	35.6	35.2
Moderate	24.5	26.4
Impaired	28.7	20.4
N = 100%	(79)	(167)

Standardization among the Irish has reduced the intergeneration
difference in impairment rates to a margin no longer statistically significant. Were such standardization possible among the Italians, there
is reason to believe that the remaining generation difference would
also fall below the level of statistical acceptability.

We have noted that the Hungarians also appeared to be an excep-
tional group. The sense of this judgment can be gathered from the
mental health composition of their two generation segments (table
18-10).

TABLE 18–10.   HOME SURVEY SAMPLE (AGE 20–59), MENTAL HEALTH DISTRIBUTIONS OF HUNGARIAN GENERATIONS I AND II

Mental health categories	Hungarians	
	Generation I	Generation II
Well	13.6%	14.8%
Mild	36.4	29.6
Moderate	31.8	14.8
Impaired	18.2	40.8
N = 100%	(45)	(26)

Here the Hungarians emerge as seeming anomalies in that the higher impairment rate for the first time is found not among the immigrants, as hypothesized, but among their second generation juniors. Standardization for SES origin and age composition is here altogether ruled out by their small numbers. Nonetheless, the picture becomes clearer if we look into the parental SES of the two generations of Hungarians (table 18–11).

TABLE 18–11.   HOME SURVEY SAMPLE (AGE 20–59), PARENTAL-SES DISTRIBUTIONS OF HUNGARIAN GENERATIONS I AND II

Parental SES	Hungarians	
	Generation I	Generation II
Lower (E–F)	22.2%	46.2%
Middle (C–D)	48.9	46.2
Upper (A–B)	28.9	7.6
N = 100%	(45)	(26)

The seeming anomaly is here seen reduced to this fact: Hungarian generation II has a representation in the low SES-origin stratum that is double that of their Hungarian immigrant neighbors. Thus, if it were feasible to standardize for parental SES, the Hungarian intergeneration divergence in impairment rates would probably be largely eliminated.

We conclude that in no national group are there intergeneration divergences in mental health composition that cannot be traced to the operation of SES-origin and age differences.

PATIENT FINDINGS

In previous chapters the number of Midtown's psychiatric patients were reported from our two field operations. From neither of these operations do the patient data on the Midtown nationality groups permit presentation here.

It is clear that variations in treatment rates can be attributed to differences in ethnic background only if analytical controls can be applied to disentangle other, more fully documented, demographic factors like age, SES origin, and generation-in-U.S. For purposes of the Midtown Treatment Census operation, the U.S. Census Bureau does not provide total population figures for subgroups analytically refined in this multifactorial fashion.

The Midtown Home Survey, in dealing with what is called the patient-history variable among its sample respondents, is not dependent on Census Bureau figures. Its patient rates have consistently been calculated relative to the Impaired mental health category only in a specific demographic group or subgroup. However, the grand total of generation I to III individuals in the several mental health categories is relatively small among most ethnic groups isolated in our sample population. This is especially the case in the Impaired category.[27]

It is not only that the distribution on the patient-history variable of each of these Impaired subgroups is statistically unreliable. It is rather that this unreliability is only one in a related series of considerations; e.g., we know that ever-patients are more numerous among the Impaired who are (1) younger (under age 40), (2) of higher socioeconomic status, and (3) American-born. Since the ethnic Impaired segments are too small to permit analytical control for these factors, differences in their ever-patient rates would be decidedly ambiguous, even as clues to the substantive connection between ethnic background and quest for therapy. Given Midtown's population scatter through many relatively small ethnic groups, the size of our sample excludes analyses of such extreme complexity.

SUMMARY

In this attempt to test the factor of national origin, we first confined ourselves to a comparison of seven ethnic groupings within the immigrant generation. With the mental health composition of generation I *in toto* serving as yardstick, we found that four ethnic groups conformed quite closely in their mental health distributions. Relative to this norm, however, the Italian-born were higher in impairment rates, and the Hungarian-born were lower—a difference exposed as largely a product of the fact that the former were more heavily type O immigrants and the latter were predominantly type N. Most deviant of all in apparent concentration of mental morbidity were the immigrant Puerto Ricans, and consideration was given to the special factors that may be operating in New York City's newest in a long procession of nationality groups.

As second step, we directed attention to intergeneration differences in mental health within six ethnic groups. In only three of these groups were such differences found. However, were control of their accompanying divergences in SES origin and age possible, these differences would very largely disappear.

This chapter sought to trace variations in mental health composition to a factor that looms large on the Midtown scene, namely, respondent differences in national culture derivations. We could discover no firm discrete variations of this kind. Whether or not other studies will confirm this finding is an entirely open question, needless to say.[28]

We would suggest that the question can be carried to the next stage of advance only if each ethnic group subsample is large enough to permit control for the obscuring effects of more powerful demographic factors. Even so, to test definitively for the links between international differences in culture and mental health, investigations will have to move to a more appropriate site than the American metropolis, namely, to the indigenous populations in the countries of origin. Among immigrants to America alone, there are too many special complications, such as subjective and objective selection, variable age at migration, familial structure in migration, differential experiences upon arrival, stage of development in the local ethnic community—as a stabilizing or disruptive influence—and stage in familial Americanization. All these intervene to becloud observation of the unencumbered factor of national culture differences and their eugenic-pathogenic potentials for mental health.

The writers now entertain the hypothesis that unencumbered observation will *not* reveal significant international differences in these eugenic-pathogenic potentials within the European continent west of the Iron Curtain. This does not blink the cultural differences existing among the countries of this continent. This *does* reflect some skepticism about the relative weight of these differences as against two other sets of likenesses that these countries share. One overarching source of likeness is their common roots in the general 2,000-year-old European-Christian tradition. In the next chapter we shall see whether the Catholic-Protestant split in the American version of that tradition registers on the mental health criterion of concern to us here.

A more specific source of intra-European likeness is the basic socioeconomic homogeneity. With corresponding SES groups in different countries apparently go similar conditions of life, values, attitudes, and behavior patterns. In this perspective, upper-class people from different countries, conspicuously joined in the "international set," probably have more in common with each other than does each national segment of that set with co-nationals in the lower reaches of the social class range. In turn, we suggest that the lower classes in the several countries, except on the point of language, have more that culturally binds than divides them. The same probably holds for the middle classes as well.

In fine, we hypothesize as follows: Comparative studies of indigenous European populations will yield conclusive findings that do not grossly diverge, in general trend, from the necessarily inconclusive comparative data for Midtown's immigrants of the several national backgrounds here represented.

It is relevant to add in closing that within the circumscribed framework of Midtown's immigrants and their European nationality subgroups, we can test a key assumption underlying the quota differences that were legislated by the congressional immigration acts of 1921 and 1924. This was the assumption that immigrants from Western and Central European countries were preferable to those who might originate in the Southern and Eastern sections of the

Continent. If mental health of immigrants (of like SES origin and rural-urban origin) is still a meaningful index of desirability in the eyes of America's policy makers (as it was in 1921–1924), then the Midtown data plainly appear to contradict that assumption.

POSTSCRIPT

Since the preceding paragraph first saw print (1962), the restrictive and discriminatory Immigration Act of 1924 has been replaced by the Immigration Reform Act of 1965 (with revisions in 1968). The latter ended the "national origins" quota system that had favored Western and Northern Europeans against immigrants from the rest of the continent. As an immediate result, by 1972 the total number of immigrants admitted annually increased by 30 percent, with striking jumps in particular from the South European countries of Portugal, Greece, and Italy of about 500, 400, and 200 percent, respectively.

NOTES

1. C. W. Mills, C. Senior, and R. K. Goldsen, *The Puerto Rican Journey*, 1950, p. 79.
2. Or 1.5 percent of the total Midtown population. However, Puerto Ricans do not figure in the Census Bureau's count of immigrants.
3. By this term we mean the complex system of more or less traditional folkways in which immigrants from a given country were bred during the childhood years before departure for the United States.
4. As a result, there was no basis for hypothesizing the degree and direction of differences in mental pathology risk that might be expected in these groups.
5. See A. R. Lindesmith and A. L. Strauss, "A Critique of Culture-Personality Writings," *American Sociological Review* 15 (October 1950): 587–600, in particular the section entitled "Oversimplification and the Homogeneity Postulate." See also, A. Inkeles and D. J. Levinson, "National Character: The Study of Modal Personality and Sociocultural Systems," in G. Lindzey and E. Aronson, eds., *Handbook of Social Psychology*, vol. IV, 1969, pp. 418–506.
6. Unless otherwise specified, data on a particular ethnic group here refer to its three generation levels inclusively, i.e., I, II, and III.
7. This group includes immigrants and generation II and III descendants of immigrants from England, Scotland, and Wales.
8. For other criteria see N. Glazer and D. Moynihan, *Beyond the Melting Pot*, 1963.
9. Mills, Senior, and Goldsen, *The Puerto Rican Journey*, p. 82.
10. Replies to question 5 above were found in all ethnic groups to be "all right" by such overwhelming consensus as to be of little discriminative value.

For all practical purposes, therefore, most respondents with a score of 1 had given "detached" replies to all four of the items preceding 5. Stated differently, a respondent classified as attached gave an affirming reply to at least one of the first four items.

11. It might be added that among the generation I adult arrivers the frequency of detached individuals is considerably larger than we had anticipated.

12. Specifically, 79 percent of the British and 44 percent of the German-Austrians are of Protestant origin.

13. Specifically, 57 percent of the Hungarians and 73 percent of the Czechoslovakians are of Catholic origin.

14. W. L. Warner and L. Srole, *Social Systems of American Ethnic Groups*, 1945.

15. See also R. T. Berthoff, *British Immigrants in Industrial America: 1790–1950*, 1953. This valuable work by a historian focuses most heavily on the second half of the nineteenth century. Comparisons with immigrants of other nationalities are drawn throughout. Special emphasis is placed on the relative ease of the British in fitting into and advancing in the American society. The importance of intercultural congruence is indicated in these observations: "In practically every American field which they entered, the British enjoyed the highest status and rose most easily. . . . With folkways and habits of thought acceptable to Americans, they enjoyed a unique advantage over most newcomers . . . the new country must have seemed rather like the old . . . settled among the Americans, [they] passed almost unnoticed. They hardly seemed to be 'immigrants' in the usual condescending sense of the word" (pp. 122–132).

The second, and perhaps more striking theme of this work is that British immigrants were accepted by Americans "as equals . . . yet they too clung to old loyalties . . . few doubted that for a proper life the old country was, after all, the only land" (pp. 139–142).

16. M. Calabresi, "The Relation of Country of Origin to Mortality for Various Causes in New York State," *Human Biology* 17 (1945): 340–365.

17. S. Graham, "Cancer, Culture and Social Structure," in E. G. Jaco, ed, *Patients, Physicians and Illness*, 1972, pp. 31–39.

18. R. W. Hyde and R. M. Chisholm, "The Relation of Mental Disorders to Race and Nationality," *New England Journal of Medicine* 231 (November 1944): 612–618.

19. That is, Selective Service Board areas.

20. A damaging limitation appears in this particular substantive phase of the Boston Induction Station studies directed by Hyde. By way of example, the 12.8 percent rejection rate reported for the Irish refer not to all Irishmen in the sample, but to all men from "Irish communities," defined as Selective Service Board districts whose selectees were in the majority Irishmen. Counted, therefore, as "Irish" were non-Irish men living in such predominantly Irish communities, and excluded were all Irish selectees who did not reside in such unusual districts.

The extent of this exclusion may be judged from the fact that the selectees living in these Irish districts totaled 2,440, or only 4 percent of the 60,000 men from the heavily Irish region of Boston.

Compounding the difficulty is the fact that we are not told how those counted as actually Irish in the Irish districts were determined. Were they only those born in Ireland? Or did they also include the U.S.-born of Irish descent?

The root difficulty is inherited from the tradition of ecological studies—here uncritically applied—where individuals living in an area are classified not according to their own characteristics but according to the average or predominant characteristics in the overall population of the area.

21. Mr. Joseph Suarez, Director, Mental Health Services Division, Hill Health Center, New Haven, Conn., and a lifelong observer of New York's Puerto Ricans, in personal communication has commented on the significance of this point. He calls attention to a powerful institution that generally tends to keep New York Puerto Ricans dependently chained to their areas of residential concentration. This is their neighborhood grocery store, which on the one hand carries indigenous Puerto Rican staples and on the other hand extends credit to fellow immigrants whenever need arises.

Thus, in leaving the areas of high Puerto Rican density, the Midtown Puerto Ricans had removed themselves from ready access to these two important services.

22. W. S. Bernard, *American Immigration Policy: A Reappraisal*, 1950, pp. 23–24.

23. The advances in general health that have accompanied the rise in the Island's standard of living are documented in C. Senior, *The Puerto Ricans*, 1961. For a descriptive treatment of a small number of Island families harboring a schizophrenic husband or wife, see L. Rogler and A. Hollingshead, *Trapped: Families and Schizophrenia*, 1965.

24. While the rear guard of poverty-stricken New York Puerto Ricans continue to manifest such instabilities, the group's vanguard is now on the upward mobility trail taken by the City's earlier ethnic groups.

25. See J. P. Fitzpatrick, "Special Problems: Mental Illness," in his *Puerto Rican Americans*, 1971, pp. 164–166. See also A. M. Padilla and R. A. Ruiz, *Latino Mental Health: A Review of Literature*, 1973.

26. Because of insufficient cases of Italian immigrants.

27. For example, there are 12 among all Puerto Rican respondents, 20 among Hungarians, 30 among the British, 34 among Czechs, 39 among Italians. Even the Irish and German-Austrian impairment cases do not exceed 54 and 78 respectively.

28. This finding on the Study psychiatrists' classification of degree of symptom formation and functional disability would not be controverted by a finding of qualitative differences in syndromal patterns among nationality groups.

CHAPTER 19

PROTESTANT, CATHOLIC, AND JEWISH ORIGINS

LEO SROLE AND THOMAS LANGNER

In the antiphony of voices that express American society, Protestantism, Catholicism, and Judaism stand out as the nation's three great religious communions. In the hypersegmented, centrifugal social structure of Manhattan, they perform a special and generally overlooked function, as the editors of *Fortune* magazine have perceptively observed:

> So what gives New York its coherence? No city could exist for three hundred and thirty-odd years in incoherence. For one thing, surprisingly enough, it hangs together on the cord of its religions. . . . From its religions the city derives much strength and character. Protestantism's vigorous social ethic, with which the city began, is still a force in New York as throughout the nation. . . . Quite apart from the fact that Jewish intellectuality and artistic appreciation give the city a special élan, Jewish philanthropy, with its deep religious base, lifts the level of the whole community. The emergence of Catholics to higher levels in the city's social structure . . . brings to New York's amalgam the ancient firmness and cultural richness of that church. For all their differences, these three faiths are united in the conviction that the community exists to serve men.[1]

The significance for mental health of personal roots in these different religious traditions[2] is the complicated and difficult question that shall engage us in this chapter.[3]

TREATMENT CENSUS FINDINGS

Due note should first be taken of the meager research literature that bears on the above question. Until recently, such research has been confined to patients of state mental hospitals, classified by religion as inscribed on the case record. Such studies have usually categorized patients only in terms of the Jewish–non-Jewish dichotomy.[4]

Nevertheless, from the largest of these investigations, Malzberg concludes: "On the basis of the estimated population in 1950, Jews had a rate of first admissions [to New York state-supported mental hospitals] of 74 per 100,000 population compared with 102 for white non-Jews. As regards the severe mental disorders which result in hospitalization, it is therefore clear that Jews have a lower rate than non-Jews. This confirms a similar conclusion which was arrived at in three separate studies."[5]

The New Haven study signaled a considerable advance beyond the foregoing literature in that it covered one-day prevalence of patients in *all* treatment sites and also differentiated Protestants and Catholics. On the basis of published New Haven distribution data,[6] we have calculated the rates per 100,000 estimated population among the several New Haven religious groups as presented in table 19–1.

In rates of *treated* psychoses and related disorders we note only minor differences among New Haven's three religious groups.[7] This is a finding at variance with previous studies of state hospital pa-

TABLE 19–1.   NEW HAVEN PSYCHIATRIC CENSUS (AGE INCLUSIVE), DIAGNOSTIC COMPOSITION (PREVALENCE RATES PER 100,000 POPULATION) OF NEW HAVEN PATIENTS BY RELIGIOUS AFFILIATION*

	Catholic	Protestant	Jewish
Neuroses and character disorders ...	140	158	442
Alcohol and drug addictions	45	36	0
Psychoses and affective disorders ...	481	414	496
Organic disorders	120	136	68
Total Patients rate	786	744	1,006

* Adapted from B. H. Roberts and J. K. Myers, "Religion, National Origin, Immigration, and Mental Illness," *American Journal of Psychiatry* 110 (April 1954): 760.

tients.[8] On the other hand, if New Haven Protestants and Catholics are also alike in frequencies of *treated* neuroses and character disorders, Jews stand out in this category with an appreciably higher patient rate.

In certain technical aspects, the New Haven study to date has had its only counterpart in the Midtown Treatment Census operation. As in New Haven's case, the latter had no United States census data on the religious composition of the Midtown population. However, from the religious distribution of the Home Survey sample we could estimate such composition, at least in the age 20 to 59 segment of the Midtown population. In addition to this intercommunity difference in the age span of the religious group rates, the one-day prevalence counts of patients in Midtown and New Haven diverge in two other respects: (1) Midtown's hospital enumeration excluded patients continuously hospitalized for five years or more, whereas this exclusion was not applied to the New Haven hospital patients; and (2) on the Midtown patients of office therapists we could secure information about neither their age nor their religious affiliation. Accordingly, in table 19–2 we can present only prevalence rates (per 100,000 estimated corresponding population in each Midtown religious group) of age 20 to 59 patients in mental hospitals and psychiatric clinics.[9]

TABLE 19–2. MIDTOWN TREATMENT CENSUS (AGE INCLUSIVE), PREVALENCE RATES (PER 100,000 POPULATION) OF MIDTOWN PATIENTS (AGE 20–59 ONLY) IN HOSPITALS AND CLINICS BY RELIGIOUS GROUPS

Treatment sites	Catholic	Protestant	Jewish
Hospitals:			
Public	659	385	250
Private	33	61	148
Total inpatients	692	446	398
Total clinic outpatients	108	103	380

Within the indicated limitations of the Midtown patient data, we see in table 19–2 that the public hospital rate is lowest in the Jewish group, half-again higher among Protestants, and higher by over 2.5 times among Catholics. With private hospital frequencies, however, the group ranking is exactly reversed. As a result, when the two sets of inpatients are taken together, the total hospitalization rates of Protestants and Jews for all practical purposes are alike, both still being appreciably below the Catholic frequency. Thus, the Jewish-Protestant difference in public hospital rates is practically wiped out when total inpatients become the measure.

Moving next to the psychiatric clinics, we observe Protestants and Catholics with identical patient rates and Jews with a frequency almost four times greater.

Among Midtown residents known on one day to all treatment facilities, the reported patients of office therapists aggregated almost half of the total reported. These patients cannot be brought into table 19–2, but it is obvious that were they included their trend could dominate the Total Patients rates. To discern the direction of this trend, we can apply one of two alternative assumptions. First, on the common element of ambulatory treatment, we might anticipate that interreligious differences in *office therapy* rates would tend to parallel the observed differences in *clinic* frequencies. If so, the Total Patients rate probably would be highest among Jews, with the Catholic rate perhaps exceeding the Protestant frequency by a relatively small margin. Or, on the common element of high treatment costs, we might anticipate that interreligion differences in office therapy frequencies would tend to parallel the observed *private hospital* rates. In this event, the Jews would again emerge with the largest Total Patients rate; but now second position in magnitude of these rates would probably be held not by Catholics but by Protestants. There are intimations in the Midtown Home Survey supporting the second assumption and suggesting that Total Patients rates among Jews, Protestants, and Catholics may stand to each other in a ratio of roughly 7:6:5, respectively. From Treatment Census evidence, this result would reflect the fact that inpatient and outpatient rates tend to vary in opposite directions among the three religious groups.

Comparisons of New Haven and Midtown Treatment Census data should of course be undertaken with caution. With this caveat in mind, attention might be called to the fact that New Haven's interreligious differences in neurosis and character disorder rates (table 19–1)—principally treated in outpatient facilities—parallel Midtown's differences in observed clinic patient frequencies (table 19–2). That is, in both communities Jews seem to emerge with higher ambulatory treatment rates and Total Patients frequencies than either Protestants or Catholics.

What is the meaning of the seemingly convergent findings from the two studies? An anthropologist's review of the literature on this general question, published a few years before the New Haven study, concluded:

The factual residue thus appears at present to be: American Jews have a lower incidence of [hospitalized] insanity than non-Jews. . . . When it comes to the matter of neurosis, psychiatric opinion holds that Jews are more neurotic or anxiety ridden than non-Jews. . . . A. B. Brill, Abraham Myerson and Israel S. Wechsler may be mentioned as exponents of this view.

The causes of Jewish neurosis are attributed by these authorities to the taboos and inhibitions of Mosaic law, to the unconscious "incest motive" resulting from exceptionally close ties within the Jewish family, to exclusion from manual activity and "seclusion into a world of life predominantly cerebral," and to the tensions of minority life.

Generalizations by practicing psychiatrists, however, invite errors resulting from the selective nature of their experience. . . . The only empirical verification comes, as usual, from studies of college students, and these studies (conducted by psychologists) are by no means in unanimous agreement on the hypothesis of neurotic Jewish personality.[10]

HOME SURVEY SAMPLE: MENTAL HEALTH DISTRIBUTIONS BY RELIGIOUS ORIGIN

To move to new ground on the inclusive question of interfaith differences in mental health, we can proceed now to the evidence provided in the sample of 1,660 Midtown adults studied by our Home Interview Survey. Here we of course apply as yardstick the Midtown psychiatrists' classification of the mental health status of each sample respondent. Although this classification scheme lacks the nosological specificity of clinical diagnosis, the Home Survey in another direction avoids a difficulty inherent in the use of institutional records, at least when religious groups are the focus of attention. This difficulty is that at institutional intake, information about religion of the patient as a rule is rather less than carefully ascertained and recorded. By contrast, in the Midtown interviews as many as 15 separate questions were asked about the individual's religious orientation, identification, and behaviors, past and present.

Discussed in chapter 7 (Book One) was the distinction between independent and reciprocal demographic variables. Obviously, the individual's religious identification can change between childhood and adulthood, and such change may be consequences of personality processes that also work themselves out in forms subsumed under the concept of mental health. Thus, adults' replies to the interview question, "To what religious faith do you *now* belong?" must be considered in the nature of a concurrent, reciprocal, and etiologically ambiguous variable relative to their mental health. On the other hand, in replies to questions on the faith that the respondent's parents grew up in, we have his/her religious origin, potentially standing as an antecedent and independent variable to the dependent variable of his/her current mental health.

We shall presently consider changes in religious identification between parents and their adult offspring. But here we first want to classify the sample adults by religious origin and to examine the mental health distribution in each of the four religious categories shown in table 19–3.

We know that among the religious groups in the sample there are differences in age composition and socioeconomic origin. We have

TABLE 19–3. HOME SURVEY SAMPLE (AGE 20–59), RESPONDENTS' DISTRIBUTIONS ON MENTAL HEALTH CLASSIFICATION BY RELIGIOUS ORIGIN

Mental health categories	Religious origin			
	Catholic	Protestant	Jewish	Others*
Well	16.1%	22.6%	16.0%	22.6%
Mild symptom formation ..	35.4	36.1	41.7	30.1
Moderate symptom formation	22.2	19.8	25.8	20.8
Impaired	26.3	21.5	16.5	26.5
Marked symptom formation	13.9	12.5	11.3	17.0
Severe symptom formation	9.0	6.9	3.8	5.7
Incapacitated	3.4	2.1	1.4	3.8
N = 100%	(832)	(562)	(213)	(53)

* Almost two-thirds of these respondents had parents who were identified as Christians of the Eastern (Greek or Russian) Orthodox Church. The remaining parents were either members of non-Western religious cults or were reported as having grown up in no known religious faith. These respondents are too diverse in religious backgrounds and too few in number to be brought into subsequent analyses in this chapter.

previously found that these two demographic factors are independently related to respondent mental health. Thus, if interesting differences appear in table 19–3, there is a decided chance that these differences are not real, but rather are spurious results of intergroup variations in age and SES origin. In table 19–4, we present the mental health distributions that could be expected were the three religious-origin groups identical in these latter respects.[11]

TABLE 19–4. HOME SURVEY SAMPLE (AGE 20–59), RESPONDENTS' DISTRIBUTIONS ON MENTAL HEALTH CLASSIFICATION BY RELIGIOUS ORIGIN AS STANDARDIZED FOR AGE AND SES ORIGIN

Mental health categories	Religious origin		
	Catholic	Protestant	Jewish
Well	17.4%	20.2%	14.5%
Mild symptom formation	34.5	36.4	43.2
Moderate symptom formation	23.4	19.9	25.1
Impaired	24.7*	23.5	17.2*
N = 100%	(832)	(562)	(213)

* $t = 2.6$ (.01 level of confidence).

This standardization almost completely levels the Protestant-Catholic differences seen in table 19–3. The impairment differences observed between Jews and the other two groups in the table remain statistically significant, however. Reference to table 19–3 locates the Jewish difference specifically in smaller Severe (3.8 percent) and Incapacitated (1.4 percent) frequencies, i.e., at the end of the impairment range rather than in the Marked category.

On the other hand, in table 19–4, Jews are also seen with the lowest prevalence of Wells at a not insignificant distance from the Protestants' Well frequency. With the lowest rates both of the Well and the Impaired, Jews of course are found more heavily concentrated than Protestants or Catholics in the large subclinical range in between, namely, in the Mild and Moderate categories of symptom formation.

We might follow the matter one step further. Suppose we look at the religious-origin groups within each of the three SES-origin strata, retaining standardization for age differences. We then find in all three strata the essential mental health picture discerned in table 19–4.

However, there are differences of degree—the most suggestive appearing in the lower stratum (E–F) of SES origin. Here respondents of Protestant, Catholic, and Jewish origin have almost identical Well frequencies, but their Impaired rates are 32.0, 30.5, and 19.4 percent, respectively.

If Jews convey the most favorable group picture of mental health in the SES stratum having the highest concentration of mental morbidity, then one possible hypothesis that can be suggested for future testing is this: Midtown respondents of Jewish parentage tend to reflect some kind of impairment-limiting mechanism that operates to counteract, or in some degree contain, the more extreme pathogenic life stresses during childhood. This hypothesis appears to be consistent with the repeatedly confirmed relative immunity of Jews to such self-impairing types of reactions as alcoholism[12] and suicide.

If such a "this-far-and-no-farther" control mechanism exists, its source is a question that here can only be a subject of speculation. One factor often hypothesized by psychiatrists as potentially pathogenic is the strong Jewish family structure. However, this factor may conceivably be eugenic on balance, in the specific sense that powerful homeostatic supports are brought into play at danger points of crisis and stress that in other groups may be unbalancing for the family and impairing for the individual.

If subsequent investigation should lend support to this inference, the mechanism involved may have historical, broadly psychosocial roots, of a kind defined by the following hypothesis: A group that for thousands of years has been beleaguered by chronic environmental threats of destruction survives by developing internal processes of resistance, deep within the dynamics of the family itself, that counteract in some measure the more extreme kinds of exogenous crises and check the more extreme forms of pathological reaction.

Also potentially relevant, although stemming from another framework, is the inference Janis draws from his classic study of surgery patients:

Arousal of some degree of anticipatory fear may be one of the necessary conditions for developing inner defenses of the type that can function effectively when the external danger materializes. . . . If a person is given appropriate preparatory communications before being exposed to potentially traumatizing stimuli, his chances of behaving in a disorganized way . . . may be greatly decreased. Thus, from the standpoint of preventive psychiatry, it is of considerable importance to determine how preparatory communications can be made to serve an effective prophylactic function.[13]

To translate this formulation for the present discussion, mobilization of anxiety about the instability of the Jewish exilic environment may historically have been established as a conditioning pattern of the Jewish family structure. In one direction, such anxiety, subsequently magnified in the adult by extrafamily life conditions, may be reflected in our finding of an unusually large concentration of Midtown Jews in the subclinical Mild category of symptom formation. On the other hand, this large component of historically realistic anxiety, as generated in the Jewish family, may function prophylactically to immunize its children against the potentially disabling sequelae of the more severe pressures and traumas of existence.[14] Later in this chapter we may see other expressions of this process.

Also to be emphasized is that, like earlier studies of patients, the Midtown Home Survey shows a somewhat higher overall frequency of mental morbidity in the Catholic group than in the Protestant group. However, this difference was found to be a wholly spurious consequence of the fact that Protestants in the aggregate are younger and of considerably higher socioeconomic antecedents than are Catholics.

HOME SURVEY SAMPLE: MENTAL HEALTH
AND PARENTAL RELIGIOSITY

In the section preceding we have been concerned with the respondent's religious origin as based on the faith in which his parents had grown up. This is a formal, demographic kind of classification, but it tells us nothing about the degree of parental commitment to the doctrines, commandments, and practices enjoined by their religious institution.

Seen in historical perspective, this dimension of individual commitment to the tenets of the faith—or "religiosity"—is extremely sensitive to changes in the environing society. The Protestant Reformation is an excellent case in point. The period in which our respondents' parents had been born roughly spanned the half century from 1864 to 1914. These, of course, were years that saw vast scientific, technological, and economic changes which made themselves felt along the entire broad front of Western institutions. Not the least of these impacts registered on the church and on the individual's anchoring ties to it.

We can hypothesize that this factor of relative religious anchorage or commitment had direct effects on parents' roles and on the home atmosphere, with radiating consequences for the development of the child as observed when he himself had grown into adulthood.

Interviewing each respondent, we asked this key question as a shortcut approach to his parents' religious orientation:[15] "How important would you say religion (belief in religion) was to your parents? For example, would you say it was: Very important? Somewhat important? Or not important at all?"[16]

We were of course aware that a reply to this question is essentially the respondent's judgment applied to his recall of observed words and deeds as they reflected parental attitude toward religious tradition.[17] We could assume that the judgment hinged in part on a norm or image of the "faithful" man that is specific to each church system and, in part, on the respondent's recall of modifications in this ideal among the parents' local contemporaries.

Within the Study's taxonomy of test factors,[18] parental religiosity certainly stands to the dependent variable of respondent mental health as a chronologically antecedent factor. But we deal with the respondent's *judgment* of such religiosity, and this "filter" is potentially open to influence from psychological processes related to the dependent variable. However, parental religiosity qualifies as an independent, as well as antecedent, test factor to the extent that the respondent's judgment took its measure from long and relatively close observations of parental behavior. We can produce no evidence to illuminate this issue. As a matter of the investigators' opinion, however, we will assume that respondents' reports of parental religiosity provide a reasonable approximation of independence from the dependent variable.

A final preparatory point must now be clarified. Earlier in this chapter, the respondent's religious origin was used, as determined by the criterion of descent through the religion of parents' upbringing (much as had national origin in the preceding chapter). This criterion was appropriate to our purposes of inclusive demographic classification at that point. With religiosity now the factor of central interest, we must gear this factor to identification of religious groupings based on a more refined criterion. That is, instead of religious origin or descent of parents, we refer to this criterion as parents' *religious-group identification*, after their marriage, as ascertained from respondent replies to the interview question: "What religious faith did *you* grow up in?"

Of course, the religion a parent had experienced during his own childhood tells us nothing with certainty about his religious identification during adulthood. However, we can be confident that the religious tradition which enveloped the child is a fairly reliable indicator of the religious-group identification conveyed, however minimally, by his parents. This criterion, of a specific religious identification *conveyed* to one's children, is the basis for our present classification of respondents' parents by religious group.

With a locus in any given religious system, individuals vary in degree of acceptance of its disciplining claims upon their thought and behavior. In this perspective, parents who had stood with the "faithful," by the light of locally modified standards of the church at large, would likely be seen by the child as having given their religion very important weight in their lives. On the other hand, parents deviating considerably from the faithful model, while remaining more or less anchored in the church, would probably be judged as holding their religion no more than "somewhat important." Finally, parents remaining formally identified as in the fold of the church but whose behavior suggested that its religious tenets were to them "not important at all" were probably at best peripheral, nominal members of the institution.

Let us first record how the sample respondents' parents are distributed on this gross scale of reported religiosity:[19]

Very important (VI) 52%
Somewhat important (SI) 37%
Not important at all (NIAA) 11%

Table 19–5 below shows next how respondents' parents located within *each group fold* are distributed by religiosity as reported to us. We need not pause to speculate on the explanations for the differences that appear in table 19–5.[20] However, they are consistent with general observations that close conformity to the normative expectations of one's religious institution characterizes more adherents of the Catholic Church than Protestants or Jews.

TABLE 19–5. HOME SURVEY SAMPLE (AGE 20–59), DISTRIBUTIONS OF RESPONDENTS' PARENTS ON RELIGIOSITY CLASSIFICATION BY PARENTAL RELIGIOUS-GROUP IDENTIFICATION

Parents' religiosity	Parents' religious-group identification		
	Catholic	Protestant	Jewish
Very important (VI)	67.4%	40.0%	31.1%
Somewhat important (SI)	28.1	45.8	48.4
Not important at all (NIAA)	4.5	14.2	20.5
N = 100%	(805)	(541)	(190)

Furthermore, if we could assume that at some not-too-distant period in the past almost all adherents of each religious faith were in the top level of religiosity, it seems apparent that this was far from the case among the respondents' parents a generation ago. Even within the relatively stable Catholic group, one in every three parents in the eyes of their offspring stood at less than a "very important" level of religious commitment. Thus, the erosions of traditional religious anchorages among adults of a generation ago can seemingly be discerned from the data presented in table 19–5.

Our primary concern here is addressed to this question: What are the detectable consequences of parental differences in religiosity for the mental health of the children they raised to adulthood? Let us first direct this question to the Midtown sample respondents of Jewish-identified parents. In table 19–6 below they are distributed on a threefold classification of the mental health continuum.

Among offspring of the several religiosity categories of Jewish par-

TABLE 19–6. HOME SURVEY SAMPLE (AGE 20–59), DISTRIBUTIONS OF RESPONDENTS WITH JEWISH-IDENTIFIED PARENTS ON MENTAL HEALTH CLASSIFICATION BY PARENTAL RELIGIOSITY

Mental health categories	Parental religiosity		
	VI	SI	NIAA
Well	8.5%	18.5%	15.4%
Mild-Moderate	76.2	63.0	64.1
Impaired	15.3	18.5	20.5
N = 100%	(59)	(92)	(39)

ents, no significant difference in mental health composition is to be seen. In the light of the relatively small number of cases in the VI and NIAA columns of table 19–6, we must consider our evidence from the Jewish segment of the Midtown sample as statistically inconclusive.

The difficulty of insufficient sample numbers is not encountered to the same degree among respondents of Protestant-identified parentage. In fact, this group is sufficiently numerous to be examined on our present test variable as subdivided by our three-way stratification of parental socioeconomic status. In table 19–7 we present the mental

TABLE 19–7. HOME SURVEY SAMPLE (AGE 20–59), DISTRIBUTIONS OF RESPONDENTS OF UPPER SES ORIGIN AND PROTESTANT-IDENTIFIED PARENTS ON MENTAL HEALTH CLASSIFICATION BY PARENTAL RELIGIOSITY

Mental health categories	Parental religiosity		
	VI	SI	NIAA
Well	26.7%	25.7%	27.0%
Mild-Moderate	56.5	55.0	56.8
Impaired	16.8	19.3	16.2
N = 100%	(101)	(109)	(37)

health distributions only for the respondents who are of upper-SES descent (A–B).

Mental health composition is almost identical in the three religiosity categories of table 19–7. However, when we similarly categorize respondents of Protestant-identified parents who had been in our middle or lower stratum of socioeconomic status, we find a rather different pattern of mental health composition. Since the pattern is quite similar in these parental strata, and the number of cases is relatively small in the lower of the two, table 19–8 below combines the respondents of these two SES-origin groups (C–D and E–F).

If the VI- and SI-reared respondents there are alike in their Well frequencies, the latter are better off in having a significantly lower Impaired rate, accompanied by a correspondingly higher frequency in the subclinical (Mild-Moderate) range of the continuum. Relative to these two groups, moreover, the NIAA-sired respondents have the largest impairment rate and the smallest Well representation.

TABLE 19–8. HOME SURVEY SAMPLE (AGE 20–59), DISTRIBUTIONS OF RESPONDENTS OF LOWER AND MIDDLE SES ORIGIN AND PROTESTANT-IDENTIFIED PARENTS ON MENTAL HEALTH CLASSIFICATION BY PARENTAL RELIGIOSITY

Mental health categories	Parental religiosity		
	VI	SI	NIAA
Well	20.9%	22.3%	12.5%
Mild-Moderate	51.3	60.4	50.0
Impaired	27.8*	17.3†	37.5*
N = 100%	(115)	(139)	(40)

* $t = 2.1$ (.05 level of confidence).
† $t = 2.9$ (.01 level of confidence).

In short, we discern the most favorable mental health picture in the SI religiosity column and the least favorable in the NIAA segment, with the VI category standing more or less intermediate. On the yardstick of impairment rates, therefore, the pattern of relationship between parental religiosity and respondent mental health can be described as being of the general J-curve type.

Of course, the generality of this pattern remains in question when we consider that it does not seem to appear among Jewish-bred respondents or among Protestant-reared people of high SES origin. However, respondents of Catholic-identified parents have not yet been examined in this respect. Analysis reveals the presence of this distribution pattern among such Catholics on *all* three SES-origin strata. However, because the number of respondents with NIAA par-

TABLE 19–9. HOME SURVEY SAMPLE (AGE 20–59), DISTRIBUTIONS OF RESPONDENTS WITH CATHOLIC-IDENTIFIED PARENTS ON MENTAL HEALTH CLASSIFICATION BY PARENTAL RELIGIOSITY

Mental health categories	Parental religiosity		
	VI	SI	NIAA
Well	17.1%	15.0%	5.5%
Mild-Moderate	56.0	63.3	58.4
Impaired	26.9	21.7	36.1
N = 100%	(543)	(226)	(36)

ents is so small in each of these strata, we can best delineate the pattern by viewing, in table 19-9, the entire Catholic-identified group as differentiated in terms of parental religiosity.

Although the intra-Catholic differences in table 19-9 do not achieve firm statistical significance, we again see the lowest Well frequency and highest Impaired rate in the NIAA column. Moreover, the SI category again emerges with the smallest prevalence of impairment; the VI respondents in turn stand intermediate in this respect.

All in all, therefore, the J-curve pattern observed among Protestant-sired respondents of lower and middle SES origins seems to be paralleled among Catholic offspring of all SES-origin strata. We can thereby infer, first, that this is a key pattern for respondents from both Protestant and Catholic childhood homes that were of lower or middle socioeconomic position. Jews of such SES origin do not seem to fit this pattern, but because of their small numbers in these strata, we lack confidence that this negative finding in their case is statistically conclusive.

Second, we can infer that a finding of no relationship between parental religiosity and respondent mental health seems to characterize both Protestants and Jews of upper socioeconomic descent. Here, Catholics of like SES origin seem to deviate, presenting instead the J-shaped curve. However, their number in this stratum is relatively small, and we cannot be sure that this positive finding in their instance is statistically stable.

Accordingly, we are left with the residual inference that in lower- and middle-class homes, parental religiosity tends to be related to childrens' adult mental health—at least if the home had been Protestant or Catholic identified.

To be sure, the affinity uncovered in these parental-SES strata is not strikingly strong. On the other hand, this relationship has come through a measure of religiosity that rests on the narrow base of a single interview question and offers only a crude trichotomous classification. Accordingly, it is a plausible expectation that with a broader base of information and more refined classification of parental religiosity the relationship may well emerge in clearer form and enlarged magnitude.

Suggestive evidence lending support to the link between parental religious behavior and offsprings' mental health comes from a study of King and Funkenstein, who report:

... there is a constellation of psychological and sociological factors which are associated with the cardiovascular reactions of healthy subjects [male college students] in acute stress. The constellation includes the immediate emotional reaction of the subject, his attitudes in the area of religious values, his perception of parental behavior in discipline, and the *church-going behavior of his parents* [italics added]. . . . We leave it to further research to spell out the manifold implications of these associations. We do suggest that they are of sufficient strength to encourage further inter-disciplinary research among the fields of physiology, psychology and sociology.[21]

The relationship seemingly discerned in the Midtown sample poses a series of questions that cannot be answered at this time. First, why is this relationship apparently specific to the lower two-thirds of the parental-SES range and seemingly nonoperative among respondents from the upper third of that SES range? What specific elements can explain why the VI type of home in the susceptible SES strata seems to be more eugenic for offsprings' mental health than the NIAA home, and why does the SI home tend to be the most eugenic type of all? Under the secularizing pressures of industrial, urban society, are different modes of religiosity chosen by parents of broadly different types of personalities? If so, the apparent consequences of parental religiosity for offsprings' mental health may partially dissolve themselves into consequences of more comprehensive aspects of parents' characters.

On the other hand, assume broad personality similarities in a group of parents who diverge in religiosity: What consequences of the latter variable alone would flow into the intrafamily processes, e.g., into performances of parental roles, and thereby into the psychological conditioning of their offspring? What effects do variations in parental religiosity have upon family stability under crisis? For children, especially in adolescence, what are the intrafamily consequences when they veer away from the religious orientation of parents under pressure of peers and larger social influences?

By the inroads made into the religious anchorages of a large segment of the population, we see one cutting edge of the vast sociocultural changes of the past century. In particular we have seen the impacts of these historical forces on the religious moorings in the generation parental to our sample adults, and we can glimpse possible residues of such forces in the mental health of these respondents.

MENTAL HEALTH AND RELIGIOUS MOBILITY

We have been concerned about presumptive changes in religiosity among respondents' parents who had been identified with a specific religious group. Here we focus on direct evidence of a more drastic kind of change—among respondents themselves, namely, a change in their own religious-group *identification*, or what we call *religious mobility*.

For respondents' religious-group lineage we shall take their religious origin, and we shall compare this with their replies to the interview question: "To what religious faith do you *now* belong?" In table 19–10 we can ascertain the relative prevalence of religious mobility in the Midtown sample population.

TABLE 19–10. HOME SURVEY SAMPLE (AGE 20–59), DISTRIBUTIONS OF RESPONDENTS' CURRENT RELIGIOUS GROUP BY RELIGIOUS ORIGIN

Current religious group	Religious origin		
	Catholic	Protestant	Jewish
Catholic	90.0%	4.1%	1.9%
Protestant	2.5	78.6	1.9
Jewish	0.0	0.4	75.6
None	5.8	14.2	16.9
Other	1.7	2.7	3.7
N = 100%	(832)	(562)	(213)

This table clearly shows that respondents of Protestant or Jewish origin have total religious mobility rates more than twice (21.4 and 24.4 percent, respectively) that of Catholic-derived people (10 percent). However, in all three origin groups most of the movement has been not into another group, but into the disidentified "no faith" or "unchurched" ranks.

Of particular relevance to us here is the mental health composition of the several subgroup segments that have sufficient numbers of cases. Given the number of these segments, perhaps the most summary indication of such composition might be in terms of the Impaired-Well ratio,[22] as presented in table 19–11 below.

TABLE 19–11.   HOME SURVEY SAMPLE (AGE 20–59), IMPAIRED-WELL RATIO OF SAMPLE RESPONDENTS BY RELIGIOUS ORIGIN AND CURRENT RELIGIOUS GROUP

Current religious group	Religious origin		
	Catholic	Protestant	Jewish
Catholic	163	57	...
N* = ...	(747)	(23)	(4)
Protestant	25	87	...
N = ...	(21)	(442)	(4)
Jewish	...	...	92
N = ...	(0)	(2)	(161)
None	200	170	120
N = ...	(48)	(80)	(36)

* N is the total number of respondents in the specific cell to which the Impaired-Well ratio value refers.

As we have just seen, Protestants who changed to Catholicism and Catholics who shifted to Protestantism are small in number. But to judge from the Impaired-Well ratios as derived from so few cases, such church-to-church changers appear in a somewhat more favorable mental health condition than do the stable Protestants and Catholics. Compared to the latter and the nonmobile Jews, however, the currently unchurched respondents from all three religious-origin groups uniformly present a less favorable mental health picture.

Since religious mobility is in the realm of voluntary behavior, it seems likely in large part to be psychologically determined. Hence, table 19–11 probably tells us more about the kinds of people who change their religious group identification than it reveals about the mental health consequences of such change.

A potential programmatic utility of the data is to highlight to metropolitan religious organizations the mental health weighting of adherents they are losing to the unchurched, unreachable condition.

HELP–NEED, THE PATIENT–HISTORY VARIABLE, AND PROFESSIONAL ORIENTATION

We turn finally to the patient-history factor as applied exclusively to the population at help-need, namely, the sample respondents who are in the Impaired category of mental health. Because religious origin is the most comprehensive criterion for classification by religious grouping, it is used with the Impaired segment of the sample in table 19–12.

TABLE 19–12. HOME SURVEY SAMPLE (AGE 20–59), DISTRIBUTIONS OF IMPAIRED RESPONDENTS ON PATIENT-HISTORY CLASSIFICATION BY RELIGIOUS ORIGIN

Patient history	Religious origin		
	Catholic	Protestant	Jewish
Current outpatients	1.8%	8.3%	20.0%
Ex-patients	19.7	24.0	20.0
Never-patients	78.5	67.7	60.0
N = 100%	(219)	(121)	(35)

Of course, the ex-patients shown in the table include people who had been hospitalized, as well as those who had used ambulatory facilities. Accordingly, if the ex-patient rates are quite similar in the three columns of the table, we can be sure—from our Treatment Census data earlier reviewed—that the exhospitalized representation in the "mix" is quite different in the three religious groups.

More clear-cut are the current outpatient frequencies. We discern that among those now at risk of help-need, Jews have a current outpatient rate more than twice that of Protestants and approximately ten times that of Catholics. This illuminates the finding earlier drawn from the New Haven Study and our Treatment Census analysis that Jews emerge with higher ambulatory treatment rates than either Protestants or Catholics.[23]

From our Home Survey sample we have already seen (table 19–3) that Jews have a lower impairment rate than either of the other two religious groups. This seemed to be at direct variance with the Treatment Census finding that Jews were the highest of the three groups in Total Patients rates. The seeming paradox is set aright by the finding that between two groups of like size a low mental morbidity rate and a strong tendency to seek therapy can bring more Impaired people to a treatment facility than a high morbidity rate and a relatively weak tendency to seek therapy.

This statement stands irrespective of the fact that determinants other than mental morbidity enter into the varying motivations that lead one to treatment—especially of the voluntary outpatient type. One of these determinants is certainly the Impaired respondent's socioeconomic status. When the latter factor among the Impaired is controlled, the interreligious differences in current outpatient rates are narrowed but by no means eliminated. In most previous studies of patient populations sorted by religious groupings, lack of control for the SES variable has obscured its contribution to the large interreligious differences in patient rates.

However, that more than socioeconomic status is involved in patient rate differences may be gathered from questions put to the Midtown sample adults bearing on a dimension that we designate *professional orientation*. This was derived from our Midtown respondents through open-ended questions that posed certain psychiatric problems in a hypothetical family. One question was: "Let's suppose some friends of yours have a serious problem with their child. I mean a problem with the child's behavior, or difficulty getting along with others. The parents ask your advice about what to do. What would you probably tell them to do about it?" A similar query was phrased in terms of an advice-seeking friend with a problem spouse.

Respondents were first sorted into those who in either or both situations would recommend consulting a psychotherapist of some kind. Sorted next were all the remaining respondents who would advise seeing a physician. In the third category were placed those who at most would refer such friends to some other kind of professional person, principally a clergymen or member of a social agency staff. The residue contained all respondents whose replies to both questions contain no suggestion of professional help of any kind.

Since professional orientation is strongly related to socioeconomic status of respondents, in table 19-13 distributions on the former variable appear standardized for respondents' own SES. The criterion of classification by religion is again religious origin.

Catholics and Protestants are alike in that within each group about half could perceive no professional help as relevant for either of the stipulated problem families, and about one in eight would refer such problems to a physician. They differ in that fewer Catholics than Protestants would recommend a psychotherapist, and correspondingly more Catholics would advise other kinds of professionals, principally clergymen.

TABLE 19–13. HOME SURVEY SAMPLE (AGE 20–59), RESPONDENTS' DISTRIBUTIONS ON PROFESSIONAL ORIENTATION SCALE BY RELIGIOUS ORIGIN AS STANDARDIZED FOR OWN-SES DIFFERENCES

Respondent recommends	Religious origin		
	Catholic	Protestant	Jewish
Psychotherapist	23.8%	31.4%	49.2%
Physician	13.3	12.5	7.9
Other professional	13.0	7.5	3.1
Nonprofessional	49.9	48.6	39.8
N = 100%	(832)	(562)	(213)

Jewish respondents, to a degree well beyond the other groups, see psychotherapists as the most appropriate source of help for the disturbed individuals outlined to them. In fact, they are the only group where this response is more frequent than the "no professional" recommendation.

Table 19–13 views the Midtown sample in its entirety, whereas table 19–12 views only the Impaired portion of that sample. Nevertheless, as observed in table 19–13, the religious groups' rank order of orientation to psychotherapy corresponds to their rank order of current outpatient rates seen in table 19–12. Independently of socioeconomic status, then, religious groups differ in their spontaneous awareness of and receptivity to the psychotherapeutic professions. Given a help-need condition and like socioeconomic status, these differences are manifested through intergroup variations in actually seeking the counsel of a psychotherapist. This generalization is consistent with the evidence provided earlier in the present chapter by both the Treatment Census and Home Survey operations of the Midtown Study.

It is now relevant to note the discussion on this point by the New Haven investigators of a patient population:[24]

It is our opinion that the acceptance of psychiatry probably accounts for the inordinately high rate of psychoneurosis among Jews.[25] The explanation for this must be considered in terms of the ethnic structure and the tradition of the Jewish group in addition to its religious organization. Among Jews it is generally accepted that there is no conflict between religious doctrine and psychoanalytic theory. This is in contrast to a partially supported opposition among Catholics. From the standpoint of community attitudes, the Jews exhibit a high level of acceptance of psychoanalytic psychiatry with a minimum of disturbance of their social values. The Jewish attitude is widely divergent from the Irish, as is substantiated by our finding that not a single patient of Irish birth was receiving psychotherapy for psychoneurosis. Although this explanation of the rates of psychoneurosis in terms of the acceptance of modern psychiatry appears plausible, we cannot definitely state that the actual occurrence of the illness is not higher among Jews.

The statement just quoted, on one point at least, finds support in the implication of Midtown data just reviewed that readiness for psychotherapy, or the "pro-psychiatry" attitude, among Jews contributes to their high patient rates. However, the explanation offered by the New Haven investigators for the Jewish acceptance of psychiatry seems to rest primarily on a contrast drawn from the Catholic group. We understand the New Haven authors to posit that official opposition of the church, at least to psychoanalysis, diverts Catholics from seeking psychotherapy of *any* kind. In the Jewish group, further, the lack of such hieratic and doctrinal opposition and a "minimum of disturbance with their social values" are essentially negative factors in the sense that they do *not* interpose barriers to soliciting psychiatric help.

In our view, this formulation is unduly simplified. First, Protestantism, at least in its metropolitan churches, if anything is more overtly active in articulating itself to psychiatry than are synagogues on the whole. On this basis, according to the New Haven reasoning, the pro-psychiatry frequencies of Protestants should be substantially larger than those of Catholics and at least approximate those of Jews. Table 19–14 reveals these frequencies by religious group as sorted into respondent own-SES strata.

In two of the three SES strata, the pro-psychiatry rates of Protestants and Catholics do not differ appreciably. In the upper stratum the Protestant frequency stands no better than roughly intermediate between those of Catholics and Jews. Accordingly, our data suggest that if there are differences in psychiatric orientation among the clergy of the three major religious groups, they appear to have no power to explain the variations in psychiatric readiness observed above among their respective laities.

The information in tables 19–13 and 19–14 enables us to question the New Haven formulation offered to explain the "high level of

TABLE 19–14. HOME SURVEY SAMPLE (AGE 20–59), PRO-PSYCHIATRY
FREQUENCIES AMONG RELIGIOUS-ORIGIN GROUPS BY RESPONDENT OWN SES*

Own SES	Religious origin		
	Catholic	Protestant	Jewish
Lower (E–F)	12.1%	13.8%	†
N = 100%	(381)	(137)	(11)
Middle (C–D)	23.6%	28.6%	41.3%
N = 100%	(322)	(168)	(46)
Upper (A–B)	35.6%	51.8%	63.4%
N = 100%	(129)	(257)	(156)

* Needless to say, a group's distribution on the own-SES range may deviate
considerably from its scatter on the parental-SES range.

† These cases are too few to present a meaningful percentage.

acceptance of psychoanalytic psychiatry among Jews." This hypothesis emphasized the absence among Jews of clerical and doctrinal
constraints to securing psychotherapy. The alternative hypothesis we
would propose emphasizes not the absence of constraint but rather
the presence of a positive motivating process, and looks for it not in
the religious institution alone but in the spontaneous operations of the
family unit as well.

Earlier in this chapter (table 19–4), we reported that in mental
health composition Protestants and Catholics are little different when
standardized by age and SES origin, whereas by comparison Jews
have a significantly lower impairment frequency and a higher subclinical (Mild or Moderate symptom formation) rate. Furthermore,
we observed that the Jewish deviation in impairment frequency was
sharpest in the SES-origin stratum that is associated with the most
pathogenic life conditions, namely, the lower class. We therefore indicated that the Jewish mental health distribution suggests the possible presence in the family unit of an impairment-limiting
mechanism that operates to counteract or contain in some degree the
more pathogenic life stresses. Consistently low rates of self-impairing
alcoholism and suicide in the general Jewish population seemed
compatible with this hypothesis.

We have since seen in the Midtown sample that, given an Impaired
state of mental health, Jews have far higher current patient rates than
Protestants or Catholics. Furthermore, Jews generally tend to deviate

from the other two religious groups of like socioeconomic status in their pro-psychiatry orientation. We would now extend the postulate of an impairment-limiting mechanism to cover its manifestations in greater Jewish responsiveness to psychotherapy as an appropriate means to limit and reverse psychopathology.

It would go somewhat outside our present framework to develop the further suggestion that this mechanism may be part of a larger survival-insurance process rooted in the Jewish family and religious tradition that has found expression in these other varying forms: (1) explicit emphasis upon health as transcending fundamental ritual prescriptions when the two are in conflict; (2) mobilization of family and kin in psychological and material support of the sick individual; and (3) pragmatism in calling upon extrafamilial healing resources.[26] The fusion of all these elements may perhaps be discerned in the millennial-long affinity of Jews for the field of medicine and, more recently, for its psychiatric branch, in the several roles of explorers, healers, and patients. The Jewish group historically can be viewed in one perspective as a culture mobilized for the prevention and, that failing, for the healing of the ailments of body and mind.

Finally, we would question the inference of the New Haven investigators that opposition to psychoanalysis (as a mode of therapy) on the part of the Catholic laity is "partially supported" by the Church.

There is no question about the Church's unequivocal reactions to the antidoctrinal aspects of the psychoanalytic literature. Overlooked, however, is the impressive movement of Church spokesmen toward explicit acceptance of Freud's scientific and therapeutic contributions.

As one churchman has put it: "A Catholic will differ radically with Freud in philosophy and religion. But such differences, radical and profound though they be, should not obscure our vision nor dim our appreciation of the many fresh and brilliant insights which he brought to the understanding of the forces moving in the subconscious areas of our mental life and exercising their pull upon us."[27] Commenting on the address of Pope Pius XII to the First International Congress on the Histopathology of the Nervous System, the Vatican's official newspaper observed: "All the systems of psychoanalysis have in common certain principles, methods and psychic experiments which are in no way contrary to rational ethics and Christian morality, and therefore are not in any way touched or reproved by the Sovereign Pontiff."[28,29]

Pope Paul VI has recently declared of psychiatry in general: "First of all we must underline the paramount importance of the branch of medicine you represent. The Church has always rejoiced in seeing scientific progress wherever such programs are placed at the disposal of mankind. Of all the branches of medicine, neuropsychiatry is a privileged branch, for this area of scientific progress is striking."[30]

From another approach we postulate that two major institutional influences, among others, may operate to restrain financially capable Catholic laymen from seeking ambulatory psychiatric care more often. Psychotherapy tends to be seen as a secularized form of a central Church procedure: the confessional. In this perspective the therapist need not be a cleric, but considerations of personal comfort in the therapeutic relationship may dictate that he should be a fellow Catholic. On this line of reasoning, the Midtown Catholics' relatively low patient rates and infrequent psychiatric readiness may partially be a function of the plain fact that Catholic clinics and office psychiatrists at the time of the Study were so few in number.

Between 1950 and 1975, the number of American psychiatrists increased many times. Data are lacking on the Catholic segment of the profession, but it is the senior author's strong impression that the proportion of Catholics among U.S. psychiatrists still lags far behind the general increase in the profession's manpower.

SUMMARY

Religious differences constitute the final demographic variable explored in the Midtown data for lines of influence leading to the several facets of mental health under review in this monograph. The principal exploratory results are as follows:

1. Despite technical differences between the Midtown Treatment Census and New Haven Psychiatric Census, intercommunity comparison revealed these parallels: (a) For the kinds of disorders usually treated in an ambulatory facility, Catholics and Protestants yielded like patient rates that were considerably below that found among Jews; (b) for the kinds of disorders usually treated in hospitals, Jews and Protestants yielded like patient rates that were below that of Catholics; and (c) taking Total Patients rates as an inclusive yardstick, Jews stood highest in both communities.

2. Clarification of these seemingly contrary directions was sought in the Midtown Home Survey sample of 1,660 representative adults. On the chronologically antecedent criterion of parental religion, the sample's groups of Jewish, Protestant, and Catholic derivation had impairment rates of 16.5, 21.5, and 26.3 percent, respectively.

Standardization for intergroup differences in age and SES origin reduced the Protestant and Catholic groups to near identity in mental health distributions. Respondents of Jewish origin retained a significantly lower Impaired rate—one wholly explained by smaller numbers in the Severe and Incapacitated subcategories of impairment. However, they were relatively underrepresented in the Well category and overrepresented in the Mild-Moderate range of symptom formation.

Analysis further revealed that the more favorable impairment rate of the Jewish-origin group was especially characteristic of its low SES-origin members. A number of hypotheses and speculations were advanced as possible explanations of these findings.

3. Within each religious-origin group we differentiated respondent parents on a threefold gradient of religiosity, i.e., commitment to and anchorage in their faith. Reflected in the data were substantial erosions in religious moorings among respondents' parents. The Midtown evidence further suggested a J-curve type of relationship between parental religiosity and offspring mental health in Protestant and Catholic families adhering to the lower two-thirds of the SES-origin range. Seemingly discernible here were the echoes in contemporary adults of the reverberating sociocultural upheavals generated during the nineteenth century.

4. Modeled after SES mobility (chapter 14) was the factor of intergenerational change in religious affiliation. The few converts to other religions were favorably constituted in group mental health, but those who had drifted into the "no religion" stream presented a relatively unfavorable picture of mental health.

5. Focus upon the patient-history variable among the religious groupings' Impaired respondents suggested this: In groups of similar size a combination of low mental morbidity rate and pronounced tendency to seek therapy can deliver more Impaired people to treatment services than a combination of high morbidity rate and slight tendency to seek therapy.

6. Representing the former combinations, Jews were also found

with a more widespread openness to psychiatry. Discussed were explanatory formulations of the readiness variable as offered by the New Haven and Midtown investigators.

NOTES

1. *Fortune*, February 1960, pp. 2–4.

2. To avoid unwieldy segmentation, we will not focus on the denominational branches within Protestantism and Judaism. Here, however, we might venture a brief look into our Midtown sample of adults for indications as to the specific denominations represented and their relative size. On the criterion of respondent's report of his own current religious identification, we find the major Protestant denominations in descending order of size to be Episcopalians, Lutherans, and Presbyterians, followed by Methodists and Baptists and a variety of smaller sects.

Similarly the three branches of Judaism are locally represented in a descending sequence by population size, namely, Reform, Conservative, and Orthodox. It may illuminate this denominational distribution to note that only 30 percent of the Jewish respondents are immigrants, almost 50 percent are children of immigrants, and roughly 20 percent are of generation III or beyond.

3. To avoid monotony of usage, we shall hereafter employ such terms as religion, faith, church, tradition, and persuasion as specific synonyms of "religious group" with which a respondent is personally identified.

4. Of course, it is necessary to have the total population figure in each group for use as the denominator in calculating its patient rate. The decennial United States census is the source of such information for many kinds of demographic groupings, but religion is not one of these. This deficiency has undoubtedly had crippling effects on epidemiological investigations of the religious factor along the entire range of diseases, somatic as well as psychiatric.

However, application of the Jewish–non-Jewish dichotomy was usually made possible by the availability of local estimates of the Jewish population. These figures were often little more than armchair estimates that by wide and unchallenged repetition had acquired an aura of universal acceptance.

5. Benjamin Malzberg, "Mental Disease among Jews in New York State, 1920 to 1952," *Yivo Annual of Jewish Social Sciences*, vol. X, 1955, p. 298.

6. B. H. Roberts and J. K. Myers, "Religion, National Origin, Immigration and Mental Illness," *American Journal of Psychiatry* 110 (April 1954): 760.

7. As in other research of this kind, the New Haven investigators lacked United States census data on religious composition of their community population. Estimates of this composition were apparently extracted from a special survey of a 5 percent sample of New Haven residents. Given the sampling error underlying these estimates and the rates derived from them, the above differences in treated psychosis rates seem sufficiently small to be a resultant of chance in the sampling process.

8. Of course, the New Haven study covered private as well as state psychiatric hospitals. If Protestants and Jews in some numbers preferred such institutions to state hospitals, then patient rates based on the latter alone would of course be understatements to the extent of such preference.

9. The absence of the office patients makes it pointless to analyze the remaining patients in each religious group by diagnostic category.

10. H. Orlansky, "Jewish Personality Traits: A Review of Studies on an Elusive Problem," *Commentary*, October 1946, pp. 377–383.

11. This is accomplished by the technique of standardization. In this method, the less-populated mental health categories in the Impaired range cannot be separately sustained. Accordingly, they are merged in table 19–4.

12. C. R. Snyder, "Culture and Jewish Sobriety," *Quarterly Journal of Studies on Alcohol* 16 (December 1955): 700–742.

13. I. Janis, *Psychological Stress*, 1958, p. 352.

14. Here may also be the seedbed of the Jewish community's proverbial gift, through its long history, for rising from adversity and for converting a handicap into an asset. Alexander King points to another possible consequence: "Jewish humor, as I learned at one of its very sources, was a racial anti-biotic, whose original cultures the children of Israel had carried out of Egypt, more than two thousand years ago, and whose health-preserving properties had been nurtured through the centuries in all the ghettoes and outposts of persecuted Judaism." (A. King, *Mine Enemy Grows Older*, 1958, p. 171.)

15. Originally also asked for this purpose was a question on parents' frequency of church (or synagogue) attendance—"when you were growing up." Subsequently, we recognized more fully that as a universal index of religiosity, frequency of church attendance had a number of serious deficiencies. Accordingly, it is not being employed here for this purpose.

16. If respondent indicated that father and mother differed in this respect, the interviewer recorded the specific nature of the difference. Later, with an eye on the parent likely to have had the larger influence on the home's religious atmosphere, we classified such cases according to importance of religion reported for the mother.

17. Whether this reply would have coincided with the judgments of the parents themselves, their clergyman, or their friends at the time, is information beyond access to us. Even if accessible, these judgments would not necessarily be of transcending relevance compared to the respondent's judgment from his personal vantage point.

18. Cf. Chapter 7.

19. If personal importance of religion is seen as a continuum ranging (1) from complete submission to the expectations of one's church to (2) more or less complete independence of one's church, it is clear that in this distribution about half of the parents stand at the VI range of the continuum. With benefit of hindsight, were we to test this factor again, we would enlarge the number of categories in the scale, perhaps to four, in order to sort out religiosity differences within the present VI category and to produce a closer approximation to a normal distribution curve.

In this direction, Fichter has applied the following fourfold classification of Catholics: "[a] *Nuclear*, who are the most active participants and the most faithful believers. [b] *Modal*, who are the normal, practicing Catholics easily identifiable as parishioners. [c] *Marginal*, who are conforming to a bare arbitrary minimum of the patterns expected in the religious institution. [d] *Dormant*, who have 'given up' Catholicism but have not joined another denomination." (J. H. Fichter, S. J., "The Marginal Catholic: An Institutional Approach," *Social Forces* 32 [December 1953]: 167–172.)

20. It might be added that parents' religiosity also varies inversely with their socioeconomic status. That is, the higher the SES level, the lower, on the aver-

age, is the religiosity reported. However, when both the SES and religious-group factors are analyzed simultaneously, religiosity varies more among religious groups within any given SES stratum than among SES strata within any given religious group.

More accurately stated, in all parental-SES strata such analytical control tends to eliminate the differences in religiosity distributions between Protestants and Jews seen in table 19–5 and tends to magnify the distribution differences between each of the latter two groups and the Catholics. For example, in the parental lower-SES stratum the "very important" frequencies of Catholic, Protestant, and Jewish parents are 74.0, 39.8, and 37.5 percent, respectively.

21. S. H. King and D. Funkenstein, "Religious Practice and Cardiovascular Reactions during Stress," *Journal of Abnormal and Social Psychology* 55, no. 1 (January 1957): 135–137.

22. It may be remembered that this expressed the number of Impaired cases per 100 Well respondents in a given group.

23. Cf. p. 433 of this chapter.

24. Roberts and Myers, "Religion, National Origin, Immigration and Marital Illness," p. 762.

25. For the New Haven data on treated neuroses and character disorders see table 19–1.—EDS.

26. Cf. L. Srole, "Social Conflicts in Relation to Health Education: Minority Groups," *Psychological Dynamics of Health Education*, Proceedings of Eastern Health Education Conference, 1951, pp. 90–99; M. Zborowski and E. Herzog, *Life Is with People*, 1952, pp. 114–115, 354–357; and M. Zborowski, *People in Pain*, 1969, pp. 120–132.

27. Rev. J. A. O'Brien, *Psychiatry and Confession*, Paulist Press, 1958.

28. *L'Osservatore Romano*, Sept. 21, 1952.

29. For the most systematic concordance bridging Catholic philosophy and Freud's contributions to scientific psychology and clinical psychiatry, see *Psychoanalysis and Personality: A Dynamic Theory of Normal Personality*, 1962, by Joseph Nuttin, Sr., Professor of Psychology at the Catholic University of Leuven (Belgium).

30. Addressed to Dr. Bertram S. Brown, Director of the U.S. National Institute of Mental Health, as reported in *Psychiatric News*, April 18, 1974.

Part VII

Epilogue

CHAPTER 20

THE CITY VERSUS TOWN AND COUNTRY: NEW EVIDENCE ON AN ANCIENT BIAS, 1975

LEO SROLE

In this data chapter, prepared for the present edition,* the author expands the focus beyond Midtown to encompass a far larger sociological terrain. I refer to the spectrum of community-habitat types defined at one pole by the relatively homogenous rural/"country"/ village/small-town scene and, toward the other extreme, by the highly heterogenous urban/city/metropolis agglomeration. Within this greatly extended framework, the present chapter will briefly review past professional assessments of urban and country milieus as polarities, and summarize recent research evidence bearing on this issue, particularly as it relates to both somatic and mental well-being.

On a preliminary semantic note, the professional literature I must draw on for these purposes largely employs the above extreme categories of settlements, and intermediate ones as well, with little more quantitative specificity or consistency than does popular usage of terms like tall, medium, and short in referring to individual stature. I have no choice except to follow the practices of the particular sources cited, underscoring that the chapter's analytic interest, by and large, is in comparing the big city at one pole with village and town at the other.

Recorded attitudes toward the city go back at least to the Book of

* In its original version this chapter was a paper read at the Conference on Cognitive and Emotional Aspects of Urban Life held in June 1972 under the auspices of the Graduate Center of the City University of New York. Subsequently revised, it appeared as an article, "Urbanization and Mental Health," in *American Scientist* 60, no. 5 (September–October 1972): 576–583. The latter has been considerably reworked and enlarged for this edition.

Genesis and its imprecations against Sodom, Gomorrah, and "the whore city" of Babylon, site of Babel, the memorable high-rise housing development that collapsed from the weight of its builders' tongues. Keynoted later by Rousseau's romantic exaltation of "man in a state of nature," the voices of antipathy swelled as the Industrial Revolution ran its accelerating course. A collection of all writings that decried, deplored, or denounced the city would probably fill a sizable college library. Heavily represented on its shelves would certainly be works of the Romantic poets. It was the English poet George Byron who wrote, "To me the hum of human cities is torture." His contemporary Percy Shelley put it more epitaphically in even fewer words: "Hell is a city like London."

There were of course U.S. counterparts. One of the fullest treatments of native-son variations on the same theme appears in *The Intellectuals versus the City* (1962), where historians of philosophy Morton and Lucia White dip into two centuries of Americans' writings about their cities.[1]

Not all men or women of letters were nettled by the American city. For example, some, like Walt Whitman, carried on an unabashed, unabated love affair with New York. Whitman communicates his extravagant image of the object of his ardor in the line, "I find in this visit to [Manhattan] and the daily contact and rapport with its myriad people . . . the best, most effective medicine my soul has yet partaken." Such solo voices aside, the Whites call particular attention to "the volume of the anti-urban roar in the national literary pantheon . . . [that has been sounded] in unison by figures who represent major tendencies in American thought."[2]

One of the giants among these figures was Thomas Jefferson, agrarian apostle of the Enlightenment and staunch preacher of the democratic canon that people are the best judges of what is best for them. Paradoxically, despite growing multitudes electing to settle places like London, Paris, Boston, New York, and Philadelphia, Jefferson in his middle years referred to them as "the mobs of great cities," which were "cancers on the body politic." He later reluctantly conceded that cities were economically necessary for a developing country like the United States. But near the end of his long life he could write: "City life offers you . . . vice and wretchedness. New York, for example, like London, seems to be a Cloacina of all the depravities of human nature."[3,4]

The Whites' cast of U.S. anti-urbanists include, among others, Emerson and Thoreau, Theodore Dreiser and John Dewey, Frank Lloyd Wright and pioneer urban sociologist Robert Park, to whom I shall return below.

The Whites note that "those figures form a body of intellectual lore and tradition which continues to affect the thought and action about the American city today."[5] Long-term observers of the proceedings in Congress or any state legislature have hardly known a year in which each of these elected bodies has not reflected this "lore and tradition," although rarely, until recently, in explicit terms.

John Lindsay has commented that "we *do* make public policy out of private prejudices," and in particular "the federal government, which has historically established our national priorities, has never really thought the American city was 'worthy' of improvement."[6] An illustration of the point is to be found in a *New York Times* editorial (April 20, 1973). It caustically noted that on the issue of appropriating already authorized funds for expanding urban mass transportation facilities, "the anti-urban forces [in the House of Representatives] succeeded in denying [such funds] to cities poisoned by exhaust fumes and immobilized by collapsing transportation systems. . . . The single-minded claque of an America of roaring highways brushed aside all rational arguments, in total lack of concern about the inescapable fact that the nation cannot prosper while its cities are being strangled."

In 1975, this congressional tendency was vented with unprecedented force on New York in particular. At the time of the city's severest fiscal crisis, and request for federal backing of its credit, the local press reported this response from the nation's capital: "A deep-rooted Congressional hostility to New York City [surfaced] in dozens of cloakroom interviews in which legislators were openly critical not only of New York's municipal management . . . but also of the city itself. . . ."

Subsequently, on a head-of-state visit abroad, the President responded to New York's crisis with a public castigation, reflecting, according to some Washington observers, that "Mr. Ford's real constituency [is] . . . anti-city Middle America." This led the *New York Times* (September 15, 1975) to comment editorially: "When a multibillion dollar private corporation is skidding into bankruptcy, alarm arouses the Administration out of do-nothingness. But when the nation's largest city is in trouble, the Administration adopts the three blind mice as its policy-making model. Indeed, Mr. Ford seems to gloat over New York's distress."

Urban sociologists and historians will doubtless mark this episode as revealing a level of animus toward the "city of cities" that was at an all-time high of explicit political expression.

A Texas writer reflected a broader view of national attitudes toward the Empire City:

New York's [fiscal] fate has inflamed a confused hostility that runs deep and bitter, that cuts across class and racial lines, that knows no geographic boundaries. Much of that hostility is a prejudice against the city's very character. Its accents are not our accents, its neighborhoods are not our neighborhoods, its life style not our life style. . . . But the hostility is more than that—it is the historic prejudice provinces have for their capital city. . . .

Like a magnet [capitals] both attract and repel, they draw from their provinces both love and hate. Although Washington may be our political capital, in every other way New York has been America's center, and we, in terms of geography and power, its provinces; it has told us what to wear, how to act, what to think, what to buy.

We need New York because it is our nation's center of excellence, the stage for the best talent in America, whether that talent be in business, the arts, communication, or finance. We also need New York because it has been our safety valve. Not only has it given our best talents their big chance, it has also taken off our hands millions of people down to their last chance. Each time some poor soul spends his last dollar on a Greyhound ticket to New York City we can cross one more human problem off our ledger books, and New York has one more person on its overburdened welfare rolls. New York is more than just any city—it is a symbol of both the best and worst in America.*

Someone else has summed up the great city as "a volatile compound of every virtue and every vice-versa known to men." Militant anti-urbanists, on the other hand, see only what is apparently wrong with the city, dismiss all that is right or excellent, and shrug off what is improving or improvable. Moreover, with anti-urbanists vocal, intellectually influential, and politically muscular, much of what has been considered wrong with the city—and in some particular ways

* William Broyle, "The Capitol Letter," *Texas Monthly*, reprinted with permission in *New York* magazine, January 12, 1976.

getting worse—may be self-fulfilling prognoses that their biases have helped to bring about. Included, by way of one more illustration, are federal failures to regulate the traffic in guns,[7] controls most heavily opposed by the rural citizenry.[8]

If the present writer here focusses on anti-urbanism as a sociopolitical ideology, it is not out of uncritical, pro-city partisanship, but to the end of tracing its relevance to central scientific concerns of this study. To state my thesis in advance: For over a century, American theory and research on the psychological consequences of small-town versus big-city life, springing from a substrate of anti-urban aversion, have sharpened ancient stereotypes that distorted national perceptions, flouted democratic values, and at times disfigured legislated policies.

I call attention not merely to philosophers like Emerson, Thoreau, or Dewey. I am referring more specifically to social scientists and psychiatric thinkers in this country and elsewhere. Almost from its beginnings as an empirical discipline, sociology was transfixed with the industrial city, its growth pains and problems and, above all, its loss of qualities believed to have been distinctively embodied in the small, pre-industrial community.

Robert Park is an especially interesting case in point.[9] He grew up in a small nineteenth-century town, became in turn a newspaperman, a student of philosophy, then of social theory, and went on to lead the University of Chicago department of sociology. In the 1920's and 1930's, that department was a colossus in American urban sociological thought and research. Park characteristically saw the metropolis as a kind of transient hotel wrought large, "a world in which man is henceforth *condemned to live*" (italics added), reflecting, say the Whites, "his disappointment over the fact that a return to the rural past was impossible."[10] Wendell Bell, a contemporary urbanologist, considers that Park and his students "gave a one-sided and partially false picture of the nature of urban life in its exaggerated portrayal of personal and social disorganization."[11] Summing up, sociologist S. H. Aronson writes: "The Chicago School brought the prestige of science to the support of an anti-urban tradition in America that long antedated the development of sociology. . . ."[12]

Park and his followers, like so many others, were misled in part by nostalgic idealization of what Marcel Proust called "remembrance of things past," and in part by Alfred North Whitehead's "fallacy of misplaced concreteness." By their central, but not exclusive, interest in the social pathology of the city, Chicago sociologists were drawn to study behavioral disorders in slums, rooming-house sections, and deteriorating areas adjoining the expanding central business district— all worthy research targets in their own right. But when they converted their findings about these problem-ridden core areas into generalizations about the genus metropolis as an entity, they were, of course, exceeding the reach of their data. This tendency probably reached its culminating expression in the thought of Louis Wirth,[13] one of Park's Chicago successors.

The anti-city bias endemic in articulate segments of American society was also in part cause and in part effect of an old and related tendency within psychiatry as well. In the United States, the tradition was started in the late eighteenth century by Dr. Benjamin Rush, "upper-crust" Philadelphian, signer of the Declaration of Independence, friend of Thomas Jefferson, and author of the first American textbook on psychiatry.[14] He there advanced his considered opinion that cities are "pestilential to the morals, the health, and the liberties of man." His psychiatric successors, medical superintendents of American mental hospitals, in the middle of the nineteenth century drew upon the premorbid social settings of their patients for empirical support of Rush's thesis.

In those years, the mental hospital population was rapidly increasing, coinciding with industrialization and urbanization in the northeastern states. Moreover, the inflow of patients from rural areas in those states lagged behind those from the cities. These trends seemed to confirm the anti-urbanists and persuade others as well that city living is intrinsically conducive to mental disorder.

Reflecting a closely related bias, antebellum southern hospital superintendents noted higher mental hospital rates among freed Negroes in northern cities than among rural southern slaves. These statistics were taken up by the anti-Abolitionists to support the position that for blacks slavery was psychologically "salutary," whereas they were especially prone to insanity in "the unnatural condition" of freedom. These ideologues neglected to mention the fact that if the northern states grudgingly admitted black patients to their mental hospitals, the southern states were adamantly opposed,[15] largely accounting for regional differences in Negro rates.

In the post–Civil War era, northern hospitals found recent Irish immigrants from seaboard cities filling their wards. Given these rising admissions, prominent hospital superintendents proposed segregation of all Irish patients in state almshouses, which of course lacked any semblance of therapeutic pretension. Mounting patient rates persuaded them that "the Irish race is especially prone to mental illness, preeminently incurable," and, moreover, they "aggravate" the condition of fellow patients of other national origins.[16]

By the early decades of the twentieth century, nativist anti-Irish fever had abated. But cresting mental hospitalizations of migrants from southern and eastern Europe prompted a political movement to bar the immigration of these newcomers in particular. Such hospital reports, reflecting their writers' "intense dislike for their immigrant patients," were used in congressional hearings "to build up the notion of the innate inferiority" of these recent settlers. The hearings culminated in the Quota Laws of 1921 and 1924 that discriminated against applicants from countries in southern and eastern Europe.[17]

Thus, mental hospitalization differentials between urban and rural populations, blacks and whites, immigrants and natives, heated up simmering prejudices, spilled into the legislative mills, and there were turned into national policies discriminatory against large segments of the American population, above all those living in cities.[18] It is no surprise, therefore, that a leading member of the House of Representatives a decade ago wrote that congressional "legislation is often a travesty of what the national welfare requires."[19]

In the light of such heavy political fallouts, it is necessary to emphasize anew that conclusions of the kind just reviewed, drawn from rates of admissions to mental hospitals, also violate a fundamental "law" of evidence. From the social characteristics of state hospital patients (those in high-cost private institutions were rarely included), generalizations were extracted about the pathological predispositions of corresponding social groups in the general American population.

Past professional prejudices and evidential fallacies aside, what is the current situation in the age-long controversy about the respective effects of small town and big city life on the well-being of their residents?

THE PHYSICAL HEALTH SITUATION

Let us start with recent research on somatic health as measured by disease-specific morbidity and mortality rates. In the past, morbidity and mortality rates of the acute infectious diseases have almost always been higher in the city than anywhere else. And it has been widely accepted, almost as a law of the urban condition, that they would continue so. However, this "law" is now being rewritten. In recent decades national morbidity studies have shown that rural-metropolitan differences in the frequencies of such illnesses have been steadily shrinking.

For example, we can refer to one of the recent National Health Interview Survey Reports (1974) on acute disorders in the United States.[20] As defined there, "an acute condition is a condition which has lasted less than three months and which has involved either medical attention or restricted activity." General types included are respiratory (accounting for more than half the total), infective, digestive, injuries, and "all others." The rate is expressed in the "number of acute conditions per 100 persons per year."

The place-of-residence spectrum is divided nationally into three U.S. Census Bureau populations: (1) All Standard Metropolitan Statistical Areas (SM),* (2) Non-SM–Nonfarm population (NF), (3) Non-SM–Farm population (F).

If we exclude the injury category (because it represents etiologically an entirely different order of malfunction than the predominantly infectious conditions), the rates for the three populations, by my calculations, are 167, 165, 142, respectively, there being no difference between the two nonfarm populations.

However, when we compare the frequencies in the SM and NF groups by age we find:

1. Below age 5, the metropolitan rate is somewhat higher than that of the NF population, as it is in the 25 to 44 range as well.
2. Within ages 5 to 24, the SM and NF frequencies are almost identical.
3. In the entire age range beyond 45, the metropolitan rates are actually somewhat *lower* than the nonfarm frequencies.

Thus, from a comparative disadvantage in the pre-school years, the metropolitan frequencies tend to become progressively more favor-

---

* The federal definition, somewhat simplified, is as follows: "The SM contains a central city with population over 50,000, and includes the surrounding county and adjacent counties that are metropolitan in character and economically and socially integrated with the county of the central city." The nation's 243 SM's in 1970 had an average population of 575,000, varying in a range from about 75,000 to over 11,000,000.

able (relative to the other nonfarm group) upward on the adult life span.

I would next turn from the acute conditions, as defined above, to those of longer duration and assigned by the National Center for Health Statistics to the "chronic" category. Since it has been widely held that physical stress and strain, wear and tear, are intrinsic to the city's tempo and style of life, we might expect the metropolis to produce correspondingly higher morbidity rates of such presumptively stress-related, "chronic" conditions as rheumatoid arthritis, hypertension, heart disease, etc.

The most recent NCHS Report (1974) covers the prevalence of all chronic conditions associated with "limitations of activity."[21] The reported age-adjusted rates (per 100 population), with community size again trichotomized, as we see in the following, fail to support the expectation:

SM 12.2
NF 13.5
F 13.2

Moreover, for the age group over 65, where the urban "wear and tear" theory would predict the greatest differences in frequencies, the theory seemingly is contradicted by these rates:

SM 40.5
NF 47.5
F 47.8

Here, the expected differences are reversed—the metropolitan population has the lowest frequency, farm areas the highest.

NCHS in the early 1960's extended its Health Examination Survey to a large national sample of children 6 to 12 years old. One of the key questions prompting the investigation was: "In general, is country living more healthful for children than city living?" Two widely accepted indicators of physical well-being were used, namely, height and weight, with analytical control for the first time applied to a most "weighty" predictor, namely, socioeconomic status of parents.

Popular images (e.g., as projected in Norman Rockwell's illustrations) have long contrasted the tall, sturdy rural lad with his shorter, stringier peer on the city streets. How closely do these images fit the present facts? The NCHS concludes: "The data very strongly suggest that for children growing up in the 1950's and 1960's in the U.S. it makes no difference on the average either in the rate of growth or size attained at any age as to whether they live in the middle of the big city, in the country, or in a suburb, as long as one takes into account the major detectable socioeconomic factors."[22]

Wrapping it all up, a definitive summary of U.S. health trends between 1900 and 1960 concluded a decade ago as follows: "As mortality from the communicable diseases shrinks to ever lower levels, differences in the general level of health and well-being between city and country have narrowed almost to the vanishing point . . . over the years, life in the cities has taken on a healthier complexion. Thus, life expectancy in New York City in 1901 was about seven years less than in the United States for males and almost six years for females. Today [1960] differences in life expectancy between residents of New York City and the entire nation are relatively insignificant."[23]

The post-1960 evidence reviewed above suggests that by measures of physical health indices the cities have pulled up to the smaller places, and among their older people have perhaps forged ahead.

For New York City in financial crisis at the time this book went to press the situation was summed up as follows in a *New York Times* editorial (January 7, 1976):

New York City in 1975 was healthier than ever before in history. For the first time, fewer than 1% of the city's population died last year. . . . Because the city is so large, has so diversified a population, and has so many of its citizens below the poverty line, the progress here is all the more remarkable.

The city's declining death rate is a particularly impressive accomplishment because the proportion of its population over 65 has been increasing steadily since 1960. . . . The forces that lengthen life are [reflected in] the latest statistics on increasing longevity in New York City.

THE SITUATION IN MENTAL HEALTH

A drug company ad in a psychiatric journal pictures a curb-side view of two looming-downward skyscrapers with the large-type caption "Anxiety Canyon," followed below by the line, "[Drug brand name] can help you control the excessive anxiety that so often accompanies the impersonal, oppressive climate of urban living."

Two psychiatrists, in a recent book for professionals, state axiomatically, without qualification or citation of a single supporting fact or source: "Psychiatric disorders occur at a significantly higher rate in cities compared with rural areas."[24]

A writer of popular works on environmental health has a chapter entitled, "The Crude Art of Cracking Up," in his book *Crisis in Our Cities: Death, Disease and the Urban Plague*.[25] He there discusses several mental health studies. Of the present investigation he writes: "The Midtown study shows that the mental illness rates in a crowded residential area of Manhattan are probably much higher than currently accepted figures for the country as a whole." Attentive reading of the original (and this) edition of the present work "shows" nothing of the kind. In fact, we explicitly warn against interpreting our data as supporting such a conclusion or inference.

The readiness to alchemize a belief into a presumed fact about the city, as manifested in the preceding examples, can take other judgmental forms. One basic limitation in the relevant research literature had been this: Mental health studies of general populations in urban and rural habitats were generally done by different investigators, using diverse kinds of methods, data, and diagnostic criteria. Thus, firm generalizations about urban-rural differences could not be made because such studies lacked sufficient comparability.

However, a series of nine independent investigations have by now been conducted, each with the distinction of having the same personnel researching mental health in both a rural and an urban place, all located, as it happens, in the Eastern Hemisphere. Although the scientific methods, concepts, and judgmental criteria applied were inadequately reported, they presumably were the same in each pair of communities. If so, a seemingly sound basis for comparing the intrapair differences is for the first time present.

Drs. Bruce Dohrenwend and Barbara Dohrenwend have performed a singular scholarly service in scanning the literature over a thirty-year period, and have summarized and assessed findings from the nine "twin" investigations they have uncovered.

These are presented in their chapter "Psychiatric Disorder in Urban Settings" appearing in the 1974 edition of the *American Handbook of Psychiatry*.[26] Table 20–1 below is drawn from that chapter (p. 428), as reproduced from my *American Scientist* article, with additions here of percentage signs and national context of each pair of studies.

The Dohrenwends offer this summary judgment about the entire

TABLE 20–1.   TOTAL PREVALENCE OF PSYCHIATRIC DISORDERS REPORTED FOR INVESTIGATIONS INCLUDING BOTH AN URBAN AND A RURAL SITE (PERCENT IN EACH SAMPLE)

Disorders in urban site	Disorders in rural site	Urban % minus rural %	Author(s)
0.8	1.7	−0.9	Kato (Japan)
1.1	1.1	0.0	Lin (Taiwan)
1.11	1.03	+0.08	Kaila (Finland)
1.28	1.07	+0.21	Kaila (Finland)
3.0	2.7	+0.3	Tsuwaga et al. (Japan); Akimotoa et al. (Japan)
13.5	11.7	+1.8	Piotrowski et al. (Poland)
45.0	40.0	+5.0	A. H. Leighton et al. (Nigeria)
18.1	13.0	+5.1	Piotrowski et al. (Poland)
34.1	20.2	+13.9	Helgason (Iceland)

set of intrapair divergences: "On the basis of this evidence—and it is the best we have available—there appears to be a tendency for total rates of psychiatric disorder to be higher in urban than in rural areas." About the perceived "tendency" of higher disorder rates among the urban sites in the set, they make this comment: "The consistency in direction of most of the urban-rural differences reported in these studies, despite the diversity of time,* place and method of assessing disorder suggest that the results be taken seriously."

The Dohrenwends ask us to take the results seriously on the criterion of consistency in direction of "most" of the intrapair differences. (In the third column a plus sign denotes the urban rate is higher, minus that the rural rate is higher.) I suggest that before fixing on the plus-minus direction of these nine differences, the analyst must first take into account their magnitude and probable statistical reliability. To do so, we can proceed stepwise down the above table and note as follows:

1. In the first pair, the urban rate is the more favorable one (i.e., has the smaller of the two frequencies), but to a degree so slight as to deny any claim to statistical credibility.

2. In the second pair, the two rates are identical.

* This refers to the fact that three of the nine investigations were published in 1942, one in 1953, and five between 1963 and 1969.

3. In the next four pairs, the urban rates *are* higher, but by margins of far under 1 percent in three instances, and by under 2 percent in the fourth case. These differences are thin to the point of being statistically ephemeral, because they certainly belong well within the range of sampling error alone. In other words, that *each* of the four differences happens to fall in the same "plus" direction is as much a matter of chance as the separate 50–50 probability that each of four successive children in a family will be female.

The inter-rate divergences between the paired Leighton communities in Nigeria (like Piotrowski's in Poland) can on the surface be viewed as of marginal statistical substance. However, Leighton warns that his urban sample numbered only sixty-four people, which "did not give us a random sample of the town's eight sample areas," together housing a population of 80,000. Impaired by an inadequately small and nonrandom sample, the Nigerian urban rate lacks credentials both of representativeness and comparability.

We are thus left with only the Helgason pair, and perhaps Pietrowski's (5.1 percent difference), to take seriously for *both* magnitude and direction of their respective rural-urban rate differences. Let us now identify and briefly describe the city in each of those two pairs. Helgason's urban site is Reykjavík, Iceland's capital, a fishing and shipping center lacking any other industry to speak of, with a population (at the time of the study) of 65,000 largely drawn from the rest of that volcanic and glacial ("fire and ice") island at the edge of the Arctic Circle. Piotrowski's urban place is Plock, a town of 37,000 in the early stages of industrialization, situated in the heartland of predominantly agrarian Poland.

How far can we legitimately generalize from these two remaining sets of twin studies? That they cover settlements in the Old World makes it hazardous to extrapolate their findings to communities in the New. This is especially so because we now know there are pronounced differences between psychiatrists of the two hemispheres in their criteria and modes of diagnostic classification.[27] Furthermore, in any typology of exclusively Eastern Hemisphere urban places, Reykjavík and Plock not only are out of the region's socioeconomic "main stream," but in size they fall into one of its classes of smaller and least urbanized cities. As for being representative of mainstream North American cities that are a primary interest in these pages, they are probably even further afield.

All in all, the "tendency" extracted by the Dohrenwends from the nine pairs of rural-urban studies falls far short of persuasive support by criteria both of statistical substance and generalizability.*

Such twin investigations of mental health in general populations have not yet been made in North America. However, there is one pair of related studies that if not "twins" may be considered "kin." I refer to the researches in Midtown Manhattan and Stirling County,† a rural area of Nova Scotia,[28] directed not by the same investigator, but by two psychiatrists with unusually homogeneous professional vitae.

Specifically, Drs. Thomas Rennie and Alexander H. Leighton had been contemporary residents in the Johns Hopkins Department of Psychiatry under the leadership of Adolph Meyer. In the early fifties, both were Cornell professors, Leighton in the Ithaca, N.Y., campus Department of Sociology and Anthropology, Rennie in the University's New York City–based Medical College. Although their investigations were administratively autonomous, staffed separately and (in terms of disciplines represented) somewhat differently, until Rennie's death in 1956 each served as an ad hoc consultant to the other's operation.[29]

The two staffs pursued independent searches for a validated series of psychopathological signs and symptoms, but both gravitated toward the same two recently reported sources of candidate symptom questions, namely the Army's (World War II) Neuropsychiatric Screening Adjunct and the Minnesota Multiphasic Personality Inventory. It is not surprising, therefore, that among the Midtown and Stirling interview instruments' two large series of psychological signs and symptoms, many were identical, some quite similar, and some were represented in one instrument but not in the other.

While Rennie and Leighton were both key members of the Meyer "school" of psychiatry, in modes of classifying mental health status

---

* For the Dohrenwends' response to this critique and my rejoinder see Appendix G.

† Stirling County (hereafter "Stirling") is a code name for an area of 970 square miles that could encompass 44 Manhattans, but in 1950 contained a population of 20,000 (96 percent white, therefore close to Midtown's corresponding figure of 99 percent). The principal sources of livelihood were fishing, lumbering, and subsistence farming. Its rural contrasts with metropolitan Midtown could hardly be more extreme. For example, in residents per square mile the latter's population density was 75,000 and Stirling's was 20.

on the basis of their overlapping sets of symptom information there were several divergences between the two, involving technicalities that, with some exceptions, are irrelevant here. The first relevant divergence was this: Under Rennie's scheme the time framework implied in almost all of his symptom questions was "in recent weeks prior to the interview." His classification therefore referred to respondent's "current" mental health status. On the other hand, Leighton's symptom time reference and classification "procedure was focussed on estimating the probability that an interviewed individual was or had been suffering from a psychiatric disorder *at any time during his adult life* [author's italics]. There is no precise way of using the evaluations to estimate the *current prevalence* [italics added] of psychiatric disorder at the time of the survey."[30]

The original use of such different time frameworks by itself would have deprived the Stirling and Midtown prevalence results of any basis for comparison. However, the Stirling psychiatrists subsequently conducted "a review inspection of our interview protocols. [This] suggests that if we went back and used these to estimate current prevalence . . . [it would be] our conclusion from all available information . . . that at least half of the adults in Stirling County are *currently* [italics added] suffering from some psychiatric disorder defined in the American Psychiatric Association's *Diagnostic and Statistical Manual* [1952]."[31] Although lacking precision, this inferential conclusion seemingly brought the two investigations to approximately similar time frameworks for sighting mental health status frequencies.

The second interstudy divergence was this: Under Rennie's scheme, classification involved placement of all sample respondents along a single six-way continuum of symptom formation, with discerned or inferred "impairment in social functioning" as the landmark defining the boundary line of mental morbidity.

As indicated in the Stirling monograph quotation given above, Leighton's criterion of mental morbidity was a "psychiatric disorder defined in the [APA] *Diagnostic and Statistical Manual* of 1952." Leighton considered this as providing landmarks for defining "a psychiatric case."[32] Rennie regarded his "impaired" category as covering symptomatic equivalents of psychiatric patients observed in his long hospital and clinical experience.[33]

Therefore, Leighton's "psychiatric case" and Rennie's counterpart of "socially impaired" psychiatric patients might be taken to approach, if hardly to achieve, approximate equivalence. Given such seeming approach, the two studies may lend themselves to cautious comparison. On this guarded assumption, we can now note that the Midtown current impairment rate was 23.7 percent and its Stirling equivalent was estimated as "at least half" of the interviewed sample. Let us accept this "least" 50 percent figure as the Stirling rate, representing a prevalence frequency about twice that of Midtown.

However, before taking that one-to-two difference seriously, we must carefully take into account disparities in the demographic composition of the two communities that yielded the difference.

1. Although French-speaking Acadians have been natives of the county for centuries, no foreign-born elements are mentioned in the Stirling publications, whereas they constitute fully one-third of the Midtown sample. Excluding the immigrant generation lowers the Midtown impairment rate to about 22 percent.

2. On the basis of scattered bits of information available in the Leighton reports I gather this decided impression: In socioeconomic class composition, about 95 percent of Stirling's adult population more or less approximate the lowest 30 percent of the SES distribution in Midtown's American-born respondents.

a. If that is so, we can take this 30 percent subsample of the Midtown native-born population, numbering 315 respondents, as a rough match of the Stirling sample.

b. The mental impairment rate of this narrowed Midtown segment is slightly over 33 percent.

3. The Midtown sample confined itself to the prime-of-life age 20 to 59 range. The Stirling sample set no upper age limit, with the result that 27 percent of its members were over the age of 59.

a. When the Stirling age 60-plus segment is excluded, the distributions of the two native-born subsamples across the 20 to 59 adult span are quite similar, as are their sex ratios.

b. By this exclusion we can match the Stirling sample to Midtown's age distribution, just as we "matched" Midtown to Stirling's nativity and SES composition.

c. The Leighton reports do not make it possible to exactly calculate the current "psychiatric disorder" frequency in the matched Stirling under-age-60 groups. However, on the basis of a Stirling volume graph[34] I estimate that excluding the elderly would probably lower the Leighton's estimated Stirling disorder rate by roughly 5 percent, i.e., from 50 percent to about 45 percent.

We started with unstandardized, estimated morbidity rates of 24 percent and 50 percent for Midtown and Stirling, respectively. By crudely matching the two subsamples to each other we have a foundation of demographic comparability in race, nativity, age, sex and socioeconomic class, and thereby have narrowed that 26 percent gap in estimation by approximately one half, i.e., to the 12 percent difference between 33 percent and 45 percent. By the test of significance of difference between two proportions, this 12 percent deviation would be statistically significant at the .01 level of confidence. On balance, taking appropriate qualifications into account, we appear to have a noteworthy residual difference in estimated mental morbidity rates, yielded by two studies that were kindred rather than twin research operations.

Compared to the nine sets of investigations reviewed by the Dohrenwends, the Midtown and Stirling studies as a pair have several advantages of their own:

1. They are both sited in North American places.
2. Midtown stands at the extreme metropolitan end of the rural-urban range, whereas the nine East Hemisphere urban sites are dispersed across cities of considerable variation along the lower end of the urban population–size spectrum. We could expect that the polar sociological contrasts between Stirling and Midtown afford an optimal test of hypotheses about the effects of community size on their residents' emotional well-being.
3. Unlike the Eastern Hemisphere set of twin investigations, the roughly comparable Midtown and Stirling morbidity rates have been here derived by conservatively estimated sample matching, a procedure applied to narrow intersample differences in demographic composition. Given the near universality of such differences between small and large localities, particularly in demographic respects relevant to mental health, analytical controls are as essential for intersample as for intrasample comparisons.

With such controls applied to data from two investigations conducted in the early 1950's, we find, perhaps for the first time in a long-tilled field, that a resident metropolitan population emerges with a lesser prevalence of mental impairment than a demographically matched sample of ruralites.[35]

However, Midtown and Stirling are each a single case drawn from a universe of communities at opposite poles of the North American continuum of local habitat types. Therefore, in the absence of independent supporting evidence, it would be inappropriate to generalize from them to their respective parent universes.

The passage of time, however, has brought us relevant independent evidence from two more recent investigations. The first is reported in the U.S. National Center for Health Statistics document entitled *Selected Symptoms of Psychological Distress* (1970). That report is based on the Health Examination Survey of a national probability sample of 6,672 adults who, in 1960–1962, were medically examined and interviewed in mobile clinics.

For the first time in any NCHS investigation, the interview included twelve self-reported symptoms of the kind used in the Midtown Manhattan and Stirling County studies. Ten were validated against the other two, namely, self-reported nervous breakdown, experienced or felt impending, and all of the ten presented "moderate to high correlations" with the two nervous-breakdown items.

Moreover, for the first time in any mental health investigation known to me, the entire community-size variable was divided into five categories, ranging from "giant metropolitan statistical areas" (cities and their fringe suburban areas with total populations of 3,000,000 and over), "other very large metropolitan statistical areas" (populations 500,000 to 3,000,000), other "standard metropolitan statistical areas" (50,000 to 500,000), "other urban areas" (2,500 to 50,000), to rural areas (of less than 2,500). It has also been possible to split the latter into predominantly farm or nonfarm areas.

Counting the actual and near nervous-breakdown items as one symptom and giving each symptom present a score of one produced a respondent score range of 0 to 11, and permitted the determination of age-adjusted mean symptom scores. These group mean scores for the rural-metropolitan variable do not appear in the report mentioned above, but have been made available to me, controlled for sex, by the NCHS. I am presenting them in table 20–2 for the white segment of the national sample to match the almost totally white populations of Midtown and Stirling.

In the men's column, a dichotomy is apparent, with the three largest (SMSA) categories of cities showing the lowest scores and the three smallest categories of localities the highest scores. The differences between the two sets of males are not wide; but they are reinforced by the identical dichotomy among the women, where the differences between the two sets of community places are substantial.

To my knowledge, the data in table 20–2 are the first of their

TABLE 20–2.   NCHS NATIONAL HEALTH EXAMINATION SURVEY (1960–1962), WHITE AGE-ADJUSTED MEAN PSYCHOLOGICAL SYMPTOM SCORES BY SEX AND POPULATION-SIZE LOCALITIES IN A SAMPLE OF THE U.S. POPULATION

	Men	Women
Giant metropolitan statistical areas	1.53	2.73
Other very large metropolitan statistical areas	1.65	2.77
Other standard metropolitan statistical areas	1.63	2.70
Other urban areas	1.98	3.26
Rural areas, nonfarm	1.90	3.14
Rural areas, farm	1.81	3.25

kinds to be drawn from a national sample with the entire metropolitan-rural spectrum delineated. Scores in the two extreme categories confirm the different morbidity rates of the matched Midtown and Stirling samples both in direction and relative magnitude.

I must add that the above scores have been standardized for age, sex, and race, but not for differences in socioeconomic mix. Relevant here, however, is that the symptom mean scores break dichotomously at the 50,000 population-size line. This suggests the unlikelihood that linear SES variations can be large enough to appreciably reduce the noteworthy parallelism between (a) the U.S. extreme locality-type symptom-score differences, and (b) the demographically matched Midtown-Stirling morbidity rate differences. Helgason's reversed crude rate findings from Reykjavík and rural Iceland hardly stand up as a credible challenge to the parallel metropolitan-rural trends here uncovered for the first time in the three largest and most analytically controlled investigations ever conducted on the North American continent.

The second investigation referred to above is of a totally new kind, involving a survey of all pharmacists in the predominantly white, Anglo-Saxon population of New Zealand, a member nation of the British Commonwealth. Each pharmacist was asked "to list every tranquilizer prescription by strength, client sex, and prescribed daily dosage . . . that he filled on an average day."[36] Webb and Collette add that the information provided was "adjusted and aggregated for each [community] to provide an index of the average number of prescriptions filled." Part of their data appeared in the above cited article; part, yet to be published, was conveyed to this writer in a personal letter from Webb.

The Webb-Collette unpublished data classify size of corporate places in six categories of population numbers from under 1,000 to over 100,000. I have the authors' permission to note this overall finding: Per capita psychotropic drug prescription rate varies inversely with size of locality, the rural rate being over twice that of the biggest cities.

On the issue of SES differences among New Zealand localities the Webb–Collette article notes previous studies that "found no association between socioeconomic status and psychotropic drug use [rates]. Furthermore, any supposed effects of socioeconomic status on physician utilization would most likely have only limited influence in the New Zealand context, for all prescribed pharmaceuticals are free and only a token charge is made for physician services."[37]

Because the NCHS and New Zealand investigations are to my knowledge the first of their respective kinds, their findings must be viewed with appropriate caution. It is suggestive, however, that the general rural-urban trends in the above two, relatively recent, surveys are similar. Moreover, as already noted, their data also coincide with the morbidity rate differences I have extracted from approximately matched demographic segments of the Midtown and Stirling sample populations, in studies conducted some years earlier.

THE SITUATION IN SUICIDE RATES

We have reviewed evidence on rural-urban differences in the prevalence of somatic and mental morbidity, with new trends visibly emerging in both. We can complete this survey by briefly scanning recent data on two forms of destructive behavior. These involve violence against the self, and crimes against others, with the frequencies of each type often regarded as indicators of differential community well-being.

Violence against the self has been measured by suicide rates, per 100,000 population, as reported by physicians on death certificates. Like other "official" statistics, this too is beset by major, and as yet refractory, deficiencies.[38]

Specifically, such figures cannot be regarded as even close approximations to the true incidence of suicide. However, if the unknown margins of underreporting have not shifted radically over recent decades, then a trend in a time series of reported suicide frequencies may roughly parallel the trend in the true suicide rates.

On that tentative, open-ended assumption, let us first consider reported suicide frequencies between 1929 and 1959. In the former year, available reported rates, as then dichotomized simply for rural and urban places, were 11.0 and 17.4 respectively. By 1959, however, the former frequency was down slightly to 10.0, whereas the urban rate had fallen by almost 40 percent to 10.7.

According to a personal communication from the Mortality Statistics Division of the National Center for Health Statistics, more recent corresponding information is not yet available. But we do have approximations suggesting further marked changes by 1967.

1. In that year, the reported age-adjusted suicide frequency for the United States was 11.1.

2. In the same year, according to the Urban Institute,[39] the average corresponding rate for eighteen large cities was 12.7.

3. However, eight of those cities had rates lower than the 11.1 national frequency, with New York's 7.7 standing as the lowest of all.

The narrow category of large cities in 1967 and the broader category of urban places in 1959 are not comparable. On the surface, however, it would appear that in 1967 at least eight of the listed large cities were continuing the falling trend of reported urban suicide rates that obtained in the period 1929–1959.

Fuller data may or may not substantiate this observation. If they do, and our previously mentioned underlying assumption is not contradicted by appropriate evidence, this conclusion would be in order: the peak rates of suicide characterizing the biggest cities since medically certified data were first assembled have been largely, if not yet completely, levelled.

THE SITUATION IN CRIME RATES

Finally, there is new evidence on frequencies of a related kind of violent behavior. For as long as police registers have been the source of national (FBI) Uniform Crime Report statistics,[40] the latter have consistently shown that cities, and above all the largest cities, have been the most crime-ridden places on the entire national scene.[41,42] This applied to both adult and juvenile delinquencies.

However, at this writing we have the first results of a pair of investigations of high school boys in Philadelphia and in a "nonmetropolitan county" in Oregon. Both followed the careers of their subjects from the age of 15 to age 18. A preliminary NIMH summary of findings reports as follows:

In the days when the United States was primarily a country of farms and small towns it was generally believed that teenage delinquency was almost entirely confined to cities. Even today many people think that teenage boys who live outside metropolitan areas get into substantially less trouble than their city cousins, and that when they do their scrapes are usually minor.

Perhaps surprisingly, studies made in recent years have shown that there is no basis for this common assumption—non-metropolitan youths have just about as many run-ins with the law as [racially matched] metropolitan youths, and the causes of these confrontations are often of roughly equal seriousness in both towns and cities.[43]

Police registers share with mental hospital records the serious deficiency that they reveal "only the tip of the iceberg." Hospital enumerations miss the disabled who are untreated or are treated as outpatients, whereas FBI compilations miss the crimes unreported to or by the police authorities.[44]

A technical advance in measuring the overall incidence of crime is being made in current surveys by the Census Bureau for the U.S. Law Enforcement Assistance Administration (LEAA). These involve not police reports, but interviews with large population samples and the confidential testimony of respondents who are surviving victims[45] of one or more crimes.

The first of these surveys is questioning a National Crime Panel of people from 60,000 households in 26 major American cities and hundreds of smaller areas. The second covers 22,000 residents and 2,000 business men in each of thirteen selected cities, varying in size from Portland, Oregon (population 383,000), to New York. Made available at the time of this writing are only the preliminary results of the investigation for the latter range of medium-to-largest cities.[46]

In announcing these findings, the *New York Times* (April 21, 1974) opened its article with the following observations:

Johnny Carson jokes about it, Europeans are horrified by it and New Yorkers are sure of it: New York is the crime capital of the United States of America. . . . Last week the nearly universal preconceptions were challenged . . . according to a Federal report, New York is significantly safer than any other major American city and some of the smaller ones as well.

To summarize the results briefly:

1. The LEAA frequencies, even with homicides excluded, on the average exceed the FBI compiled rates by 260 percent.

2. With specific reference to crimes of violence against persons, i.e., assault, robbery, attempted rape and rape, the annual "victim report" rate per 1,000 residents (age twelve and over) was at a low of 36 in New York and at highs of 59, 63, 67, and 68 in Portland, Philadelphia, Denver, and Detroit, respectively.

3. New York was also lowest of the covered cities in frequencies of "household victimization" (breaking and entering for thefts of property) per 1,000 households.

Further results and technical assessments of the two ground-breaking surveys will be issued in the years ahead, in particular with findings from small urban and rural places. At this writing, however, "nearly universal preconceptions" about heaviest frequencies of force-involved criminal incidents, at least in the middle-to-top size range of cities, seem to be approaching resemblance to Humpty Dumpty's "great fall."

It has been implicit in anti-urbanist thinking that the larger the community the higher the rates of such overlapping forms of pathology as somatic illness, mental disorder, suicide, juvenile and adult crime. To be sure, serious reservations have long been registered about the accuracy of measurement techniques applied to all of these manifestations of individual and community dysfunction. However, in recent years methods applied to four of these indices have been appreciably improved.

We must assume that varying margins of underreporting remain in all of them. Even so, it is a striking fact that all five indicators are sounding the same *new* message in *unison*: The traditional linear correlation—the bigger the place, the worse it is—seems "no longer operative." In the face of this unanimity, it seems the time has come to redraw the contrasting millennia-old city versus country images to fit the recently emerging facts.

Parenthetically, it is ironical that this historical turnabout in the apparent well-being of American city dwellers has surfaced at a time of deepening crisis in the fiscal affairs of their municipalities. The current political responses at the federal level to this widespread crisis have potentially important sociopsychological and policy implications for the future of the city. These are being held for discussion in concluding chapter 23.

The traditional image of rural and small-town America seems also in process of being redrawn. In the past decade a little noticed series of nonfiction works have appeared[47] documenting that our smaller places (both here and abroad) are not, and probably never were, benign havens of untroubled "serenity, tranquility, and stability." One disillusioned ruralite among the many who did not escape to the city speaks of "shattered cherished myths." Another deflates "the fantasy of the city dweller about the superiority of rural life over urban life." A third, foreshadowing the New Zealand study discussed just above, notes: "Our drug stores sell a lot of tranquilizers and pep pills." A distinguished historian-reviewer of one of these books comments on its revelations as follows:

The reality of rural life, and it comes through in this book with authenticity, is harsh. Discomfort, isolation, dependence on the whims of nature, the bare revelations of life and death, the inevitable predacity of living beings, the need for social intercourse but the treachery of social pressure, the unrelenting rhythm of hard work—all these form the other side of the coin of which we prefer to see only the side showing the image of the noble savage. Many people cannot tolerate this kind of life. Mental illness is often high in rural areas.[48]

Another reviewer of the same book sums it up succinctly: "On the whole, I'd prefer hell. Or even Philadelphia."

At both ends of the rural-metropolitan continuum we seem to be breaking through ancient stereotypical barriers and confronting current existential realities that, on the whole, big cities are no more Shelley's "Hell"[49] than our open places are Rousseau's approximation of "Paradise Regained."

NOTES

1. See also the subsequent works: A. L. Strauss, ed., *The American City: A Sourcebook of Urban Imagery*, 1968, and J. B. Quandt, *From the Small Town to the Great Community: The Social Thought of Progressive Intellectuals*, 1970.

2. M. White and L. White, *The Intellectuals versus the City*, 1962, p. 2.

3. Ibid., p. 19.

4. Jefferson was of course a Virginia aristocrat, and according to his biographer Dumas Malone: "He was a highbrow, built his home on a mountain top, didn't like to rub shoulders with people. . . ." (*New York Times*, January 9, 1975).

5. White and White, *The Intellectual versus the City*, p. 3.

6. *The City*, 1969, p. 5.

7. The Federal Gun Control Act of 1968 (banning mail-order sales) "has failed . . . to reduce the illegal use of firearms. . . . the appalling slaughter [a threefold increase in homicides since 1968] so plainly attributable to the uncontrolled traffic in firearms will not abate until ownership of guns is effectively regulated by Federal laws which can and will be enforced." (*New York Times*, editorial, January 3, 1975.) On the same issue, one New York City Congressman expressed the view that "we are literally out of our minds to allow 2.5 million new weapons to be manufactured every year for the sole purpose of killing people."

8. Recent opinion polls have shown 75 percent of adults favoring a law that would require a police permit to buy a gun. Regardless of size of community only about one in five opposed such a law—except in rural areas where the opposition was almost twice as large.

9. R. H. Turner, *Robert E. Park: Selected Papers*, 1967.

10. White and White, *The Intellectuals versus the City*, p. 162.

11. "The City, The Suburb, and a Theory of Social Choice," in S. Greer et al., eds., *The New Urbanization*, 1968, p. 136. See also E. Mayo, *Human Problems of an Industrial Civilization*, 1933, p. 141.

12. "The City: Nostalgia, Illusion and Reality," in I. Howe and M. Harrington, eds., *The Seventies*, 1972, p. 432.

13. L. Wirth, "Urbanism as a Way of Life," *American Journal of Sociology* 44, no. 1 (1938): 1–24.

14. B. Rush, *Medical Inquiries and Observations upon the Diseases of the Mind* (1798), 1972.

15. N. Dain, *Concepts of Insanity in the United States: 1789–1865*, 1964, pp. 105–108.

16. Ibid., pp. 99–104.

17. W. S. Bernard, *American Immigration Policy: A Reappraisal*, 1950, pp. 23–24. Bernard notes that "the use of out-dated population statistics was the most flagrantly discriminatory device of any employed in quota calculation, and it made particularly obvious the motives which were behind the quota legislation."

18. For exploitation of a related form of institutional statistics, see K. Weis and M. E. Milakovich, "Political Misuses of Crime Rates," *Society* 11 (July–August 1974): 27–33.

19. H. Bolling, *House out of Order*, 1965.

20. National Center for Health Statistics, *Acute Conditions, July 1972–June 1973*, series 10, no. 98, (1974).

21. National Center for Health Statistics (NCHS), *Limitation of Activity and Mobility Due to Chronic Conditions 1972*, series 10, no. 96 (1974), p. 6. See also NCHS, *Rheumatoid Arthritis in Adults*, series 11, no. 17 (1966), table 7, p. 20, and NCHS, *Hypertension and Hypertensive Heart Disease in Adults*, series 11, no. 13 (1966), p. 17.

22. National Center for Health Statistics, *Height and Weight of Children*, series 11, no. 13 (1966), p. 17.

23. M. Lerner and D. W. Anderson, *Health Progress in the U.S.: 1900–1960*, 1963, pp. 105–106.

24. P. M. Insel and R. H. Moos, eds., *Health and the Social Environment*, 1974, p. 8.

25. L. Herber, *Crisis in Our Cities*, 1965, p. 140.

26. S. Arieti, ed., 1974, pp. 424–447. The authors generously made available a prepublication draft of their chapter.

For earlier summaries of the relevant literature see A. R. Mangus and John R. Seeley, *Mental Health and Mental Disorder*, 1955, pp. 209–214; Eleanor Leacock, "Three Social Variables and the Occurrence of Mental Disorder," in A. H. Leighton et al., eds., *Explorations in Social Psychiatry*, 1957, pp. 308–340; and S. C. Plog, "Urbanization and Psychological Disorders," in S. C. Plog and R. B. Edgerton, eds., *Changing Perspectives in Mental Illness*, 1969, pp. 288–311.

27. Diagnostic differences of this kind exist even between two psychiatric communities having so much in common, and so advanced, as London and New York. See J. E. Cooper et al., *Psychiatric Diagnosis in New York and London*, 1972. See also M. Kramer, "Cross-National Study of Diagnosis of the Mental Disorders," *American Journal of Psychiatry*, Supp. (April 1969): 1–11.

28. D. C. Leighton et al., *The Character of Danger*, 1963. See also A. H. Leighton, *My Name Is Legion*, 1959, and C. C. Hughes et al., *People of Cove and Woodlot: Communities from the Viewpoint of Social Psychiatry*, 1960.

29. Leighton was named director of the Midtown Study in 1956, when the latter's data gathering and mental health classification processes were both completed. He continued as director of the Stirling investigation.

30. D. C. Leighton, et al., *The Character of Danger*, p. 356.

31. Ibid.

32. Ibid., pp. 46–47.

33. In Rennie's clinical view, being in outpatient psychiatric treatment was by itself no necessary sign of "impairment in social functioning."

34. Ibid., p. 260.

35. For the Leightons' comparison of the Stirling and Midtown studies see their chapter "Mental Health and Social Factors" in A. M. Freedman and H. I. Kaplan, eds., *Comprehensive Textbook of Psychiatry*, 1967, pp. 1520–1525.

36. S. D. Webb and J. Collette, "Urban Ecological and Household Correlates of Stress-Alleviative Drug Use," *American Behaviorial Scientist* 18 (July 1975): 752–772.

37. Ibid., p. 755.

38. For a full critique see J. M. Henslin and J. C. Campbell, "Sociology and the Study of Suicide: Issues and Controversies," in P. M. Roman and H. M. Trice, eds., *Explorations in Psychiatric Sociology*, 1974, pp. 159–184.

39. M. J. Flax, *A Study in Comparative Urban Indicators*, 1972, p. 39.

40. For a fuller discussion of the shortcomings of police reporting of crimes, see Weis and Milakovich, "Political Misuses of Crime Rates," pp. 27–33.

41. Personal observations suggest that in the absence of competitive press, radio, and TV coverage of crimes, nonreporting of such events, both to and by the local police, is substantially greater in small places than in the metropolis.

42. *Social Indicators, 1973,* published by U.S. Department of Commerce, Social and Economic Statistics Administration, 1974, pp. 45, 55.

43. NIMH Research Report No. 5, "Teenage Delinquency in Small Town America, 1974," 1975, pp. 1–7. Also, M. E. Wolfgang, "Crimes in A Birth Cohort," *Proceedings of the American Philosophical Society* 117, no. 5 (1973): 404–411; F. L. Richmond, "Rural Delinquency and Maturational Reform: Extent and Character of Official Deviancy" (unpublished report of Marion County Youth Study, 1974).

44. Recent studies have shown that the high overall correlation between city size and (FBI-reported) rates of violent crime is almost entirely accounted for by intercity differences in such census-type indices as unemployment rate, racial composition, and proportion of families with female heads, all three closely associated with poverty. These findings suggest that high crime rates are not intrinsic to the city as such, but rather to the poverty that tends to be more densely concentrated within it.

45. According to NCHS latest age-adjusted figure (1970) the U.S. annual homicide rate of 7.6 per 100,000 population, while the largest in the world, is too small to significantly affect the findings of the LEAA surveys.

46. U.S. Department of Justice National Crime Panel Surveys, *Crime in the Nation's Five Largest Cities,* advance report, April 1974, and *Crime in Eight* [Other] *American Cities,* advance report, July 1974.

47. I would cite the following in particular: Page Smith, *As A City Upon A Hill: The Town in American History,* 1966; R. Blythe, *Akenfield: Portrait of an English Village,* 1969; E. Morin, *The Red and the White: Report from a French Village,* 1970; E. Rosskam, *Roosevelt, New Jersey: Big Dreams in a Small Town and What Time Did to Them,* 1972; and Raymond Williams, *The Country and the City,* 1973.

48. Lawrence Wylie in *Trans-Action,* May 1970, p. 59.

49. In B.J.L. Berry, *The Human Consequences of Urbanization,* 1973 (The Making of the Twentieth Century Series), the author identifies himself (pp. 32, 58) with the revisionist view of the city as formulated in an earlier version of the present chapter. Berry joins in a critique of the long tradition of unfavorable evaluations of the metropolis that preceded and followed the Park-Wirth-Chicago school of thought.

CHAPTER 21

SUMMING UP, 1975

LEO SROLE

Whatever their separate particularities of time, place, characters, and reporting styles, a novel like James Joyce's *Ulysses*, for example, and a research monograph like the present one, are each, in Émile Zola's phrase, "a study of humanity." Their overarching subject matter is accompanied by a common undergirding framework. To illustrate:

1. His *Ulysses*, Joyce indicates, is the odyssey of Stephen Dedalus, Leopold Bloom, and their familiars as they criss-cross each other's paths through the central sections of Dublin on one noteworthy but unsingular day of their lives. To be sure, the Midtown investigation randomly corralled a far larger company of characters; and what we learned emerged during our encounters as we joined each in his or her Manhattan home for several hours of one particular, seemingly commonplace day.

2. Joyce, like his contemporary, Sigmund Freud, plumbed each of his character's interior, meandering streams of affect-laden ruminations. Ours was a somewhat related two-pronged quest, that of the psychiatrist's diagnostic inquiry into manifestations of underlying emotional distress and that of the sociologist delineating the landscape contours of the respondent's past and present family and community environs.

3. Both sets of "explorers," to use the term Freud applied to himself, wrestled with problems of synthesis—to extract larger patterns of coherence and meaning in the volatile confluences at the junctures of their subjects' interior and exterior lives.

4. Joyce cast himself as his own protagonist in the character of Stephen Dedalus. Except for the preformulated stimuli-questions conveyed through our interviewers, the Midtown researchers were strictly sideline observers

of our sample respondents. In turnabout, however, one or another of us could well have written a "documentary" novel on the investigators working through a host of procedural issues and interdisciplinary strains as they confronted so many diverse kinds of subjects, on matters at once so intimate, so psychologically complex, and so broad in social scope.

5. Novelists and behavioral scientists are all dedicated to serving illuminating social purposes. But in the course of observation, synthesis, and report writing, both sets of professionals themselves undergo subtle and sometime significant changes. The observers in the end, like Joyce-Dedalus, are altered by immersion in their subjects as representatives of large classes of human beings. Certainly the present author can testify, at least for himself, to the following effect: When the 1962 edition of this volume was at last in hand, he recognized that his research experiences in Midtown had penetrated to deeper personal levels than the purely cognitive.

In the above senses, then, the two kinds of craftsmen tend to move through a parallel but largely tacit sequence of stages. I suggest, therefore, that this covert agenda would have been shared little differently had Joyce in his time happened to place his characters on the east bank of the Hudson River rather than on the River Liffey, and had we later chosen to conduct our study in Midtown Dublin instead of Midtown Manhattan.

This monograph has crowded a large canvas with the minutiae of many research concerns and findings. It is now time to step back from our pointillistic closeup of that canvas to highlight its major motifs in an equivalent of the short coda that closes a long and intricately woven musical composition.

Unlike most previous investigations of the same general kind,[1] this report, in data chapters 4 to 6, has sketched the huge amphitheater in which our studied subjects were engaged as natural actors. There they projected themselves both as individuals and as a social aggregate with multiple interlocking lines of collective identity.

New York is a leviathan among world cities, and Midtown is a large and integral segment of the photogenic island-hub of that metropolis. In synoptic form we delineated (1) the high-density, compact features of Midtown as a residential habitat; (2) the enormous diversity in the socioeconomic, cultural, and geographical origins of its all-white population; and (3) the great complexity in its network of institutions and in its psychosocial qualities as a community. Midtown, in these and other specific respects, was found at time of study to be a close counterpart of Manhattan's non–Puerto Rican, white population, numbering some 1,250,000 people, and to resemble high density, "gold-coast-and-slum" sections of others of our biggest cities.

Nor, Senator Goldwater to the contrary notwithstanding,[2] can the city in any way be perceived except as one of the most vital organs of the entire national body sociopolitic. On the contrary, emphasizes one novelist, "The island of Manhattan . . . touches all of us on the surface, but also lies at the buried, troubled questioning center of American life."[3]

TECHNICAL ACCOUNTABILITY

The scientist is required to be as forthright and critical in describing the working methods he has applied, and their limitations, as in reporting his findings. Scientists tend to be silent about the paths on the way to and from their final blueprint design and to make the final route look smoother and neater than was actually the case. False leads, miscalculations, obstructions, blind alleys, and other forms of waste motion are often unacknowledged, although inevitable to exploratory research in still partially dark areas. Moreover, even when tidied up and selectively telescoped, such brief working accounts are often relegated to the "back room" of the report's appendixes.

In this monograph, three early chapters (7 to 9) have devoted some sixty-five pages to setting out our technical problems, dilemmas, and reasons for our resolving decisions. We there emphasized limitations in our methods that we were aware of from the start, steps taken to counteract or at least estimate the effects of potential sources of error, oversights we discovered only in the rear-view mirror of hindsight, and the hedges we had to plant around the generalizations extractable from our findings.

Such accountings and caveats there, and in subsequent chapters, were intended to serve our readers further, so far as we could do so objectively, by making them parties to the role of "our own most persistent critics." That the hardcover edition of this monograph has been assigned as a case study in graduate courses on research methodology suggests that perhaps our section "Strategy and Tactics" is serving as an example of technical openness and self-criticism.

One reviewer of the original edition seemed to support that inference: "The authors are at some pains—they seem almost obsessive compulsive—to examine the weaknesses and biases of their procedures honestly. Indeed, it may well be as a case study in self-conscious research methodology that this book will have its greatest value; the chapters on [research] design are as subtle in their self-questioning as the musings of a Dostoevsky character."[4]

We need only add here that the Midtown Study has been among the first investigations in its field to make the following combination of advances in operating methods:

1. A shift in focus from an inpatient aggregate to a large sample of a community's general population, although we also covered Midtown's inpatients and outpatients in our Treatment Census Operation.

2. In primary mode of data gathering, a change from census-type counts of institutional case records to multihour, face-to-face interviews with sampled subjects.

3. A shift from incidence to prevalence as the more defensible measure of frequencies of mental morbidity.

4. From reliance on psychiatry's embattled diagnostic categories of disorder, a turn toward classifying mental health on an innovative, inclusive gradient of degrees of symptom formation.

5. In breadth of statistical analysis, a shift from the traditional cross-tabulation of one or two potential predictors of mental health toward controlled analysis of up to five of such explanatory variables simultaneously.

MENTAL HEALTH IN THE MIDTOWN SAMPLE AS ENTITY

Skimming the top layer of the Home Interview findings, how did our sample of the Midtown population "shape up" on the Study psychiatrists' continuum of mental health differences? Compressed into a single sentence, the subclinical forms of symptom formation (the Mild and Moderate categories) constituted almost a 60 percent majority of the sample adults, and on either side of this modal group were the segment of Well individuals, approximating somewhat under

20 percent of the sample, and the morbidity segment of Impaired people, representing somewhat more than 20 percent of the sample. It was impossible, however, to judge the significance of this distribution except in the comparative perspective of findings from other relevant populations. Unfortunately, no other urban study known to us has tried to estimate the frequency of Wellness or of the subclinical forms of symptom formation, ruling out comparative analysis on these levels. However, several investigations have reported on the overall (i.e., untreated and treated) frequency of mental disorder, and these offer at least the potential for comparison with the Midtown morbidity findings.

Such comparison was especially indicated, given that previous studies of patients, i.e., treated morbidity only, could seem to imply that the Midtown overall morbidity rate was inordinately high. If so, one ready interpretation might be that the assessment "screen" applied by the Midtown psychiatrists to identify the Impaired individuals had been unduly coarse.

Seeming to support this view were previous investigations of the overall prevalence of mental disorder in rather less than representative samples of Baltimore and Boston. Both of these studies reported overall morbidity frequencies of about 11 percent, representing half the Midtown sample's Impaired rate of 23.4 percent. Suffice it to recall that when known gross errors in underreporting mental disorder cases were corrected, and differences in population composition had been adjusted, the Baltimore and Boston frequencies were shown to approximate the Midtown sample's rate.

However, if these corrected rates from Baltimore and Boston did not stand as a challenge to the credibility of Midtown's estimated impairment frequency, neither could they be read by themselves as lending support to the plausibility of the Midtown estimate. All in all, the Midtown sample's roughly 2:6:2 distribution among the Well, the subclinical, and the Impaired bands of the mental health spectrum had to be tentatively considered specific to *this* sample population, as screened through the particular methods, data, and psychiatric judgments brought to bear in this investigation. It must be added, however, that in the years since publication of this monograph's original edition, the consensual tendency in the psychiatric literature has been to regard the Midtown sample's Impaired rate, given our criteria of impairment, as a scientifically credible estimate.

MENTAL HEALTH IN MIDTOWN'S COMPONENT GROUPS

To the present researchers, the Home Interview Survey "held out the ultimate hope of uncovering clues to the differential quality of various group environments" (Book One, p. 10). For this purpose we systematically combed through an array of constituent groups within the Midtown Home Interview sample, including the following classes of groups:

Age levels—four (20–29, 30–39, 40–49, 50–59)
Genders—two
Marital statuses—four (never married, married, separated-divorced, widowed)
SES-origin strata (i.e., SES of respondent's childhood family)—six
Own-SES strata in 1954—six
Own-SES mobility types—three (upward, downward, stable)
Generation-in-U.S. aggregates—four (immigrants, children of immigrants, grandchildren, and great-grandchildren)
National-origin groups—eight
Religious-origin communities—three
Degree-of-religiosity subgroups within each religious community—three

In searching through these nine categories and their forty component segments, the test yardstick we applied to all was of course the compositional distribution of each group segment on the psychiatrists' mental health gradient scale—in particular, intergroup differences in relative number of Impaired per 100 Well.

The most clear-cut and pervasive finding raked out from this meticulous search was this: Respondent SES-origin and current age level share almost equally strong input relationships, independent of each other, to adult mental health make-up. Specifically, age 20 to 29 and high SES-origin respondents were most heavily loaded with the Well, whereas the age 50 to 59 and the low SES-origin respondents, especially those from poverty-level childhoods, were most heavily weighted with the Impaired.

Interestingly, the powerful trinity of age, SES, and mental health composition came through in consistent fashion when we pieced together four independent sources of age-fragmented evidence. One was based upon psychiatric observation of the national college population universe (age 18 to 22). The second emerged from a large sample of American enlisted men in the age range 18 to 37. The third derived from an investigation of "senior citizens" (over 64) in an upstate New York city. And the most recent is reported from a large national cross-section sample in which frequency of "nervous breakdown" varied simultaneously with both age and years of schooling (an SES indicator). In effect, therefore, the Midtown Home Interview sample, together with these four highly contrasting sources of evidence, suggests that the triadic constellation of SES origin, age, and adult mental health may well be a generalized phenomenon in the national population at large.

At first scan, similar links to mental health also appeared within the Midtown generation-in-U.S., national-origin, and religious-origin categories. But these relationships, with two exceptions, largely "washed out" when intergroup comparisons were made with the effects of age and SES origin analytically controlled. The two exceptions were (1) respondents from Jewish families whose impairment rate was somewhat below those of like age-and-SES non-Jews, and (2) immigrants from impoverished, rural places abroad, whose Impaired-Well ratio was the highest of any group or subgroup of like age in the entire Midtown sample.

Stated differently, within the age 20 to 59 Midtown sample's population universe there appear to have been two relatively eugenic group settings during childhood, namely, families in the upper third of the SES-origin spectrum and Jewish families across the rest of the SES range, and one setting during "prime of life" adulthood, i.e., the age 20 to 29 decade of that forty-year expanse of the life cycle. On the other hand, the most pathogenic group environments in childhood seem to have been families in the lower third of the SES-origin range, especially those in the lowest sixth of that range, and above all those originating in poverty-stricken rural areas overseas, with the single most pathogenic group during the "prime of life" years appearing to be those in the last decade of that span (i.e., age 50 to 59).

THE STUDY'S MASTER HYPOTHESIS

From this capsule overview, we might now reexamine the following statement on page 119 (Book One):

The Midtown Study phrases the following general proposition as its most fundamental postulate: Sociocultural conditions, in both their normative and their deviant forms, operating in intrafamily and extrafamily settings during childhood and adulthood, have measurable consequences reflected in the mental health differences to be observed within a population.

This hypothesis, in far simpler form, dates to at least the end of the eighteenth century, but then and since the postulate has largely been restricted to contextual conditions operative during *adulthood*. Our findings on Midtown's four adult age levels seem to be consistent with the proposition so delimited.

However, our hypothesis was broadened to also include sociocultural influences on adults that had operated decades before, during their formative *childhood* years. This early life-history emphasis of the postulate was tested, perhaps for the first time in a general population, within the Midtown sample and, as already noted, was confirmed in our mental health findings on respondents' SES origin, overseas-rural provenience, and religious origin. No subsequent study known to us has attempted to replicate coverage of the latter two childhood factors.

POST HOC HYPOTHESES

Mechanisms that might partially explain these empirical results have been suggested in the appropriate data chapters above. Hypothesized on the pathogenic side were the following three overlapping, but not coterminous, sets of social processes:

1. The multiple, interwoven deprivations imposed on children of indigent parents. In the past decade notable investigations pointed on this front have been reported by a number of social scientists.[5]

2. The stigmatize-rejection mechanisms rooted in the evaluative apparatus of the society's prestige rewarding and penalizing system. From childhood onward, these have been directed in most extreme forms at blacks, but they comprise a pathogenic pattern that cuts across all color lines and there ensnares and demeans the poor, the disabled, the aged, and other nonmainstream categories. Recent work has appropriately focused upon the "self-esteem" consequences of such systemic tendencies for their outcaste objects.[6]

3. Role-transitions and their potentially jolting impact on vulnerable

personalities among children as well as adults. These transit points have been incorporated into the focus of a fast growing literature on "life events" as potential psychological stressors.[7]

All three processes stand arraigned as social system dysfunctions, exacting a huge human toll and economic price, and calling for societal self-correctives, such as are discussed in the closing chapter.

DISCLAIMERS AND CLAIMERS

To be emphasized here are the following further observations. Nowhere in this monograph have the Study's social scientists regarded the above three noxious intrusions into the individual life stream of millions of people as precluding the simultaneous operation of pathogenic somatic factors, either as primary or secondary contributions to the emergence of mental disorder. No less emphatically, these intrusions are far from encompassing the entire universe of exogenous sociocultural factors that can be implicated as potentially damaging for the personality development of the child. Nevertheless, they represent discernible orders of social experience that together may account for a substantial portion of dysfunctional inputs into family units. There they can strain or dislocate the intricate balancing mechanisms of parents—strain that can ultimately yield mental disturbance in their children. Underlying this observation is our basic formulation that mental morbidity is in part immediate manifestation of an impaired ego, damaged by an earlier malfunctioning intrafamily structure that, in turn, had been rendered defective, at least partially, by disruptive intrusions from or defaults by mainstream community and national social networks.

"This may be," to quote the poet, "the unkindest cut of all."

REVIEW ON MENTAL HEALTH SERVICES

Chapters 10 to 18 above included Study information secured both from our Home Interview and Treatment Census[8] operations on delivery of mental health services to Midtown's residents.

Having uncovered a frequency of mental impairment far beyond that estimated by earlier investigations, the above-mentioned Midtown information exposed (1) the enormous disparity between this previously unmeasured reservoir of need for therapeutic help and the gross quantitative inadequacy of the services available, and (2) the discriminatory dimensions of that disparity. In brief, we emphasized, "those *most* in need of such services had by far the *least* access to them."

It is now appropriate to ask: What has since happened on this front? In the years just before the Midtown Study was launched, an estimated annual total of one million Americans had one or more contacts (as a patient) with a mental health professional in a hospital, clinic, or office. A decade later the number had doubled, by 1970 it had doubled again, and by 1975 it probably reached a total of five million. This represents a jump in a quarter century from 0.7 percent to 2.4 percent of the national population, largely made possible by NIMH-supported tripling in the number of practicing psychiatrists and allied professionals per 100,000 people.

With the advent of psychotropic drugs in the mid-fifties, followed by the establishment of community mental health centers in the decade since 1965, came large-scale shifts in the sites of treatment. In 1955 about 77 percent of what the NIMH Biometrics Division calls "patient care episodes" were attended in mental hospitals, predominantly state supported. By 1975 that figure had fallen to about 40 percent, with over half of these now treated by the psychiatric inpatient services of local general hospitals.

In the latter year, new, tax-supported, community mental health centers probably accounted for over 20 percent of all patient care episodes, with the remaining 40 percent treated principally by the enlarged cadre of office therapists and to a relatively small extent by privately supported outpatient clinics.

The simultaneous expansion of the system, and large-scale shift of primary treatment sites from distant state institutions to accessible local facilities, for the first time brought such services close to home for millions. These developments were made possible by the combined backing of the electorate, their congressional representatives, leaders of the mental health professions, and federal, state and community authorities and agencies.

According to NIMH directors previously cited, researches of the early 1950's, including the Midtown Study, provided evidence that helped to spark, support, and accelerate these unprecedented developments. Melvin Sabshin, Medical Director of the American Psychiatric Association, addressing the APA's 1975 Institute on Hospital and Community Psychiatry, made the following further observations relevant here: "The need to rectify imbalances in this country's mental health delivery system provided the moral fuel and force for the community mental health legislation of the 1960's. These imbalances . . . discriminated against the poor, the old, the very young . . . ,"[9] and, the Midtown Study had added, the foreign-born.

The huge and rapid transformations mentioned did not happen without adaptational strains, resistances, and slippages. These are still rife in 1975 and may be further exacerbated if federal funding in the years immediately ahead continues to drop below the level legislatively set as national goals in the late 1960's.

On a closing note about community mental health as a social movement, Sabshin concluded that it "has a history now, rather than being a hope, a prayer, and a vague plan, as it was in 1963."

It was the Midtown Study's unanticipated privilege to have contributed to that history and, hopefully, to continue that role in the future.

NOTES

1. An outstanding exception in this genre is C. C. Hughes et al., *People of Cove and Woodlot: Communities from the Viewpoint of Social Psychiatry*, 1960, volume 2 in the Stirling County Study series of monographs.

2. The Senator from the last continental state to join the Union, a state harboring a population less than one-fourth of New York City's, has offered the Procrustean proposal that this metropolis in its entirety "should be sawed off the continent and set adrift in the Atlantic."

3. H. Gold, *Salt*, 1963.

4. E. Z. Friedenberg, *Commentary*, December 1962, pp. 545–547.

5. See in particular: J. G. Eisenberg, T. S. Langner, and J. C. Gersten, "Differences in the Behavior of Welfare and Non-Welfare Children in Relation to Parental Characteristics," *Journal of Community Psychology* 3 (October 1975): 311–340; V. L. Allen, ed., *Psychological Factors in Poverty*, 1970; R. Sennett and J. Cobb, *The Hidden Injuries of Class*, 1972.

6. S. Coopersmith, *The Antecedents of Self-Esteem*, 1967.

7. One of the early delineations of this focus was offered by J. S. Tyhurst, "The Role of Transition States—Including Disasters—in Mental Illness," in *Symposium on Preventive and Social Psychiatry*, Walter Reed Army Institute of Research, 1958, pp. 149–172.

For one of a number of recent investigations in this area see G. W. Brown, et al., "Life Events and Psychiatric Disorders: Nature of Causal Links," *Psychological Medicine* 3, no. 2 (1973): 159–176.

8. For our critique of previous patient enumeration investigations based on the Midtown Study's Treatment Census operation results, see Appendix H.

9. M. Sabshin, quoted in *Psychiatric News*, November 19, 1975.

CHAPTER 22

PSYCHIATRIST'S COMMENTARY

STANLEY T. MICHAEL

This monograph was written by sociologists and is based on sociological data gathered in a random sample of the community. But it is a sociological study with medical orientation. The central reference point is an estimate of mental health; its central theme the etiology of mental illness; its programmatic concern the amount, quality, and adequacy of psychiatric treatment. Although conducted by psychiatrists and clinically oriented sociologists, the Study was not clinical. Subjects were not seen by trained medical personnel, nor were medical and laboratory examinations performed in a clinical setting. Nevertheless, the fundamental orientation toward psychiatric problems has resulted in a significant contribution to the psychiatrist who, bearing down on the individual case, may formulate only a general impression of the total social and epidemiological setting of his patient.

Not infrequently, the clinician recognizes psychopathology in relatives and other significant persons related to his patient. He may not know the extent of the psychopathology, but he is aware that most of these persons have never had psychiatric care. How severe is this unknown psychopathology? What behavior is the psychiatrist to expect from these other untreated significant persons in relation to his patient? Can he treat his patient as though everyone else around him were mentally well? The clinician has to formulate pragmatic answers to these questions. He will have to continue to meet the impact of the environment on the psychopathology of his patient. In this respect the findings of the Midtown Study can be of significant assistance by providing information not only on the prevalence of psychopathology in the community as representing his patient's broader environment, but also by estimating the frequencies of psychopathology in specific demographic situations and circumstances.

The design of the study provided for simultaneous estimates of treated and untreated psychopathology as well as the enumeration of known patients in psychiatric treatment. The information was gained from two sources: the respondent himself and the treatment facilities —hospitals, outpatient clinics, psychiatrists in private practice and psychologists. Through this integrated approach, information about prevalence of clinical morbidity, previously available only from clinical studies, assumed a new dimension in its relatedness to the total psychopathology in the community. Not only are we beginning to recognize the distribution of treated and untreated psychopathology, but also the various conditions which were previously only vaguely implied or suspected of being related to psychopathology and treatment are becoming more clearly understood. Reference is here made particularly to the relationship between socioeconomic status and the prevalence of psychopathology and its treatment. The relatedness of attitudes toward psychotherapy and such sociocultural factors as socioeconomic status, religion, or generation-in-U.S. is an enlightening contribution.

The concept of sociogenesis of mental illness deserves special comment. In the discussion of the conceptual design of the Study in chapter 8, it was suggested that mental illness is multidetermined; however, since such factors as constitutional predisposition, biological determination, and psychogenesis are not fully understood in their theoretical preconceptions, nor accessible as data pertinent to this particular study, it was decided to report and analyze only sociogenic factors. There is no intention to disavow or conceal the etiological importance of the non-sociogenic factors, but the influence of these would remain largely undetermined and open to speculation. As a consequence of the decision to cover only the sociogenic factors, the reader who is not mindful of the formulation and design of the report may be impressed with a sense of sociogenic overdeterminism. This impression is further strengthened by the fact that the manuscript was written by sociologists whose orientation pervasively influenced the terminology and structural composition of the language of the book. The selection and formulation of concepts to be analyzed, the data suitable for such analysis, the framework of presentation, the arguments relevant to the claims, the supporting data in the tables, the new hypotheses extracted, and the form and outline of the book were all contributed by the sociologists.

The proposition presented in chapter 8 that sociocultural conditions may "have measurable consequences" for mental health is a plausible hypothesis and worthy of testing. The method of choice for this investigation consisted of description and enumeration of demographic variables which carried an etiological potential relative to mental health. In the conceptual formulation, the mental health of the respondent (as represented by the psychiatrists' ratings) was considered the outcome and therefore was made the dependent variable. Conditions prevailing earlier in the life history were assumed to possess a potential for influencing adult mental health.

The caution and reservations necessary in the interpretation of pathogenic potential in a matter as complex as the etiology of mental illness impose severe limitations on generalizations from the findings, especially if these should be interpreted as constituting the total information. The pitfalls involved in statistical correlation of two or several biological variables are numerous not only because of the nature of the biological phenomena themselves, which in their complexity pose formidable sampling impediments, but also because of the multiplicity of interpretations of the implied associations, which may be spurious even when statistical validity is beyond question.

The partial applicability and incompleteness of the sociogenic hypothesis may be best demonstrated by analysis of an example. It has been shown in chapter 14 that parental socioeconomic status as an antecedent factor is related to the mental health of the offspring, the best mental health occurring in respondents whose parents were in the high SES groups, and relatively unsatisfactory mental health in respondents whose parents were of low SES. The inference is presented that "these differences [in mental health] were predominantly implanted during the preadult stage of dependency upon parents." If one chooses to be oblivious of constitutional factors, this hypothesis might be acceptable, cautiously as it is worded. However, there are other possible interpretations:

1. The parents of the upper-SES groups had good mental health, which was passed down to their children—our respondents—by inheritance of a

constitution promotive of good mental health. In contrast, the parents of low SES had poor mental health, which was passed on to their descendants through hereditary predisposition to poor mental health. Such a hypothesis, not proved, nor necessarily exclusive of other factors, offers a satisfactory interpretation of the data based completely on constitutional heredity.

2. A second hypothesis, sociogenic in nature, might be derived from a biological hypothesis that living organisms tend to return to homeostasis and from deviation and pathology toward normal physiology. It is not the parents' low SES which is pathogenic in the direction of poor mental health; rather, respondents are born in all SES groups with equal potential for good or poor mental health, but the conditions in the families of high SES tend to favor the evolution of the positive potential in the offspring, which in the families of low SES remains unexploited.

3. The statistical correlation may be interpreted by still another hypothesis, as may be inferred from the data regarding social mobility and mental health (chapter 14, pages 331 ff.). It would seem from the data presented that respondents who are upward-mobile in SES have better mental health than respondents who are downward-mobile. Mental health, as represented by the Impaired-Well ratios of the various socioeconomic groups, has a greater direct correlation with the respondents' own SES as compared with the SES of the respondents' fathers. This may be demonstrated by the steepness of the regression curve of the Impaired-Well ratios correlated with the respondents' own SES, which is greater than the curve of the Impaired-Well ratios related to parental SES (Figure 14–4). These two observations would seem to suggest the possibility that a respondent's mental health determines his SES. In other words, and in the terminology used in the design of the investigation, the SES of the respondent becomes the dependent variable and a consequence of the respondent's own mental health, which thus becomes the antecedent variable. The same would apply to the respondent's parents, resulting in the observed correlation between parental SES and respondent's mental health.

4. The statistical correlation between parental SES and the mental health of respondents could be interpreted also as contingent upon the fact that respondents' SES and parental SES are highly intercorrelated. Given that respondents' mental health is closely related to own SES as a primary phenomenon, then parental SES may be tied to the former by its own relatedness to respondents' current socioeconomic status.

It is not intended here to estimate the extent to which each one of these hypothetical factors contributed to the relatedness of SES and mental health, nor is it possible from the available data. However, accepting the premise established in chapter 8 that this report will be confined solely to the sociogenic findings, we must never lose sight of the ever-present alternative interpretations which, even though indeterminate and unknown, may be potential modifiers of the sociogenic impact.

The association of increasing severity of mental symptomatology with increasing age of the respondents is a finding which must also be hedged with numerous qualifying, cautionary, and conditional statements. The age of the respondent was known to the rating psychiatrist. It would have been very difficult, indeed frequently impossible, to gauge the significance of certain symptoms without the knowledge of the age milieu in which the symptoms operated. The age factor was taken into account and was represented in the psychiatrists' rating judgments. If on statistical count the symptoms of the older respondents still averaged to be more severe and more incapacitating, it can be inferred that on the basis of symptoms alone, without knowledge of the age of the respondents, the mental health ratings of the older respondents would have been even worse, as the respondents would not have been credited with the compensations with which they countered the insidious decline in health due to aging.

The possibility must not be overlooked that the symptomatology on which the mental health rating was based was not necessarily of the same quality in the various age groups. Part of the matrix which formed the basis of the rating scale consisted of psychosomatic symptoms and illnesses. By definition, psychosomatic conditions were rated as moderate symptoms and were not considered adequate to elevate the rating beyond the designation "moderate symptom formation," even though the psychosomatic illness might be in a terminal phase as, for example, hypertension complicated by cerebrovascular disease and hemiplegia, conditions which certainly interfere with life adjustment. However, the presence of a psychosomatic condition did not preclude a more severe rating if other symptom complexes so indicated.

In early adulthood, psychosomatic conditions are not necessarily taken seriously. In contrast, the impact of recurring incidence with age, the unrelenting progress of relapse and remission, the chronic and increasing residues after each attack, as for instance in arthritis, impresses on the older respondents the extent of their incapacity, which in turn is more readily reported to the interviewer as age increases.

Psychosomatic symptoms increase with advancing age and no

doubt contributed substantially to the more severe average mental health ratings in the groups of more advanced age. The prevalence of respondents whose psychosomatic symptoms were considered to be primary contributors to the mental health rating, outbalancing all other symptoms, and who were consequently designated as psychosomatic types was 5.2 percent in the age group 20 to 29, 11.8 percent at 30 to 39, 11.6 percent at 40 to 49, and 17.9 percent at 50 to 59. While undoubtedly change in role function, especially that of a parent respondent in relation to growth of children and their departure from the home, may contribute to conflict and stress and to the development of psychopathology in the older age groups, decline in biological vitality with concomitant loss of ability to cope with adversities, increasing physical debility, and illness cannot be disregarded as significant determinants of the increase in mental symptomatology observed in the respondents of advancing age.

There is, in addition, the question of differentiation of the types of psychiatric symptoms according to age level. Is there a difference in the quality of symptoms in respondents of the youngest age group as compared with those of the oldest? Reports attesting to a high incidence of neurotic symptoms in the twenties with steeply falling curves in the next decade[1,2] raise the question whether the greater morbidity of the older age groups may not be based on symptoms of a more severe quality, perhaps even psychotic, in addition to the already mentioned psychosomatic symptoms. The problem of the quality of symptoms as related to age raises a challenging issue for future research.

The higher incidence of psychosomatic conditions in the older age groups of the community sample leads yet to additional speculations in relation to psychiatric therapy. The more advanced medical clinics accept psychotherapy as the treatment of choice in psychosomatic conditions. However, the populace in general is more likely to consider its psychosomatic conditions physical and seek treatment with a general practitioner or a specialist in internal medicine. Indeed it has been estimated that 30 to 60 percent of patients seeking medical help for presumed medical conditions[3] are essentially afflicted with psychosomatic or psychoneurotic illness and consequently should receive psychiatric treatment. If the proportions of our respondents who had psychosomatic conditions increased with age, is it not possible that these respondents are receiving therapy for their psychosomatic conditions from general practitioners and other medical specialists? If so, our statistical evaluation, which indicates that respondents of the older age group are receiving less psychiatric therapy in relation to their need than are respondents of the younger age groups, may have to be reevaluated by further investigation. These respondents may be in a therapeutic relationship which, though ostensibly consisting of medicinal and physical therapy, is basically psychotherapy in disguise in the form of relationship therapy, directive encouragement, and supportive therapy. The presence and importance of such nonspecific, auxiliary psychiatric therapy must not be underestimated, even though from the viewpoint of the psychiatrist such treatment may be deemed inadequate because of its inability to provide understanding of the psychodynamic causes of the illness.

There are still other considerations which may contribute to the interpretation of the abrupt decline in rate of outpatient therapy in the older age groups of our respondent population. As has been cited,[4] the national annual frequency of chronic somatic disorder increased from 9.4 percent of the age 20 to 24 population to 31.1 percent of the age 55 to 64 population. The rate of somatic illness increases threefold from young adulthood to late middle age. Not only does frequency of illness increase with age, but so does the severity of incapacity resulting from such somatic illness. In youth somatic illness is not the rule and is not usually anticipated as a source of interference in life adjustment. It is also overcome with reasonably assured expectancy of early recovery because of the relatively vigorous physiological defense forces of the young patient. In contrast, with advancing age somatic illnesses, especially those with a chronic and recurring course, become increasingly important as a factor around which the patient must modify his life. Indeed, lapses in conformity in social behavior which would be ill tolerated in young adults are readily excused in the aged if attributable to somatic illness. Both the patient and society are apt to seize on somatic disability for explanation of social malfunction rather than dwell on psychoneurotic interpretations. Since the emphasis shifts with age to somatic disability, which in its own right is increasingly more threatening to social and even physical survival, it is likely that the resources, time, and effort of the patient will be preferably oriented toward somatic therapy rather than psychotherapy.

The data presented in this volume seem to be unequivocal in their indication that certain demographically defined groups of the population are influenced for or against psychotherapy by sociocultural factors. Age is essentially a somatic factor grossly related to somatic development and illness. But in our study it is also a sociocultural factor, especially in relation to psychiatric therapy, as the era of psychotherapy is relatively recent, and the older age groups have not been exposed to its impact at a time when their emotional pliability might have allowed for its acceptance. It would seem that with the sociocultural influences established as factors affecting the quest for psychotherapy in the various age groups, the next step for investigation is the unraveling of the complex relationships between age, sociocultural factors, and somatic illness—all these bearing on psychiatric symptoms and their treatment by psychotherapy.

The uncovering of mental and emotional symptoms in four-fifths of the sample representing an urban population suggests that either a degree of psychopathology is the norm in the statistical sense of population average or that mental mechanisms which by psychodynamic derivation can be considered pathological may be a mode of normal adjustment.

The individuals in the Impaired category of mental health, derived from the original psychiatric ratings containing the suffix "with interference in life adjustment," are represented as being analogous to patients in psychiatric therapy. Such a designation clearly demonstrates the difficulty in dissociating the hitherto clinical approach to mental health from concepts necessary or desirable for the estimate of mental health in a nonpatient community population. When it is urged that the mental ratings "Marked" and "Severe" are comparable to the clinical conditions of patients in ambulatory treatment, and the rating "Incapacitated" to the clinically hospitalized, the distinction is presented only as an attempt to anchor our conceptualizations in relation to known degrees of psychopathology.

If the degree of severity of psychopathology in the above ratings of the community sample is comparable to that of patients, what are the factors which sustain these respondents in the community and prevent them from succumbing to the load of symptoms which drives their peers into ambulatory treatment or a hospital? Do the symptoms of these untreated respondents have an unusual protective quality? Do these respondents have compensatory devices which counteract the pressures of the symptoms? Are they equipped with special, socially motivated assets or symptoms which prevent them from seeking

therapy? A well-organized defense mechanism, a systematized paranoid state, or a devotion to a system of physical culture or to a religious healing cult may possibly be sustaining individuals with large loads of psychopathology in the community. On the other hand, passive-dependent tendencies; depressive, hypochondriacal, or hysterical symptoms; or introspective rumination may incline others to collapse of defense and to the seeking of therapy. The number of symptoms or their severity may provide an indication of severity of psychopathology, but the degree of interference in life adjustment or the appearance as a patient for psychotherapy is determined also by a socially directed quality of the symptoms in both their positive and their negative senses.

The proposition that those in the Impaired mental health category are in risk of needing help evolved during the analysis of the data. It was not one of the criteria in the original rating process—indeed no estimate was made of the need for therapy of the respondent during the rating process. It may not have been possible to estimate the need for therapy from the data available to the rating psychiatrist, but this investigation does indicate that it is desirable that any future study of psychopathology in an untreated community population be designed to provide more definite answers on the need for therapy, the desirability of therapy, and its acceptability to the respondent.

The data and interpretations reported here are committed in the direction of revelation of etiological relationships between selected demographic variables and mental pathology. As the data evolved, we learned too that certain demographic variables influenced attitudes of the respondents toward psychiatry and psychotherapy. Undoubtedly psychopathology and demographic variables also influence the respondents' attitudes which are related not to psychiatry directly, but rather to all social interactions and ultimately to the structure of the social order itself.

Psychopathology is destructive to the individual and may interfere in his enjoyment of life. Psychopathology of the individual may also interfere in the lives of others. In order to understand and cope with these noxious forces with adequacy and appropriateness, we must know more about them. This volume is intended as a contribution toward that needed understanding. The data presented provide new knowledge and a springboard for future research in social psychiatry, and hopefully will lead to the redefinition of some of our psychiatric concepts and insights.

NOTES

1. M. Shepherd, "The Epidemiology of Neurosis," *International Journal of Social Psychiatry* 5, no. 4 (1960): 276.

2. M. Shepherd and E. M. Gruenberg, "The Age of Neuroses," *Milbank Memorial Fund Quarterly* 35, no. 3 (1957): 258.

3. R. Kaufman et al., "Psychiatric Findings in Admissions to a Medical Service in a General Hospital," *Journal of Mt. Sinai Hospital* 26, no. 2 (March–April 1959): 160–170.

4. S. D. Collins, K. S. Trantham, and J. L. Lehmann, *Sickness Experience in Selected Areas of the U.S.*, Public Health Monograph, 1955, pp. 8–21.

CHAPTER 23

SOCIOLOGIST'S PERSPECTIVES: PAST AND FUTURE, 1975

LEO SROLE

Further important social implications in the Midtown findings emerge when they are placed in historical perspective.

W. H. Auden, in a work of poetry, indelibly viewed the twentieth century above all its predecessors as "The Age of Anxiety," an imputation that has found few challengers even in the ranks of psychiatry. That historical tag is actually a contemporary version of the older notion that the Industrial Revolution and its corollaries were responsible for a continuing deterioration in general mental health from a presumed high level in the presumably carefree pre-industrial period.[1] On the American scene, the seeming increase of state mental hospital patients after the industrial quickening of the mid-nineteenth century was widely regarded as supporting that nostalgic view of the period preceding.

The most sophisticated research to challenge the reality of a temporal trend surmised from raw totals of mental hospital patients is that of sociologists Goldhamer and Marshal, in a study conducted several decades ago.[2] Using first admissions of psychotics to Massachusetts hospitals, and applying age-specific rates, the investigators found no increase between 1840 and 1940 in these frequencies among those below the age of 50. In other words, for the largest category of hospitalized disorders by far there was a flat (i.e., unchanging), rather than an upward, trend of rates within the 90 percent of the population who, through most of the century covered, were under age 50.

This report did discernibly little to diminish acceptance of the long-standing axiom about the historical increase in the frequency of mental disorder. However, the Massachusetts hospital patient finding, for reasons already demonstrated above, itself lacks credibility as an indicator of the trend in overall frequencies of emotional disability within the population at large.

For trend discernment purposes, a time series of studies of such populations is needed. Unfortunately, investigations of this kind have been few in number, technically diverse, and, even if they had been comparable, they were conducted over too short a period to permit sighting of longer range trends. Yet authoritative calls for such information continue to be made. For example, the Director of the National Institute of Mental Health has recently observed that the effects of NIMH programs since the agency's establishment in 1948 "could be best assessed if we could state clearly whether there is [now] more or less mental disorder in the population [than in 1948]."[3]

A point of departure toward responding to such questions may be found by taking another look at our own Midtown respondents. This monograph, in chapters 14 and 15, has documented that parents' SES during one's childhood has pronounced consequences for mental health. If that is a firm fact, as other investigations have since confirmed, then we may have the basis for a retrospective extrapolation of the direction of previous changes in general mental health. To be specific: the latter is the "unknown" in an algebra-like equation for which we have "known" trends of two other related kinds, documented on a national basis in government reports of the past 35 to 45 years.

The first "known" is the historical trend in the economic and other components of socioeconomic status. The second "known" is the direction of long-term changes in the physical health of the American people.

If we demonstrate in the following pages that socioeconomic and physical health trends are concordantly linked, and if we accept the view that a population's mental health tends to be interwoven with its somatic health, then the temporal trend in our unknown could reasonably be extrapolated from the direction of like changes in the two "knowns."

To restate the equation in statistical terms: If three variables are correlated with one another at a given point of time, and the previous known historical trends of two of these are found to be parallel, then the undocumented course over time of the third variable can be plausibly extracted from the similar trends of the other two variables.

The *overall* expansive direction of America's recent economic evolution has been personally observed by every perceptive adult. But the longer sweep of that movement may not have been generally or accurately appreciated. In the following capsule review I am necessarily dependent upon such details as are reported in available government and other publications, often in less comprehensive coverage than the reader and I would have preferred.

In the national economic domain let us start, by way of accessible illustration, with the average annual salary paid full-time, mainly skilled, employees in the bellwether durable-goods manufacturing industry. In inflation-free, constant (1973) dollars such wages ascended from $1,600 in the pre–World War II year of 1940 to over $10,000 in 1973.[4] Supplemented in recent decades by working wives, the gross *real* income of such families has multiplied by about seven times. Looking at family income in the *entire* labor force, excluding the substantial boost in fringe benefits, and subtracting the growing take of taxes (partially flowing back in expanded public services and subsequent income supplementing payments), the remainder can be translated into "disposable income per capita." In the same constant dollars, such work-generated income climbed from $2,000 per *man, woman, and child* in 1940 to about $4,800 in 1973, a total jump of 140 percent, or an average annual increase in spendable money of 4.1 percent. At the same time, the hours of work needed to pay for standard items of consumer goods and services fell between 1939 and 1973 by about 50 percent.

Accompanying these strides has been the secular contraction in the proportion of American families with incomes "below the minimum adequacy level," as defined in constant dollars by the Social Security Administration.[5] From 45 percent in 1935, this figure fell to 28 percent in 1950, to 15.6 percent in 1965, and to an estimated 12.7 percent in the economic recession year of 1975.

The cumulative gains in real income in part reflect shifts within the occupational hierarchy. Large-scale unionization of blue-collar industries in the 1930's and 1940's carried their skilled and semi-skilled workers' wage levels up to (or above) those of lower-white-collar families. Moreover, there have been broad shifts in the proportion of the labor force (1) holding white-collar jobs, up from 31 percent in 1940 to 50 percent in 1975, and (2) doing unskilled work, down from 40 percent to 22 percent in the same period.

One effect of the wide gains in buying power on the standard of living can be read on a crude but representative gauge like stability and quality of housing. The heavy investment in home ownership rose between 1940 and 1973 from 43 percent of all families to 65 percent. And in the same period the proportion of households living in qualitatively substandard units fell from about 49 percent to 7 percent.

Another large part of the increase in family discretionary spending has been salted into additional increments of children's education. The climb between 1940 and 1973 in years of schooling completed has been steep. For example, the proportion of persons 20 to 24 years old who had graduated from high school almost doubled from 44 percent to 84 percent. Similarly, the proportion of persons 25 to 29 years old with college degrees more than tripled in the same period, going from about 6 percent to almost 20 percent.[6]

The above advances were of course already under way, if at a lesser annual momentum, in the first three decades of the century.[7] Thus the overall effects of such long-term socioeconomic strides in education, occupation, working conditions, and disposable income on the standard and quality of family living have been predictably profound.

To sight one such effect, let us turn to our second "known," namely the domain of physical health, where available data in some instances go back to 1900. The best known yardstick here is of course average life expectancy at birth. In 1900 it was 46 years for males and 48 for females; by 1974 the corresponding figures were 68 and 76, a phenomenal jump of 22 years and 28 years respectively.

Part of these gains are explained by a drop in the infant mortality rate during the same period from 140 (per 1,000 live births) to 19. (In 1870 it had been 300.) But the increments in lives saved continued far beyond the first twelve months after birth. For example, we might look at the average years of life remaining to those who have achieved age 30. In 1900 their further life expectation if male was 33, if female 35. By 1971 the corresponding figures were 40 and 47, respectively, an average life-extending dividend for men of seven extra years over their own grandfathers' expectancy at age 30, and for women of twelve years over their own grandmothers' at similar age!

These increases in years of expected life of course reflect drops in a number of major disease-specific death rates. For example, the TB death rate fell from 46 per 100,000 population in 1900 to 1 in 1973. Especially noteworthy is that most of this drop came well before the initial large scale use of anti-TB drugs, when the annual rate had already descended to about 10.

As for mortality from the chronic disorders of later life, it has been generally assumed that these have been continuing to increase. However, between the only available baseline year of 1949 and 1973, the age-adjusted rate of cancer mortality, excluding cancers sited in the cigarette-vulnerable respiratory tract, has receded, just as death rates for heart disease have fallen back from 292 to 248, and for stroke from 87 to 64.[8]

V. R. Fuchs, an eminent medical economist, has accounted for these long-term changes in the mortality picture in the following broad terms:

For most of men's history life was short and uncertain. It depended primarily upon such basic economic conditions as adequate supplies of food, water and shelter. . . . [In particular] from the middle of the eighteenth century to the middle of the twentieth century rising real incomes resulted in unprecedented improvements in health in the United States and other developing countries.[9]

Fuchs adds however that the long link in the general population between per capita income—"above a certain minimum [i.e., poverty] level"—and life expectancy has recently largely disappeared. And surprising perhaps is that education has now apparently displaced income as a primary influence on physical well-being. He notes:

One of the most striking findings of recent research on the socioeconomic determinants of health in the United States is the strong positive correlation between health and length of schooling. This result holds for several types of health indexes ranging from mortality rates to self-evaluation of health status. It also holds *after allowing for the effects* [italics added] of such other variables as income, intelligence, and parents' schooling.

This relationship may reflect a chain of causality that begins with good health and results in more schooling. In the most detailed investigation yet undertaken of this subject, however, Michael Grossman has shown that the reverse hypothesis—that more schooling leads to better health—stands up well under a number of critical tests. One of Grossman's most interesting findings concerns the relationship between schooling and premature death. Suppose you were studying, as he was, a group of white men in their thirties and you wanted to predict which ones would die in the next ten years. According to his results, educational attainment would have more predictive power than any other socioeconomic variable—including income and intelligence, two variables that are usually highly correlated with schooling.[10]

We shall have to await publication of Grossman's report[11] to assess his arresting findings on these facets of socioeconomic status.

In any event, it is beyond question that rising standards of living and improvements in physical health are trends that are joined and have marched together since the turn of the century, and long before. Fuchs emphasizes further: "During most of the period medical care (as distinct from public health measures) played an insignificant role in health, but, beginning in the mid-1930's, major therapeutic discoveries [e.g., antibiotics] made significant contributions independently of the rise in real income."[12]

A broad spectrum world history of the twentieth century, sponsored by UNESCO, elaborates:

Improvement in the economic situation, living conditions and nutrition of the masses of the people must be credited with much of the reduction in mortality and improvement in health. . . . Inadequate diets not only meant deficiency diseases in extreme cases, but general lack of resistance to [other] diseases. . . . The advances [in health] achieved in the industrially developed countries during the years under review were intimately bound up with the rising levels of real income enjoyed by the people of these societies.[13]

Deprivations of elementary creature necessities and debilitations of physical health add up to a form of slavery[14] that cripples and locks personality development of the young into chains cutting off subsequent escape from that state. Coles documents the full force of this point when he refers to "the frightened children [of the poor] who years later are adults plagued by defeat, futility, hate and loss of the *freedom* [italics added] to change with changing circumstances."[15]

In this light it seems little less than an unarguable inference that the historically documented progress of a very large part of the population from poverty and near poverty toward higher standards of living and physical health carried with them similar changes in mental health over time.[16]

The Midtown data, although gathered in 1954, can be viewed as supporting this inference. Specifically, in the light of the known socioeconomic strides of the past century, we can assume that the parents of our D-origin respondents (p. 321 above) had in the main come up from E- and F-like childhood family backgrounds. We can also assume that had these D-origin sample members themselves been reared in E or F stratum settings, then their mental health composition would likely have approximated that of their E and F class-origin contemporaries in the Midtown sample.

On these assumptions we can hazard the estimates that our 384 D-origin respondents of 1954 had numerically about 20 percent fewer Impaireds and 40 percent more Wells than they otherwise would have had. These estimates must be assessed in the light of several additional considerations. They are based on inferrable socioeconomic movements among Midtown respondents' parents above poverty and near-poverty levels in the decades just preceding and following 1900. However, such gains were appreciably slower and smaller than those that are known to have followed in the decades after 1935.

Thus, it can be argued that the above estimated mental health improvements in our D-origin respondent group would have been significantly larger had the post-1935 socioeconomic and physical health changes been under full steam at the turn of the century. If so, our estimated mental health gains may be understatements of the probable mental health trend in children of the post-1935 years, and in any case, would represent the progress of only *one* parent-to-child generation in the past hundred-year processional of the generations.

Although it contradicts a long and predominant train of professional and popular thought, the position buttressed by the circumstantial evidence presented above is not without other knowledgeable advocates.

For example, confronting the characterization of our era as preeminently an "age of anxiety," a distinguished contemporary historian of the eighteenth century onward documents that "within this last [i.e., twentieth] century enormous burdens of anxiety have been lifted off the shoulders of men and women, particularly in the industrialized West, *to a degree that they can scarcely appreciate* [italics added]."[17] And from a cross-cultural perspective, an eminent anthropologist similarly rejects that characterization in an article pointedly entitled "One Vote for 'This Age of Anxiety.' "[18]

Reinforcing the position joined by such advocates is the fact that the intertwined scientific, technological, and democratic revolutions launched in the eighteenth century and accelerated in the two centuries following, powered a series of advances in facets of the human condition other than those discussed above. Among other thrusts they (1) forced the legal emancipation of American blacks from slavery; (2) freed women to a large, although still incomplete, degree from their dependent, constricting domestic role and de jure status as chattels; (3) transformed American society from the European model once relatively closed to spacial and vertical SES mobility into one open for unprecedented degrees of self-actualizing movement in both dimensions; (4) expanded the time and means for self-recreating leisure; (5) turned around a laissez faire state to provide public funding for a variety of social programs, targeted principally at persons in need;[19] and most recently (6) raised the scientific foundations of general medical and psychiatric care.

It is almost a truism, however, that there can be no new benefits without new costs. With the above massive humane gains have come a number of secondary side effects, including psychological strains inherent (for some) in adapting to rapid change, tensions generated by the heightened competitiveness and insecurity of a more fluid status system, erosions in the doctrinal and moral areas of the religious sphere, and loosening in the cathected qualities and supportiveness of interpersonal relations. To this incomplete list must be added overpopulation, economic and social devaluation of the aged, and uncontrolled technological defilement of the natural environment.

The many who have embraced the traditional view of a "decline and fall of mental health in the West" did so in part because of almost exclusive fixation on such adverse side effects, which they saw as particularly rampant in the expansive city. Conspicuous among those manifesting such preoccupations have been both sociologists and psychiatrists. In contrast have been two other sets of professionals. First have been the economists, who were themselves preoccupied with charting the primary socioeconomic movements of the Industrial Revolution, without regard, until recently,[20] for its adverse secondary effects. Second are a small number of diverse kinds of observers who have emphasized the sociopsychological gains accompanying socioeconomic advances. For example, A. H. Raskin, an editor of the *New York Times*, speaking of post-1935 developments among newly unionized skilled and semi-skilled blue-collar employees, saw their economic advances as bringing "a new sense of economic emancipation and dignity to millions of workers."

The most powerful leverage for improving human health is exemplified in the macro-economic evolution reviewed in this chapter and was distilled in the axiom of journalist-statesman Theodore Herzl near the turn of the century, namely, that "whoever would change men must first change the conditions of their lives."

Among health professionals there has long been a division of labor between those who work directly with the individual sick, primarily physicians, and those who address themselves to focal points in the community environment that contain health hazards, primarily milieu-altering, disease-preventing public health specialists.

In his "Message to Congress on Mental Illness and Retardation" (February 5, 1963), President Kennedy extended the reach of the latter specialty into the mental health field in these words:

An ounce of prevention is worth more than a pound of cure. For prevention is far more desirable for all concerned. It is far more economical and it is far more likely to be successful. Prevention will require both selected specific programs directed especially at known causes and the *general strengthening of our fundamental community* [italics added], social welfare, and educational programs which can do much to eliminate or correct the harsh environmental conditions that often are associated with mental retardation and mental illness.

Twelve years later what can be said about movement in the interim toward preventing mental disabilities? A number of recent innovations fall under the rubric of "secondary prevention," generally defined in the public health field as "early case finding" and intervention at the first manifestations of a potential disability.

Chapter 11 (Book One) discusses social role transit points as hurdles in the life cycle where vulnerable personalities experience distress and difficulties in effecting the transition. An example is the child first entering school, when reading, learning and related emotional problems may first be visible to a professional, i.e., the first grade teacher. Early malfunctions manifested here tend to have "snowballing" effects on subsequent learning failures, dropping out of school, work handicaps, and spiraling emotional disabilities across the entire life span.

Imaginative experimental interventions at this level in the school system have been demonstrated by psychiatrists Kellam and Schiff in a Chicago poverty area.[21] The professional skills required for such intervention have been illustrated by the innovators mentioned. But training for such secondary prevention specialists seems to be lagging far behind the needs calling for them.

At the other end of the schooling cycle are the local programs that help young people with problems or special needs through the transition from school to work. One impressive example is to be found in the broad social spectrum of sixteen sponsoring community organizations that have joined to form a coalition called "The Industry-Education Coordinating Council of New York City." Operating the programs under this federation are a total of sixty-eight school system bureaus and other nonprofit agencies, government or private. An illustration is the High School Redirection project that "offers students who may be potential dropouts an alternative work-study program format leading to a regular high school diploma, and including individual and group counselling."

Still farther into the life cycle is the point at which an adult worker's emotional-behavioral tendencies are disrupting both his productivity and relationships with his associates and supervisor. Isolation from his disaffected coworkers aggravates his condition until he is usually suspended from his job. Dean H. J. Weiner has developed an innovative strategy of intervening in the unionized work setting, through the on-the-spot shop representative of the union involved.[22] On the basis of a demonstration try-out, the New York City Central Labor Council and the Columbia University School of Social Work are conducting training courses for union counsellors, shop stewards, and other officers of 500 constituent union locals having a combined membership of 1.25 million workers.

Such union personnel have had the sole responsibility of communicating worker grievances to management. Now they are also charged with addressing themselves to the worker whose behavior is placing his/her job in jeopardy. They do so by providing the worker with emotional support, counselling, mediation with management to avoid suspension, and, if still necessary, referring him/her to an appropriate mental health service. This intervention strategy has also been adopted by the United Automobile Workers' union locals in Detroit and by several other unions on a national basis.

The common element in all three of the above resourceful developments is that they reach out to people at risk where they are still functioning in their regular extrafamily settings, arresting, if possible, the need to see a therapist, and facilitating, if necessary, referral to such a specialist. In working through established institutions like the school and the work place, they represent secondary prevention at its best, and offer models for other kinds of community institutions to constructively serve their members in new ways.

The above three illustrations of secondary prevention in action are of narrow-gauged dimensions in that they reach out in pinpointed fashion to help already distressed individuals in an early stage of maladaptive behavior.

Broad-gauged *primary* prevention, on the other hand, is directed toward correcting what Knowles has referred to as our persisting "great social problems." He continues:

In attacking the causes, rather than simply trying to alleviate the symptoms, of these problems, [we] have learned that what lies at the root of most social pathology is human *powerlessness*—the powerlessness of the poor, of the undernourished, of the uneducated, and of those who receive unequal treatment because of their race, color or sex—to claim a fair share of life's opportunities and rewards. Promotion of social justice should be a concern—as long as we have a society [still] characterized by severe inequities.[23]

Fundamental to the power sharing called "freedom of choice" is a social system that universalizes these elementary ingredients of self-actualizing personality development: the right to equal respect for the inalienable dignity of all individuals without exception, no less than the right to more equitable fulfillment of the creature essentials and amenities of the human estate. Both ingredients call for top-priority attention to that 12 percent powerless segment of the American population which, a decade after the trumpeted and short-lived "War on Poverty," is still hanging onto the ledge below the minimum subsistence line.[24] That segment, estimated 27 million in absolute number of individuals at this writing, is increasingly concentrated in urban and rural enclaves that exacerbate the already epidemic prevalence of emotional and behavioral disabilities documented in chapter 14. These handicapped millions clearly present the most serious challenges to our socioeconomic inventiveness, to our psychotherapeutic ingenuity, and to America's two-century-long claim to being above all a moral society.

Two recent and promising developments toward ending the pariahdom of poverty have been (1) the "income maintenance" proposal, still languishing in Congress, to place an adequately supportive income floor under the substandard earnings of "the working poor"; and (2) the West European concept of "supported work," now being programmatically demonstrated, tested, and evaluated in thirteen American states. The latter program provides subsidized employment to the many "nonworking poor" now caught in the "welfare trap," i.e., those unemployable in the competitive labor market because of physical, educational, mental, or emotional disabilities.

Answering to the call for improvers of the human condition have been the social *macro-changers*, preeminently the ideological, scientific, political, and technological innovators who in modern times sparked and propelled the Western democratic and industrial revolutions. Recently a new breed of macro-changers has emerged, concentrating not on solutions to immediately pressing problems but on identifying and catalyzing public discussion of alternative solutions to large, long-range social problems, imminent and forseeable. One manifestation of this development is to be seen in the formation of the World Future Society,[25] which has issued a ground-breaking report: *The Next Twenty-five Years: Crisis and Opportunity*.[26]

Joining the recognized macro-changers have been a growing establishment-shaking army of activists who have mobilized in an array of advocacy groups like the civil rights, women's liberation, environmental conservation, mental health, senior citizen, and consumer-protection movements. Their already discernible impacts on change are in various degrees accelerating, although a sociologist would parenthetically remark that they have not been joined with comparable activism from their natural allies, our religious institutions.

Finally are the unsung, anonymous legions of lay *micro-changers* who, on the model of Alcoholics Anonymous, manifest in their daily lives the person-to-person approach, "I actively care."

Macro-changers, organized activists, and "on my own" micro-changers are all indispensable to a society of concerned citizens who contribute to making a community that cares,[27] one that incorporates the common core of all psychotherapies, and that in the aggregate can energize the "critical mass" of what can freely be called "a layman's health-enhancing, therapeutic community."

There are many promising indications for the future that this care-sharing personal orientation is part of a changing humanistic ethic that has struck new roots, among other places, in the current generation of young people. For example, social psychologist Kenneth Kenniston notes that the overall educational composition of American young adults today is "absolutely unprecedented in world history. . . . No one can guess the full impact of these wide educational gains. But they certainly mean that a large segment of society will be more capable of dealing with complexity . . . and *more concerned with the society around them*" (italics added).[28]

Taming and bending the physical environment to sustain and enhance the human estate has fully engaged man since he acquired the art of making fire hundreds of millennia ago. From a state of passive, fatalistic, total obeisance to social arrangements as an immutable given, the average man, collectively speaking, has now progressed far in his power to remake his society, a development that can be measured in the span of a few short centuries. Most noteworthy is that the sweep of this movement has recently accelerated enormously, above all in the decade since 1965.[29]

If the Midtown investigation has in any way illuminated the need for and realistic potentials for an activist lay society committed to individual and collective well-being, it will have partially repaid the debts owed to all the micro-changers who made the study possible. This would include most conspicuously the 1,660 Midtowners, in the aggregate and each in his or her own individual way, who for us opened the vistas to both the past and the future that are sketched in this and successor study monographs.[30]

NOTES

1. One mid-nineteenth-century thinker dated the turning point from the democratic revolution, rather than the industrial. He proclaimed: It is our "free institutions which promote insanity." (D. C. Hayden, "On the Distribution of Insanity in the United States," *Third Literary Messenger* 10 [1844]: 178.)

2. H. Goldhamer and A. Marshal, *Psychosis and Civilization*, 1949.

3. Bertram S. Brown, "A National View of Mental Health," U.S. Department of Health, Education and Welfare Publication no. (NIH) 74–661, 1974, p. 5.

4. All of the 1940–1973 income and occupation figures below are derived from *Fortune* magazine graphs, April 1975, pp. 92–96.

5. W. J. Cohen, *Social Policy for the Nineteen Seventies*, U.S. Department of Health, Education and Welfare Indicators, May 1966.

6. Schooling figures are from *Social Indicators, 1973*, U.S. Department of Commerce, Social and Economic Statistics Administration, 1974, pp. 100 and 107.

7. A medical observer has written, "Let it be recalled that there were all sorts of improvements in general socioeconomic status in New York City, as in other cities, between 1900 and 1930." (W. McDermott, "Medical Institutions and Modifications of Disease Patterns," *American Journal of Psychiatry* 122 [June 1966]: 1398–1406.)

8. Graph in *Fortune*, April 1975, p. 94.

9. V. R. Fuchs, *Who Shall Live?* 1974, pp. 30, 31, 54.

10. Ibid., pp. 46–47.

11. M. Grossman, "The Correlation between Health and Schooling," Conference on Research in Income and Wealth, *Household Production and Consumption*, National Bureau of Economic Research, forthcoming.

12. Fuchs, *Who Shall Live?*, p. 54.

13. Caroline F. Ware et al., *The Twentieth Century*, 1966, p. 472.

14. A Belgian playwright identifies the malaise usually accompanying poverty as rooted in the "feeling that . . . without money, one is someone who, in a sense, does not quite have the right to live; someone who, in a sense, does not exist; someone who fluctuates between being and nothingness." (Félicien Marceau, quoted in the *New York Times*, February 28, 1960.)

15. R. Coles, "What Poverty Does to the Mind," *Outlook*, April 1968.

16. Lest a simplistic theory of economic causation be read into this formulation, the view expressed is an elaboration of an ancient Jewish proverb: "It is not that a full purse is necessarily good [for mental health] as that an empty one is almost certainly bad." Bronowski offers us an apt paraphrase: "The good life is more than material decency, but it must be based on material decency." (*The Ascent of Man*, 1973).

17. J. H. Plumb, *In the Light of History*, 1973, p. 199.

18. Margaret Mead, *The New York Times Magazine*, May 20, 1956.

19. Data on federal expenditures for "selected programs for low-income persons" in the U.S. are a relevant yardstick. Information as to the magnitude of such outlays in 1929 is not at hand, but predictably they were minuscule. Data are available for the years 1968 and 1973, and they show outlays of $13 billion and $32 billion, respectively. When social security and other benefits for the general population are added under the rubric of "total social welfare programs," the corresponding figures are $60 billion and $122 billion, respectively. (A. M. Skolnik and S. R. Dales, "Social Welfare Expenditures, 1971–72," *Social Security Bulletin*, December 1972; and A. M. Skolnik and S. R. Dales, "Social Welfare Expenditures, 1972–73," *Social Security Bulletin*, January 1974.)

20. See A. M. Okun, *Equality and Efficiency: The Big Tradeoff*, 1975.

21. S. Kellam et al., *Mental Health and Going to School*, 1975.

22. H. J. Weiner et al., *Mental Health Care in the World of Work*, 1973.

23. J. H. Knowles, *Rockefeller Foundation Annual Report for 1973*, 1974.

24. For the definitive work on poverty alleviation in the decade since 1964

see R. D. Plotnick and F. Skidmore, *Progress against Poverty*, 1975. See also M. Pillsuk and P. Pillsuk, *How We Lost the War on Poverty*, 1973.

25. The Society is an association of a wide spectrum of professionals that defines itself as "an impartial clearinghouse for a variety of different views and does not take positions on what will happen or should happen in the future." See *The Futurist: A Journal of Forecasts, Trends and Ideas about the Future* 10 (October 1975).

26. Edited by A. A. Spekke, 1975.

27. That ever-refreshing octogenarian and psychiatric missionary Karl Menninger recently told a conference on "Toward a Caring Society": "We must help people learn to care more for one another, personally and through institutions like government, the mass media and business. . . ." (Reported in the *New York Times*, November 13, 1975.) Dr. Menninger might have added this pragmatic note, provided in a 1975 report of the National Institute of Mental Health (Office of Program Planning and Evaluation, June 1975): Mental impairments that in greater or lesser measure arise from the "care-lessness" of others exact a heavy price in direct and indirect costs that in the United States added up to a $36.5 billion estimated total in 1974.

28. K. Kenniston in a *New York Times* interview, February 4, 1971.

29. Manifestations of the power of this current is that it swept two American presidents out of the land's most powerful office by nonelectoral processes of resolute public opposition.

30. T. S. Langner and S. M. Michael, *Life Stress and Mental Health*, 1962, and L. Srole and Anita K. Fischer, eds., "Mental Health in the Metropolis Revisited: The Midtown Manhattan Restudy, 1954–1974," work in progress. For a preliminary technical and data report see L. Srole, "Measurement and Classification in Socio-Psychiatric Epidemiology: Midtown Manhattan Study (1954) and Midtown Manhattan Restudy (1974)," *Journal of Health and Social Behavior* 16 (December 1975): 347–364.

Part VIII

Appendixes

ERRORS, ARTIFACTS, AND BIASES IN THE MENTAL HEALTH DISTRIBUTIONS AMONG SES–ORIGIN GROUPS

Several potential sources of error in the research process may conceivably have contributed to the Well and Impaired trends reported in table 14–1.

One potential source of error could intrude from the interviewers if, for example, they performed their inquiring role in such fashion that the information secured tended to make upper SES-origin respondents look better in mental health than they actually were, and lower SES-origin people worse than they were. We can adduce no direct evidence offering a guarantee that this kind of systematic bias was absent.

However, given that we had fully anticipated this possibility we can outline the steps we took to control and minimize it. It will be remembered that our interviewers were all professionals highly experienced in the interviewing art and thus aware of its fallibility.

Moreover, in their own social class origins (or SES group served in a professional capacity), the interviewers were chosen to cover almost the entire status spectrum. Thus, so far as it was practicably possible, it was our policy to assign each interviewer to respondents of the SES range and ethnic background closest to his family or professional experience. It is our opinion, based on our supervision of the interviewers, that the special leaning they harbored was a rather consistent one, combining both empathy for and clinical objectivity toward the respondent.

Hardly serving to dilute this predilection was their knowledge that according to a blueprint of our research design we intended to reinterview a subsample of our respondent population. Although the blueprint did not finally work out in the form originally anticipated, it was foreseen by the interviewers as affording a technical opportunity to check the respondent information they were reporting.

On several grounds, therefore, it seems unlikely that our carefully selected and specially trained staff of professional interviewers had, wittingly or unwittingly, systematically or significantly, distorted the essential facts of the case about their respondents.

Another potential source of bias in the data may be sought among the respondents themselves. That is, to explain the SES connection uncovered (table 14–1) in these terms, it would have to be assumed that high SES-origin respondents tended to censor their answers to the symptom questions, whereas the lower SES-origin respondents in turn were more truthful in replying to these queries.

However, two considerations argue against this assumption. The first is the general observation that denial of symptoms, somatic as well as mental, tends to be a conspicuous mechanism among individuals of lower-class background; whereas people of higher-class rearing are able in a professional setting to confront and report their symptoms more readily and fully. Indeed, Hollingshead and Redlich have observed that "denial or partial denial of psychic pain appears to be a defense mechanism that is linked to low status."[1]

Second, we have reason to believe that several aspects of the Midtown Study's own public image—i.e., its sponsorship by a nationally known medical college and its "community health" focus—carried greater weight with higher SES-origin people than with lower-status respondents. Thus we sensed that the former, more often than the latter, accepted the interview in terms of its medical framework and conscientiously gave candid replies to its questions as a matter of both personal and civic responsibility. These orientations also become manifest when we examine the interview protocols. There it is quickly apparent that compared with their lower-status fellow respondents the sample's higher-SES people more often volunteered or elaborated revealing sensitive material about themselves.

The possibility we posed for evaluation here is that higher-SES people on the whole underreported their symptoms to a greater extent than did their lower-status fellows. The two considerations just presented suggest, on the contrary, that *lower*-SES respondents on the whole underreported their symptoms to a larger degree than did their upper-status neighbors.

In this light, if sample respondents as a source of error have skewed the SES-origin trend reported in table 14–1, they may well have done so by understating the frequency of mental morbidity not at the *top* of the SES-origin range but at the *bottom*. If so, the association between parental SES and respondent mental health is larger (not smaller) than table 14–1 bears witness.

A third possible source of SES bias must be considered, one emanating from the Study's evaluating psychiatrists who judgmentally classified all sample respondents on a gradient scale of symptom formation. To measure the effect of this and related kinds of sociocultural bias, a two-stage mode of rating respondent mental health was devised for the psychiatrists. In formulating Rating I for each respondent, the psychiatrists had all symptom information except data about his functioning in sociocultural settings that might demographically identify him. In deciding Rating II, the psychiatrists additionally had the information so excepted and all other demographic data about the respondent, including those revolving around his socioeconomic status. Thus, if the sample's Rating II distributions, when compared with the sample's Rating I distributions, showed that the Rating II changes in certain SES-origin groups tended to be more favorable than those in other status groups, the presumption would have to be credited that the socioeconomic information had perhaps contaminated the psychiatrists' judgments. Actual comparison of the "before SES knowledge" ratings (I) and the "after SES knowledge" ratings (II) reveals no status differentials in the direction of the rating changes made by the psychiatrists. We can accordingly infer that the trends in the SES-origin distributions observed in table 14–1 are not to a perceptible degree an artifact of bias on the part of the Midtown psychiatrists.

Of the three potential sources of bias in the SES-origin mental health trends, evidence has been presented that one left no discernible trace of intervention. For two other possible sources of such error evidence is not available. For one of these sources of error, namely, the interviewing staff, the possibility was likely reduced by measures of control that appear to have been more or less effective. As to the respondents themselves as a source of error, there are reasons to believe that their differentially incomplete reporting of symptoms may have operated in a direction of *understating* the SES-origin differences recorded in table 14–1.

All told, therefore, the chances seem large that the association there observed between parental SES and adult mental health is genuine, rather than a spurious result of errors and biases unlocked by the measurement process itself. Confirming findings from other investigations, presented elsewhere in this volume, seem to further enlarge these chances.

NOTES

1. A. B. Hollingshead and F. C. Redlich, *Social Class and Mental Illness*, 1958, p. 176.

RURAL–URBAN DIAGNOSTIC ISSUES*

LEO SROLE

Responding to my critique of the nine sets of rural-urban investigations presented in earlier formats, the Dohrenwends have drawn attention to another tabulation they extracted from six of the nine collected pairs of investigations. In a personal communication relating to my original paper (read to the 1972 CUNY Conference, identified on page 465 above), Dr. Bruce Dohrenwend commented: "We emphasize the consistency in the direction of the differences in table [20–1]. You emphasize their magnitude. Our general feeling, given the problems of measurement, etc., in these studies is that [such] consistencies tend to be important—but you are right that there is room for argument and difference of opinion on the matter—especially if you restrict yourself solely to the findings in table [20–1]." The latter point was subsequently amplified in a reply to my *American Scientist* article (September 1972) by Dr. Barbara S. Dohrenwend, that appeared in the January–February 1973 issue of the same journal.

She indicated there that "the results presented [in the first table] are illuminated by considering data on three broad types of psychological disorder" set forth in the second table of the Dohrenwends' *Handbook of Psychiatry* chapter (p. 429). Her letter continues: "Dr. Srole commented that the differences between percentages of all types

* See chapter 20, pp. 475–478.

of psychological disorder [combined] were very small in some of the nine studies, and suggested that these small differences probably represented nothing more than chance outcomes."

With reference to the second table alluded to above, Dr. Dohrenwend added: "A different interpretation is suggested by the inconsistency in the direction of the differences between rural and urban rates for psychoses, for neuroses, and for personality disorders. Specifically, in the clear majority of studies, psychoses were found to be more prevalent in rural areas, whereas both neuroses and personality disorders were found to be more prevalent in urban areas. Such inconsistency across different types of disorder might well be expected to result in small differences when all types are combined [as in table 20–1].

"On this reasoning I suggest that we should not dismiss differences in results for rural and for urban communities as due to chance. Instead, I think that these epidemiological findings justify the hypothesis that rural areas have higher rates for the most severe type of disorder, psychoses, while urban areas tend to have an excess of the less severe but nevertheless debilitating neuroses and personality disorders."

At the request of the editors, I submitted a rejoinder published in the same issue of the *American Scientist* that carried the above-quoted letter. One paragraph in that rejoinder read as follows: "In my article, I explicitly avoided discussion of the sub-rates of psychoses, neuroses and personality disorders . . . in part because psychiatric criteria for differentiating these three nosological types are beset with unsatisfactory margins of unreliability."

Before going on to the rest of the rejoinder, I would here make explicit the nature of the nosological difficulties just alluded to:

1. Psychoses, neuroses, and personality disorders are of course the three broadest categories in psychiatry's framework of nonorganic disorders, each subdivided into a series of diagnostic classes.

2. Unlike the readily delineated, "hard" types of etiologically specific physical disease entities, these categories of mental disorder are "soft," in the sense that they symptomatically overlap and are etiologically non-specific, leaving no clear diagnostic lines marking off one "disorder" from the others. M. H. Miller puts it that "all combinations and permutations of symptomatology are seen in clinical experience."[1]

3. Miller continues: "Compounding the effort to [differentiate] inclusive categories of neurotic versus psychotic individuals is the clinical pic-

ture presented by a *large group of patients* [italics added] who have been variously labelled 'borderline'—or 'pseudoneurotic psychotics.' "[2]

4. Others have also identified "pseudo" types among the personality disorders (e.g., "pseudopsychopathics") that present elements characteristic of neuroses and/or psychoses.[3]

5. Brill cuts more deeply when he refers to "the conventional wastebasket of the personality disorders, where much of our current lack of knowledge is gathered in one place."[4,5]

6. Such irregularities in psychiatrists' usage of the profession's conventional nosological rubrics prevail under optimal, intensive clinical explorations of patients' case histories. Spitzer and Wilson marshall the most recent research evidence as to inter-psychiatrists' agreement in applying current diagnostic categories, under *optimal* circumstances, and conclude: "In only three categories does the level of [interjudge] agreement reach satisfactory levels: mental deficiency, organic brain syndrome and alcoholism. Only fair agreement is reached for psychosis and schizophrenia. For the remaining [thirteen] categories the agreement is clearly poor."[6]

7. Babigian and associates point to an overlooked set of extraneous sources of diagnostic disagreements: "No matter how the nosological system is improved, the setting in which the diagnosis is made, the focus of the psychiatrist (diagnostic versus therapeutic) and the attitudes toward mental disorder, particularly psychosis, will continue to be major factors in the classification procedure."[7]

8. On the international level, R. M. Spitzer notes that "psychiatrists throughout the world use the same diagnostic terms [in clinical practice] when they have entirely different concepts and definitions of those terms."[8] This consideration adds an additional cloud overhanging the comparability of diagnosis-specific rates yielded by the psychiatrists of different countries whose results the Dohrenwends have called to our attention.

9. In field studies of general populations, usually involving one interview session, such accumulated diagnostic difficulties are magnified many times over. Indeed, in the Midtown study, Rennie considered the traditional psychiatric categories to be inappropriate for the kinds of symptomatic information gathered in our respondents' home interviews. Karl Menninger, one of the giants in contemporary psychiatry, has gone farther and denied their appropriateness or usefulness even in optimal clinical circumstances. He refers to them as "obsolete handles which have been so long used, arranged, rearranged, reordered, disputed and at last, we hope, discarded."[9]

10. For community population studies that *do* apply the three main diagnostic rubrics of clinical psychiatry, the above listed difficulties open the door "wide as a barn" to the play of judgmental bias, and especially to long-standing stereotypes about psychological differences between rural and city people. In historical perspective, the psychiatric literature abounds

in such preconceptions, with mounting evidence that social characteristics of examinees artifactually influence the diagnoses assigned by their examiners.

11. To control such biases in twin field studies of the kind reviewed by the Dohrenwends the obvious, if hardly perfect, solution is to have each subject's interview protocol assessed by psychiatrists who are "blind" to his or her place of residence and related identifying data.

Despite the cumulative weight of the above diagnostic difficulties, I have followed the Dohrenwends' suggestion to reexamine the second table in their *Handbook of Psychiatry* chapter. That tabulation presents the separate rates of psychoses, neuroses, and personality disorders reported for each rural and urban site.

Of course, the number of subjects in each of these nosological categories is a fraction of the number of "total disorders" presented in the Dohrenwends' first table. With smaller numbers in each category, greater differences between the two studies in each linked pair of investigations are required if they are to be viewed as statistically meaningful.

In this light, my *American Scientist* rejoinder summarized the Dohrenwends' second table as follows: "For none of the three mental disorder types, in my judgment, do the separate rural-urban rate differences of the [six pairs of] reviewed studies fall outside the range of probable chance variations, with the exception of the Helgason investigations in Iceland."

It continued: "Professor Dohrenwend urges 'the hypothesis that rural areas have higher rates for . . . psychosis, while urban areas tend to have an excess of . . . neuroses and personality disorders.' This hypothesis has been with us for some time. Yet I must submit that the comprehensive evidence corralled by the Dohrenwends, the isolated Iceland case excepted, supports only the null 'no difference thus far' conclusion."

I am most grateful to the Dohrenwends and to the editors of the *American Scientist* for stimulating the above interchanges on an issue central to chapter 20.

NOTES

1. H. M. Miller, "Neuroses, Psychoses and the Borderline States," in A. M. Freedman and H. I. Kaplan, eds., *Comprehensive Textbook of Psychiatry*, 1967, p. 590.

2. Ibid., p. 591.

3. O. Kernberg, "Borderline Personality Organization," *Journal of the American Psychoanalytic Association* 15, no. 3 (1967),: 641–685.

4. H. Brill, "Nosology," in Freedman and Kaplan, eds., *Comprehensive Textbook of Psychiatry*, p. 582.

5. An extreme position in the perennial professional controversy swirling around the usefulness of this particular category has been taken by Drs. Richard Schwartz and Ilze Schwartz. In a paper delivered to the 1975 meeting of the American Psychiatric Association entitled "Are Personality Disorders Diseases?" they replied in the negative and urged "that personality disorders be removed from the standard [official APA] nomenclature."

6. R. L. Spitzer and P. T. Wilson, "Nosology and the Official Psychiatric Nomenclature," in A. M. Freedman et al., eds., *Comprehensive Textbook of Psychiatry*, 2nd ed., vol. 1, 1975, pp. 831–833.

7. H. M. Babigian et al., "Diagnostic Consistency and Change in a Follow-Up Study of 1215 Patients," *American Journal of Psychiatry* 121 (March 1965): 901.

8. Book review in *American Journal of Psychiatry* 132 (August 1975): 881.

9. K. Menninger et al., *The Vital Balance*, 1963, p. 48.

MIDTOWN CRITIQUE OF PREVIOUS PATIENT ENUMERATION STUDIES

We here briefly review and assess what the Study's Treatment Census operation in particular had for the first time clarified. Our specific interest in the Treatment Census had been in two different facets of the patient traffic. The first had to do with the demographic sources and institutional destinations of those who have found their way to psychiatric attention. This we call the "logistic" problem, to which we shall return presently.

The other aspect is the logical problem besetting generalizations drawn from file data by enumerative studies of mental patients, principally those hospitalized. An incomplete inventory of investigations reported in English-language publications listed fifty-five of this kind that had appeared in a twenty-five-year period.[1] With few exceptions, these researchers took the characteristics of their patient aggregates as more or less accurately reflecting the characteristics of the psychotic population, untreated and treated. However, Robert Felix, the leading mental health authority in federal government at the time, declared this unequivocal view of that assumption:

The large number of prevalence and incidence studies of hospitalized psychotics are inadequate for our purposes on many counts. First of all, they deal with only part of our problem, the seriously ill. Secondly, they deal only with that portion of the seriously ill which becomes hospitalized. Third, they can deal only with those socio-environmental factors which are included on hospital records. These studies are in no sense carefully designed experiments to explore relationships or test hypotheses by means of original data. The researchers have no control over the case-finding process, over the record keeping, or even the diagnosis. Rather, they are dependent upon (1) the public's uneven willingness to give up its mentally ill members and to support them in institutions, (2) the hospitals' unstandardized record-keeping activities, and (3) the hospital staffs' varied training and skill in classifying disorders. Finally, the studies have not always been made with much perception of sound methodological principles.[2]

Several years later Gruenberg amplified this position: "I don't think that it [hospital admission] is a good definition of illness. . . . The more we get into it, the more clear it becomes that it doesn't have any substantive meaning."[3]

Despite these pointed criticisms, enumeration studies of patient records continued to be made for the express purpose of testing hypotheses that were predicated on the relationship of the entire aggregate of mental disorders (not its treated cases alone) to its general population universe.

For example, one researcher used hospital admission rates to test (and "confirm") this hypothesis: "The emotional security and social stability afforded by married life make for low incidence of mental illness. . . ." Offered in explanation for the use of *hospitalized* mental patients was this reasoning: "Data on the total incidence of mental illness are almost non-existent. The best available measure of incidence is admission rates to mental hospitals. Whether or not the proportion of the mentally ill who are hospitalized differs by marital status from the total [of] mentally ill is purely a matter for speculation. . . . Since there was no alternative, hospital admission rates were employed . . . to test the hypothesis. . . ."[4]

Here, "best available measure" narrows down to one assumed to be the *only one* available. Moreover, the suitability of this forced choice for the stated hypothesis is left dangling as a matter of pure speculation.

The New Haven investigation[5] marked a definite step forward in two respects: (1) It covered ambulatory as well as hospital patients, and (2) it framed three of its five major hypotheses in terms appropriate to the use of patient frequencies as the test yardstick. However, two of the five hypotheses referred to the totality of people in "psychiatric difficulties," and then proposed to use mental *patients* as the test population.

The New Haven monograph is exemplary in the numerous reiterations that its unit of observation is the psychiatric patient. Sporadically, however, it slips into the implication that it is studying the universe of "mental illness." Of particular interest is its claim that in comparing patients and nonpatients in each social class, "broadly speaking we compare the mentally 'sick' with the mentally 'well.' "[6] Seemingly implied is the two-part proposition: (1) All or most of the "sick" are patients, and (2) all or most of the nonpatients are well. The proposition thus offered is strictly speaking not an axiom that can be accepted as if it were self-validating on its face.

Even more striking is the New Haven conclusion: "We are impelled to infer some subtle connection between class status and psychotic illnesses that we cannot explain away by questioning whether the data are for all cases or only for those in treatment."[7] This is a clear instance of begging the question.

The inference may or may not be correct as stated in a form referring to the totality of psychotic cases. However, to suggest that the specific nature of the population from which the inference has been extracted is an irrelevant matter reflects a somewhat free reading of the laws of evidence. Such a reading is apparent in most of the literature of patient enumeration studies.

Despite the absence of supporting evidence and ample indications of face invalidity, such studies have often claimed, tacitly or explicitly, that treated cases are a valid measure of what epidemiologists want to know about the mentally impaired as a whole. Moreover, their generalizations from the former to the latter have moved from the pages of an extensive literature into the stream of scientific knowledge. Notwithstanding several dissenting voices of considerable authority, this claim, by a process of selective inattention, continued until recently to be widely if not universally accepted.[8]

From the beginning of the Midtown investigation, the writer fully shared the critical views of Felix and Gruenberg quoted above. With the Midtown Treatment Census and Home Survey operations juxtaposed, it was possible to put these views under empirical scrutiny.

As a major point of approach to our Treatment Census, we reviewed Midtown's patients in the care of clinics and office therapists. Midtown's *clinic* cases of this type exceeded New Haven's rate at the time by a margin of 2.5:1, a difference illuminated by the fact that Midtown's home borough had 2.2 as many clinics (per 100,000 population) as did New Haven. In turn, Midtown's *office* patients outnumbered New Haven's by a ratio of 4:1. Of relevance to this difference is that compared to New Haven, Manhattan had 4.4 times as many office therapists per 100,000 population.

Also pertinent is that in both communities treatment capacities of clinics and office therapists were far from meeting *manifest* demands for their services. Similarly, the state mental hospital systems serving these two communities were known to be overcrowded at the time by 25 to 30 percent above their official bed capacities.* In the light of such conditions, it was plain that hospital and ambulatory patient rates reflected intercommunity differences *not* in overall frequencies of "mental illness" but in bottleneck limitations of available professional personnel and their treatment capabilities.

If the Midtown Treatment Census could tell us nothing beyond the population of patients, the companion Home Interview Survey could elicit rough approximations of the volume of unmet need for such services. In the Impaired mental health category of the Home Survey sample we had a resident community group that entailed a risk of need for professional help. To this sample group we applied the broad criterion of "patient history"—defined by the minimum of spending one or more sessions with a psychotherapist. Among these Impaired respondents, only 26.7 percent had ever been patients in this particular sense during their lifetime. The remaining 73.3 percent had never been to such a specialist.

The latter included 29.1 percent who appeared ready to accept psychiatric or other professional intervention—offering a rough estimate of unmet and apparent readiness for helping services. Another 44.2 percent of Impaired respondents were never-patients who seemed to reflect no immediate awareness of professional help as relevant to problems of emotional disability, and thus were unlikely to enter the market for such services, at least of their own accord. In fine, the large problem of unmet need seemed to hinge in part on shortages in the supply of treatment capacities to meet ready demand and, in part, on a latent demand that is still dormant.

To generalize from studied psychiatric patients to the total population of mentally impaired, investigators should have evidence that one of two conditions obtain: (1) The untreated among the latter are

---

* In the intervening years, both hospital populations have fallen far below the overcrowding point.

relatively few in number and therefore cannot significantly affect the generalizations drawn (the 1880 national census of psychotics[9] and the Midtown Study 75 years later both offer suggestive empirical grounds for rejecting this first possibility); or (2) the untreated are indeed numerous, but are nonetheless similar to the patients in demographic and other characteristics. In tacitly accepting one or other of these possibilities as valid, previous investigators operated without a visible foundation of evidence. Here also the Midtown Study could throw some suggestive light.

In the Home Survey sample of adults, impairment rates tended to *increase* with age. Among the Impaired, on the other hand, we found that ever-patient rates tended to *decrease* with age.[10] On the scale of socioeconomic status, the Midtown Treatment Census reported that Total Patients rates (in hospital, clinic, and office facilities) *increased* upward with SES. Nevertheless, the Midtown Home Survey found that impairment frequencies *decreased* upward on the SES ladder.

This seeming contradiction was clarified by the finding *among the Impaired* that ever-patient rates *increased* upward on the SES scale. That is, at the bottom of the SES continuum, relatively many Impaired people yielded relatively few patients, whereas at the top of the continuum relatively few impairment cases yielded relatively many patients. Essentially the same countertrends of impairment frequencies and patient rates emerged from our analyses of the age, generation-in-U.S., and religious-origin variables.

In Midtown at least, the various social groups yielded mental morbidity rates that were almost the reverse of the trends in the frequencies with which help-needy people in those same groups managed to cross the threshold of a psychiatric setting. In other words, here the treated were a small and (except for sex and marital status composition) a completely unrepresentative segment of the Impaired people. Relative to the logical problem posed above, therefore, generalizations from the patients' data to the latter people were fallacious in almost topsy-turvy fashion.

As for the logistic problem raised earlier, Midtown relative to other communities was (and still is) especially favored in the size of its treatment facilities. Nevertheless, the clogged bottlenecks that actually described these services forced the splitting of the help-needy into two different traffics. More likely to appear in the patient traffic were adults who in age were younger (20 to 39), in own SES were of the upper or middle brackets, and in nativity were American-born. More heavily concentrated in the untreated stream were adults older (40 to 59), of lower SES, and of foreign birth.

In part, the demographic divergences between the two traffics seemed to be a function of self-selection, arising from their differential awareness of, orientation to, and means to secure the services of a therapist. But in some part, and here we stand entirely on the New Haven investigators' observations,[11] these demographic differences may also be a function of professional selection based on questionable assumptions about treatability, prognosis, and sociocultural congeniality.

For public policy in planning the expansion of treatment facilities, we have suggested that continuing systematic assessment of the untreated traffic is indispensable.

NOTES

1. A. M. Rose and H. R. Stub, "Summary of Studies on the Incidence of Mental Disorders," in A. M. Rose, ed., Mental Health and Mental Disorder, 1955, pp. 87–116.

2. R. H. Felix and R. V. Bowers, "Mental Hygiene and Socio-environmental Factors," Milbank Memorial Fund Quarterly 26 (April 1948): 127–128.

3. E. M. Gruenberg, "Problems of Data Collection and Nomenclature," in C. H. Branch et al., eds., "The Epidemiology of Mental Health," mimeographed (University of Utah), 1955, p. 67.

4. L. M. Adler, "The Relationship of Marital Status to Incidence of and Recovery from Mental Illness," Social Forces 32 (December 1953): 185. See also R. M. Frumkin, "Marital Status as a Categoric Risk in Major Mental Disorders," Ohio Journal of Science 54 (July 1954): 274.

5. A. B. Hollingshead and F. C. Redlich, Social Class and Mental Illness, 1958, p. 11. In the present volume, we take critical exception to technical epidemiological points in four chapters (1, 2, 7, 8) of the New Haven monograph. These exceptions in no way detract from our view of the remainder of the latter book as a definitive turning-point work on the unwitting intrusion of social class elements in the operating methods of psychiatric facilities.

6. Ibid., p. 197.

7. Ibid., p. 244.

8. Since publication of the present monograph in 1962, the prevalence of the claim in the literature has considerably diminished, but by no means disappeared (illustrating the lag in fully correcting scientific error). Whereas the frequency of psychiatric patients had previously been almost always equated with the freqency of "mental illness," the latter term now is generally qualified as "treated mental illness."

9. Referring to the national census of mental patients made in 1880, Malzberg reports that "there were 40,942 patients with mental disease in hospitals. In

addition, through the cooperation of physicians, a total of 51,017 patients were found outside of hospitals." (B. Malzberg, "Important Data about Mental Illness," in S. Arieti, ed., *American Handbook of Psychiatry*, vol. 1, 1959, p. 161.)

In a more recent publication, it is reported that "in 1961 for every person hospitalized for a mental disorder in England and Wales, there were two seriously disturbed people [known to general practitioners] in the community, a conclusion that is consistent with previous [British] research." (A. Little, "An Expectancy Estimate of Hospitalization Rates for Mental Illness in England and Wales," *British Journal of Sociology* 16 [1965]: 221–222.)

10. In chapter 22 (p. 508) coauthor S. Michael has advanced the possibility that older Impaired people more often than their younger counterparts secure help for their mental health problems from general practitioners. There is relevant evidence available to assess this suggestion: In the American adult population generally, the average number of physician visits per person per year varies little with age below age 65. Specifically, these reported averages are: age 25 to 34, 4.4; age 35 to 44, 4.1; age 45 to 54, 4.3; age 55 to 64, 5.1. (National Center for Health Statistics, *Health Statistics: Volume of Physician Visits*, series 10, no. 75, 1972, p. 17.)

This trend assumes added significance in light of the further national fact that the proportion of adults with one or more activity-limiting, chronic medical conditions *does* increase in the relevant NCHS categories from 7.6 in the age 17 to 44 group to 19.5 in the 45 to 64 age range. (National Center for Health Statistics, *Health Statistics: Limitation of Activity and Mobility Due to Chronic Conditions*, series 10, no. 80, 1973), p. 19.) If an age trend of mounting frequency of chronic somatic conditions is accompanied by little rise in the frequency of "doctoring," the implication is that with advancing age (in the indicated range) both primarily somatic and primarily psychological conditions tend increasingly to go unattended.

11. Hollingshead and Redlich, *Social Class and Mental Illness*.

INDEX, BOOK TWO